ENDORSEMENTS

For many years we wanted to tell the story of how God helped our family through persecution. When God laid this desire on our hearts, we simply wanted to give testimony to His faithfulness. We had no idea that times would change and that religious freedom in America would erode. It is our hope that Christians in the west will learn from our experience, and know that when persecution comes, it is possible to walk with the Lord and serve Him. Circumstances may change, believers may live in freedom or persecution, but Jesus is always the same. We are grateful to Evelyn Puerto for reliving the era of persecution with us, so that others can be encouraged to be faithful to the end.

—Igor and Lena Yaremchuk

This is the moving story of a precious believer in Christ, who remained faithful despite extreme, government-sponsored persecution. More than that, it is the story of God's faithfulness to His beleaguered people, showing once more that even the most evil intentions of sinful men can be employed by God to bring about great good. Irpin Biblical Seminary is a monument to that great truth, and the life of Dr. Alexei Brynza is a testimony to the immeasurable grace of our omnipotent God, who is able to make all things (including our hardest trials) work together for good.

—John MacArthur

At long last you have the opportunity to read the inspiring story of my friends Lena & Igor Yaremchuk. You will be fascinated to see what opened Igor's aesthetic eyes to recognize the existence of God. And you will be inspired by the heartrending story of a family's struggle for survival amidst crushing persecution. This book will bless your life.

—June Hunt
Founder, CEO, CSO (Chief Servant Officer)
Hope for the Heart

"Beyond the Rapids" is a gripping story of a family that demonstrated courage and faith in their "bitter struggle" against atheistic communism.
Evelyn Puerto tells of God's intervention and the demonstration of His hand of comfort through answers to prayer in the midst of great fear, deprivation, and uncertainty. The historical content lends great credence to the events and helps us understand the tremendous struggles followers of Christ, living in an oppressive society, experience. The reader will be captivated by the "lives" of the Brynza children, the difficulties they encountered because they were from a Christian family, the "romantic intrigue" they experienced, and God's protection and grace in their lives. It is a wonderful story of God's faithfulness to a family dedicated to His glory.

—Dr. Bob Evans
International Representative
BCM International

BEYOND THE RAPIDS

ONE FAMILY'S TRIUMPH OVER RELIGIOUS
PERSECUTION IN COMMUNIST UKRAINE

EVELYN PUERTO

Pleasant Word
A Division of WinePress Group

© 2010 by Evelyn Puerto. All rights reserved.

Pleasant Word (a division of WinePress Publishing, PO Box 428, Enumclaw, WA 98022) functions only as book publisher. As such, the ultimate design, content, editorial accuracy, and views expressed or implied in this work are those of the author.

No part of this publication may be reproduced, stored in a retrieval system, or transmitted in any way by any means—electronic, mechanical, photocopy, recording, or otherwise—without the prior permission of the copyright holder, except as provided by USA copyright law.

Unless otherwise noted, all Scriptures are taken from the *Holy Bible, New International Version*®, *NIV*®. Copyright © 1973, 1978, 1984 by Biblica, Inc.™ Used by permission of Zondervan. All rights reserved worldwide. WWW.ZONDERVAN.COM

Scripture quotations marked NKJV are taken from the *New King James Version*®. Copyright © 1982 by Thomas Nelson, Inc. Used by permission. All rights reserved.

ISBN 13: 978-1-4141-1605-1
ISBN 10: 1-4141-1605-5
Library of Congress Catalog Card Number: 2009909161

CONTENTS

Foreword..ix
Introduction and Acknowledgments......................xiii

PART I: IN THE RAPIDS
1. Grandpa and the Firing Squad........................1
2. Unlikely Heroes......................................5
3. You Can't Believe Everything You Learn in School....9
4. Papa's Search for God...............................17
5. Advice for Finding a Wife..........................21
6. A Powerful Earthquake..............................27
7. Our Illegal Sunday School..........................33
8. Prayers That Insult God............................41
9. Give Us This Day Our Daily Bread...................49
10. Receive All from God's Hand.......................53
11. I Meet the Bone Eater.............................59
12. Persecution at Home and Work......................65
13. Joy in Spite of Terror............................71
14. Papa's Promotion..................................79
15. The Soviets' Hammer and God's Hammer..............87

PART II: SEEKING AND FINDING

16. Can Frog's Skin Cure Cancer? 101
17. Ambition and Faith Collide 105
18. I Challenge God 109
19. An Enemy of the Established Order 113
20. Trapped in a Cage 117
21. Refining Like Silver. 121
22. Surrender Brings Victory. 127
23. Fighting to Avoid Conflict. 133
24. Foolish and Wise Choices. 139
25. God Protects and Provides 153
26. A Skeptical Scientist 159
27. On a Helicopter in Afghanistan. 169
28. How God Used the Atheists to Help
    Me Find Him. 179

PART III: BITING MY ELBOWS

29. A Scandalous Romance. 189
30. Instead of a Camel, I Rode the Bus 197
31. All Good Wives Can Make Borscht. 205
32. I Propose Marriage 211
33. Biting My Elbows 223
34. Testing God. 231
35. A Smooth Courtship?. 235
36. "We Can Tell Igor to Go Away". 241
37. I Still Have Time 251
38. A Premonition of Death 261
39. If You Fly, You Die. 271
40. Igor Meets a Witchdoctor 279

PART IV: COMING HOME

41. The Terrible Rabbit 285
42. Saved by a Communist 291

43. Cards, Crime, and the Army 295
44. The End of the Soviet Union. 301
45. A Childhood Dream 305
46. God's Plan Revealed 311

Epilogue 317

Endnotes 323

FOREWORD
A LEGACY THAT KEEPS ON GROWING
FOR THE GLORY OF CHRIST

*B**EYOND THE RAPIDS* is a riveting treatise of Dr. Alexei Gavrilovich Brynza's exemplary life and his powerful eternal legacy. It is the true story of an authentic Isaiah 66:2 servant of Christ who, along with his beloved helpmate, Valentina, and their four children, faithfully served the Lord. It takes place principally in the region of Zaporozhe in southeastern Ukraine during the cruel oppression of all believers by the savage communist regime of the Union of Soviet Socialistic Republics. But it concludes gloriously under post-communist freedom in Irpin, a suburb of Kiev, with the development of a wonderfully fruitful theological seminary.

This is the story of a faithful Christian family that stayed true to the Lord, despite the severe consequences that Christians faced during the brutal communist persecution over several generations. When our Heavenly Father answered the prayers of countless Christians throughout the globe and brought the godless regime down, He raised up Alexei Gavrilovich Brynza to lead in the training of faithful men to advance His Kingdom across the lands of Russia. Through many adversities, God had shaped Brynza into a man bearing His special qualifications that He set forth through the pen of the prophet Isaiah, one "who is humble and contrite of spirit, and who trembles at My word" (Isaiah 66:2).

Dr. Brynza was raised in a loving but severely persecuted Christian family. His father, Gavril Brynza, was exiled to a work camp in harsh Siberia. Alexei grew up believing the Bible as God's Word, committed his life to Christ at a young age, and began preaching the Gospel as a teenager. Baptized at age twenty, he became a Baptist pastor at thirty-seven, and was elected regional pastor for the Zaporozhe oblast at the age of forty-three. In 1990, when Pastor Brynza was fifty-eight, the Union of Evangelical Christians-Baptists (UECB) selected him to lead the development of a new seminary for the training of pastors and church planters.

I first met Pastor Alexei in 1990. While not tall in stature, he was a giant in his knowledge and understanding of God's Word. Growing up in a Baptist church at that time was akin to growing up in a Bible institute. In a typical week, there were five services and three sermons from the Scriptures in every service. Young Alexei loved the Lord, was faithful in church attendance, and studied God's Word at every opportunity. In spite of having no formal training in the Bible or in theology, he became a self-taught Bible scholar and a Christ-like pastor.

When the Lord brought the Iron Curtain crashing down in 1989, Pastor Yakov Kuzmich Dukhonchenko, the leader of all UECB churches in Ukraine, was deeply concerned that the sudden burst of freedom would attract a flood of false teachers, who could bring great harm to their precious churches. Many had given their lives and others—including Dr. Dukhonchenko—had endured extended prison terms for the crime of preaching the Gospel of Jesus Christ. They had stayed faithful no matter how severe the oppression became. The communist opposition had unwittingly served to purify their faith and make them strong.

However, these humble believers, who knew how to die quietly for their Lord without resistance, were unaware there were people in the free world who called themselves Christians but didn't believe the Bible as God-breathed, inerrant, and all-sufficient. Dr. Dukhonchenko determined to establish a seminary to train faithful pastors, who in turn could equip their churches to stand against the myriad of theological errors that began to pour in through well-intentioned missionaries and guest preachers from Western nations.

Pastor Alexei Brynza was a humble, faithful shepherd, who loved the church and revered God's Word. He was precisely the type of shepherd that Dukhonchenko and the UECB Council wanted their new seminary to produce. In Luke 6:40, Jesus said, "A pupil is not above his teacher; but everyone, after he has been fully trained, will be like his teacher."

Pastor Dukhonchenko and Pastor Brynza, with help from the UECB Council, determined that church leaders would select married men ranging in age from 25-35, who were serving as preachers on the basis of faithfulness, giftedness, and fruitfulness. Those who met the criteria and passed a written exam on Bible knowledge would be invited to come to the seminary for oral and preaching exams. In February, 1991, fifty-five men were sent by their regional pastors for these exams.

It was a remarkable several days. Each man underwent an oral examination concerning his testimony, personal life, ministry experiences, and Bible knowledge. Thirty UECB pastoral leaders sat in a semi-circle questioning each candidate one-by-one. Then all fifty-five candidates preached a fifteen minute message.

Then Pastor Dukhonchenko came to me with a very worried expression. He said, "Brother Robert Robertovich, we have a very serious problem. We have thoroughly evaluated fifty-five candidates and find all of them qualified to study at our new seminary. What shall we do? Our budget can accommodate only twenty-five." I replied, "Brother Yakov Kuzmich, if you are saying that the Lord has sent fifty-five instead of twenty-five, then we will trust Him to provide what will be needed for fifty-five." Trusting the Lord for the necessary resources, the seminary began. Grace

Community Church of Los Angeles sent three Master's Seminary professors—Dr. Richard Mayhue, Dr. George Zemek, and Professor James Stitzinger—to conduct the initial classes.

Pastor Alexei Gavrilovich provided wonderful leadership, taught many classes, and personally discipled hundreds of students. His beloved Valentina was a constant blessing to the wives of the students and the women enrolled in the Christian Education and deaf ministries programs. Greg White, Bruce Alvord, and Brian Kinzel, also sent by Grace Community Church of Los Angeles, began to teach in 1992. As of 2010, they are still teaching and have raised their children in Ukraine.

Graduates are serving churches in every oblast of Ukraine, in many parts of Russia, and in the Commonwealth of Independent States. Several graduates have become the directors of regional Bible institutes in Ukraine, Azerbaijan, Kazakhstan, and Moldova. A number are serving as regional pastors in Russia and Ukraine and in the leadership of the Ukrainian UECB. In recognition of his outstanding faithful service, The Master's Seminary granted an honorary Doctor of Divinity to Alexei Brynza. Indeed, he was a valiant warrior dedicated to upholding the truths of the Word of God at any cost. No error that caught his attention ever escaped without his taking measures to see that it was corrected.

On October 3, 2008, the greatly loved and highly revered founder-president of Irpin Biblical Seminary went home to heaven to be with His Lord and Savior Jesus Christ. The words of the apostle Paul concerning himself serve also to describe the life and ministry of Alexei Gavrilovich Brynza... *"for to me, to live is Christ and to die is gain"* (Philippians 1:21). Our beloved brother had fought the good fight, finished the course, and kept the faith. This outstanding book about Alexei Gavrilovich and his family will greatly bless and strengthen the faith all of who read it.

—Dr. Robert W. Provost
President, Slavic Gospel Association

INTRODUCTION AND ACKNOWLEDGMENTS

I'M VERY GLAD you will write my father's story, about how God helped my family. But I hope no one dies this time." This was not the reaction I was expecting from my Ukrainian friend, Lena.

I first met Lena and her family when I traveled to Ukraine, from Russia, where I was serving as a missionary. Fatigued by the long trip, I could barely pay attention to Lena's tour of the seminary where her father served as rector. "Here are my father's books. During the years of communism, they were illegal. Most of them were buried in the yard in a metal chest. My father dug them up at night if he wanted to use them. My parents never told us that they even had these books."

Lena's father, Alexei Brynza, was a Baptist pastor during the final twenty-five years of the Soviet Union. The Great Terror of Stalin's years had long been over, but fear still controlled the population. However, the difficulties Alexei faced pale compared to what his parents endured: Stalin's Terror and the Great Famine in the 1930s, as well as the horrors of Nazi occupation during World War II. The communist party, intent on creating an atheist state, never ceased its efforts to stamp out all religious belief. Alexei and his wife,

Valentina, struggled to raise their four children as Christians in a society that was overtly hostile to Christianity. Set in the city of Zaporozhe (which means "beyond the rapids"), the narrative spans the years from early in the 20th century to shortly after the fall of the Soviet Union, covering three generations of the Brynza family.

Lena and her three brothers grew up knowing they were different from most of their classmates. As they grew older, they each faced distinct challenges and were tempted away from following Christ. They each take a turn narrating their own story, as do Lena's husband, Igor, and her youngest brother's wife, Ruslana, both of whom were raised as nonbelievers and came to faith later in life. Relying on interviews with the family, I have attempted to compile their recollections into an account as faithful as possible to the actual events of their lives. Some names have been changed out of respect for persons who still may be living.

I was not the first person to be struck by the amazing way God worked in the lives of the Brynzas. During the early 1990s, novelist Scott Taylor met Lena and Igor when they were living in the United States while Igor attended seminary. Intrigued by the way God drew Igor to faith and brought Lena and Igor together, he set out to write their story. Sadly, cancer took his life before he could finish.

In 2002, shortly after my return from Russia, I was approached to write the story of Lena and her family by Pat Grace, who herself had been inspired by the victory God had given the Brynzas. After some reluctance, I agreed. Lena's comment about people dying didn't help; at that time, she had no idea if any of Scott Taylor's work was available or how to contact his relatives.

Two years later, while I was visiting Ukraine for some follow-up interviews with Lena and her parents, Igor received an email from Erika Taylor. She had promised her father on his deathbed that she would finish his book, and was prepared to make good on her promise. Erika generously gave me all of her father's interview notes and drafts. These provided much of the material for the sections on Igor and his courtship with Lena. Erika herself, over the course of weekly phone conversations that often lasted late into the night, provided much guidance on structure and writing and helped me shape the book from what would have been a dull documentary into something much more readable. She also contributed greatly to the structure and tone of the section about Yakov, demonstrating what a fine writer she is. Her encouragement kept me going through many difficult times, and her friendship is one of the joys that have come to me through this project.

All people in Russian-speaking countries have a middle name, or patronymic, which is their father's first name with an ending of –ovich or –evich for men and –ovna or –evna for women. Use of the first name and patronymic when speaking to someone shows respect, like using Mr. or Mrs. Most first names have a familiar form, such as Yasha for Yakov, which is similar to using Bob for Robert.

I am grateful to all the Brynzas for sharing their stories and for their time and willingness to be interviewed. Lena and Igor were especially helpful in answering many questions and translating drafts for her brothers. It was a privilege to get to know Alexei and Valentina, and to witness lives that are truly dependent on God.

Pat Grace was an encouragement and cheerleader through this entire project, and she and her husband, Wayne, provided valuable financial support, as did Central Presbyterian Church. Randy Mayfield's support and encouragement are also deeply appreciated.

Tanya Gavrilova Bougie performed the first round of interviews, and I am deeply grateful for her help at that stage of the project. Thanks to Priscilla Gunn for allowing the use of her house while reviewing the draft with Lena and Erika.

Many people provided feedback on various drafts or pieces of drafts of the book: Margie Diebold, Ellen Schmidt, Terra Ayers, Eileen Pheiffer, Gary Woodward, Greg and Mickey Button, Carlos and Leigh Iwaszkowiec, Paul Reising, Joyce Lindstrom, Jenny Whitman, Carol Myers, and others. Brenda Nelson's copywriting expertise and thoughtful advice were especially helpful. Robert Provost of Slavic Gospel provided some very welcome corrections.

My husband, Tony, wholeheartedly loved and encouraged me, gave me thoughtful criticism and advice, and never let me give up. He and my stepdaughter, Kristina, also deserve appreciation for letting me talk about this book night after night over dinner. Thanks, Kristina, for helping me over a few places when I was stuck.

And mostly I am grateful to our Lord and Savior, who works all things for good for those who love Him.

PART I
IN THE RAPIDS

Lena, the daughter of the Brynza family, weaves her memories of growing up in a Christian family in a society that blatantly mocked and oppressed believers with the stories of her grandparents' and parents' struggles to remain faithful to Christ despite persecution, famine, and hardship.

CHAPTER 1

GRANDPA AND THE FIRING SQUAD

Stone walls do not a prisone [sic] make.[1]
—George Bernard Shaw

Then you will know the truth, and the truth will set you free.
—John 8:32

As told by Lena

MY PARENTS DIDN'T allow my three brothers and me to play with the other children in the neighborhood. They built a wood fence around the yard and installed a gate, which Mama locked every morning after Papa left for work. Then she let us amuse ourselves in the yard while she was cooking or planting potatoes or taking care of the goats. We often stood at the gate, peeking through the bars, stretching our hands into the air, rejoicing that our hands were free, even if we were not, waving at the neighbors passing by, neighbors who laughed at us, remarking we were like prisoners in jail.

Maybe the neighbors were joking; maybe they remembered that our grandfather had been imprisoned during the Great Patriotic

War. Many Ukrainians rejoiced when our country was invaded. Some greeted the German army with bread and salt, the traditional symbols of welcome, hoping the Nazis would rule more humanely than the iron-fisted communists. After two years of German occupation, the Soviet Army drove the Nazis out, fighting so fiercely around Zaporozhe that the Dniepr River ran red with the blood of the dead.

The Soviet Army rounded up all the men who survived the occupation to take to the front. My grandfather, Gavril, was among them. He refused to fight. The Baptist church left decisions about participating in war or bearing arms to each person's conscience. For Grandpa, it was clear. "I am a Christian," he said, "and I will not kill anyone."

To the Soviet authorities, this was traitorous. How could any citizen shirk his duty to defend the Motherland from the fascist invaders? The Nazis treacherously attacked our country, plundered wantonly, slaughtered millions of people, and carried off thousands more to slavery in Germany. Maybe my grandfather would have been more willing to help a regime that had not been so cruel to believers. He certainly wasn't going to compromise his principles to help the Communist Party complete its Five Year Plan. He would remain true to his faith and convictions no matter what.

For many years the authorities sought reasons to arrest Grandpa for his faith; now they had grounds to execute him. He was tried, sentenced to death by firing squad, and thrown into the death cell with others condemned to die. There he sat for an entire month. The guards distributed almost no food and offered no medical care of any kind to these prisoners, reasoning that the inmates were going to die anyway. Why waste good food or medicine on traitors and criminals?

Every morning, as the pale winter sun peaked through the tiny window high up in the wall of the unheated cell, the cell's door grated open and a guard appeared. As he probed the faces of the condemned with his flashlight, the prisoners waited, resigned, knowing what was about to happen—one of their number would be called out never to return, and each one hoped to be spared one more day. But the guard's light would finally settle on one weary face. "You. Let's go."

One morning the light drilled into Grandpa's face. He calmly said good-bye to his cellmates. After a month in the death cell he still wasn't sure why he had been arrested. Was it for refusing to fight in the army, refusing to kill another human being? Or was it simply for his faith? Now his sentence was about to be fulfilled; it didn't matter why he was to die. He staggered to his feet, lightheaded from hunger, stiff from inactivity.

The weak light of the winter sun pierced Grandpa's eyes when he left the cell. Each step was a struggle, every muscle protesting, pain shooting through his feet as he walked to certain death, his heart at peace. He knew that in a few minutes he would be rewarded for his faith and enjoy eternal life with God. The guards marched Grandpa along the muddy streets of the camp. As they passed the headquarters, an officer came out. "Where are you taking this man?" he asked.

"To the firing squad."

"What has he done?"

"He's a Baptist leech who won't fight."

"My mother was a Baptist," said the officer. "I can't allow you to kill him. Give him another trial."

At the second trial they sentenced Grandpa to ten years hard labor in a concentration camp in Siberia. Grandpa's suffering was only beginning.

CHAPTER 2

UNLIKELY HEROES

[Stalin]—Greatest Genius of All Times and Peoples
—Soviet banner[2]

Glorify the Lord with me; let us exalt his name together.
—Psalm 34:3

As told by Lena

"LENIN LIVED, LENIN lives, and Lenin will live forever," we chanted with our classmates. Lenin, the great builder of the revolution, was a hero for all time, our teachers told us. Of course they idolized Yuri Gagarin, the first man in space, not only for his courage, but because he proved the superiority of our communist technology over America's. And they urged us to imitate Pavlik Morozov, the boy who fulfilled his duty to the state by denouncing his father to the police for being anti-Soviet.

However, my Baptist family honored different heroes; people we met through the stories of our parents and grandparents. Nearly every day my brothers and I wandered across the yard to our grandparents' house to see what Grandma and Grandpa were up to. Whatever the job, they worked together in tandem. I can see burly Grandpa peeling potatoes, his balding head bent over the task, the knife dwarfed by his muscular hands. Tall, skinny Grandma prepares the borscht, carefully pouring off the ruby liquid, keeping only the pale remnants of the beets that had lost their color through long boiling, adding pieces of carrots and cabbage she'd slivered to precisely equal sizes. As she moves from table to stove, she hunches over a little from long habit. She started stooping when she married a man shorter than herself—she did not want to appear dominant. Like a good Baptist wife, she always covered her hair with a dark colored scarf, except on Sundays, when she wore her white one. In those days, there was one way to wear the scarf, and the husband was the head of the household. That Grandpa turned his wages over to Grandma every week never seemed to bother anyone.

Across the years I feel Grandpa's massive forearms circling me as I sit on his lap, his muscles rock-hard from a lifetime of manual labor. His green eyes light up as he tells and retells stories of faith: David defeating Goliath, Daniel escaping uneaten from the lions' den. As we grew older, the heroes of the stories changed from biblical figures to my grandparents and their acquaintances, people whom God had miraculously rescued. Grandpa's escape from death by firing squad was just one of these stories, and my brothers and I marveled at what God had done for him. Not wanting to scare us, my parents didn't tell us the details when were small. When we were teenagers and learned the truth, our kind and funny grandpa took on a whole new persona. We began to understand why this tough man cried when he spoke of God's protection on his life; he became an inspiration to us.

My grandfather, Gavril Brynza, never wanted people to think of him as a hero; he never saw himself as anything but a simple man. He was born in 1904 into an unbelieving family. That is, his mother was a believer but his father was a drunk. My great-grandmother, Yana, living in fear of her husband, did not attend the Orthodox Church as often as she would have liked.

For most of his life my Grandpa Gavril lived in Upper Khortitsa, a small village on the west bank of the Dneipr River, opposite the city of Zaporozhe. In his youth, Gavril tended a herd of sheep, working with descendants of the German settlers who carried their Protestant faith to Ukraine. He saw the Germans' faith and how it made their lives different from most of the Ukrainian peasants. The Germans were hard-working, prosperous, and sober; the Ukrainians were poor, and often drank up what little money they had. Now and then my grandfather would visit the German Mennonite church because, as he would tell us with a laugh, "I liked to look at the girls." In 1923, he came to believe and was baptized. Three years later, he married a woman who had also come to faith. Even well into his eighties, he was still working as a manual laborer, performing menial jobs or herding animals.

Sometimes he made jokes of his stories. Sitting at the kitchen table, drinking tea with apricot jam, he would ask, "Lena, did I ever tell you how the pig saved Ukraine?"

"How could a pig save Ukraine, Grandpa?"

"It really happened, Lenichka. Many years ago, when the Tatars came through and conquered our land, they took everything there was to eat: cows and chickens, grain and fruit. Being Muslims, they didn't take the pigs. So the pigs were all the people had to eat. By giving their lives those pigs saved the people from starving. There's even a monument to the pig in Ukraine. It's true."

No matter the season, or the work that went with it, the stories never stopped. Out in the yard, with the spring breezes tousling the new leaves on the oak trees, Grandpa and Grandma planted potatoes. "Grandpa, why are there so many Germans here in Zaporozhe?" Grandpa turned over a spade full of black soil, damply smelling of spring. He stepped back from the hole he was digging, leaned on his spade, and wiped his face. "They've been here almost 200 years, Lena. After the war with the Turks, there weren't enough people left to farm the land."

Grandma tossed three tiny potatoes into the waiting hole. "The Tsarina, Catherine, invited German farmers to come, making many promises of all kinds of help."

Grandpa covered the potatoes with dirt and started tamping it down. He didn't tell us the rest back then when we were small. Catherine II wanted to repopulate her southern lands and to show the locals the ways of productive German farmers. Knowing Mennonites were persecuted in Germany, she lured many to Ukraine with the promise of religious freedom. Her promises weren't kept for more than a generation or two. The government began persecuting believers with beatings or arrests, punishing those who converted an Orthodox person into a Protestant with many years in a labor camp or exile in Siberia. In 1905, new laws were passed, easing some of the persecution, giving people the right to choose their own beliefs and even to leave the Orthodox Church.

"Think about it, Lena," Grandpa told me. "Those settlers came here with nothing. There were no houses or barns or tilled fields or gardens waiting for them. All they had was their faith. They had to rely completely on God and trust Him, even when times were hard." In later years, I had many opportunities to trust God: in illness, in fear, in doubt.

CHAPTER 3

YOU CAN'T BELIEVE EVERYTHING YOU LEARN IN SCHOOL

If it is necessary for the realization of a well-known political goal to perform a series of brutal actions then it is necessary to do them in the most energetic manner and in the shortest time.
—Lenin, in March 19, 1922 letter to Molotov[3]

He has sent me to bind up the brokenhearted, to proclaim freedom for the captives and release from darkness for the prisoners.
—Isaiah 61:1b

As told by Lena

SOMETIMES WE CAME home from school and told Grandma and Grandpa our own stories, stories we learned in school. We thought we knew everything.

"So, then, Grandma, there was the Great October Revolution of 1917. Lenin saved the people from oppression by the tsar and created a system where everyone is equal. Now workers are not exploited and we live better than anyone else on earth."

Grandma's brown eyes smiled sadly into Grandpa's before she turned back to chopping cucumbers. Grandpa gazed thoughtfully at his work-worn hands, stained red from the beet he was slicing. It wasn't until many years later that I realized how carefully my grandparents and parents avoided contradicting what we learned in school, only correcting us when the teachers told us there was no Creator, or made other statements that directly opposed the Bible. Otherwise, they waited until we were older and could be trusted with the truth to tell us what the teachers left out.

So in time they told us that, yes, life was brutal for the common people under the tsars. At first, many Christians thought the Revolution was God's tool for liberating them from the oppression of the tsar and the Orthodox Church. Some helped the Bolsheviks, reasoning that under a new regime, Protestants would be more likely to gain religious freedom.

"Why did they think that?"

"They forgot that if you feed a raven, he will peck out your eye," Grandpa told us. "They believed the Bolsheviks' slogan "All power to the soviets!"

This meant each factory, organization, or collective farm's soviet, or council, would have the power to make its own decisions. No longer would there be a central government issuing edicts and supporting one national religion.

But it didn't turn out that way. In practice, "all power to the soviets" meant all power to councils controlled by the Communist Party, and the Party planned to control all aspects of people's lives. At first Lenin was busy making a peace treaty with the Germans so he could extricate our country from World War I. Then a civil war consumed his attention. For the most part, churches were free to do as they pleased.

But in 1922 Lenin determined to make a quick end to any resistance from the Orthodox Church against the Soviet government. Confiscating all valuables from the churches and monasteries, claiming they were needed to provide help for famine victims, Lenin plundered the wealth of the Orthodox Church and diluted much of its power. He sapped what remained by ordering that church leaders be seized, judged, and destroyed. Anyone who protested was tried in court for interfering with the construction of a socialist society. The idea was to suppress opposition in so brutal a manner that people would not forget about it for a long time.

While Lenin was concentrating on the Orthodox Church, Protestants like my grandparents enjoyed five or so years of relative peace. After Lenin's death, Stalin used Lenin's tactics against Protestant leaders. The Atheist Five Year Plan began in 1928 and was supposed to end all religion in the Soviet Union. The next year, Stalin created government agencies like the Committee for Anti-Religious Propaganda and the Department for Victory over Religion.

While the main targets were people of influence, ordinary church members were not spared, and they faced imprisonment for the most trivial offenses. One man told his children not to use a red pencil. Since red was a symbol of the revolution, the authorities accused him of holding a belief against Communist power, and sentenced him to ten years in prison.

In spite of this, my grandparents did not waver. They continued to meet with other believers and to worship God; Stalin's laws and repressions did not stop them. These were the horrible years of the 1930s that my grandparents would not tell us about when we were small, the years when the Baltic-White Sea Canal was built on the bones of the workers; workers sentenced to labor camps for believing in God or not believing in Stalin; workers who constructed the canal with wheelbarrows and their bare hands—a canal which for many became their grave. The thousands of prisoners who died during the winter were simply stacked up in piles; their burial would have to wait until the ground thawed in the spring. When we asked about their younger years, all my grandparents said was that times were difficult and God helped them. "You see, children, the Lord preserves the faithful. He will always be faithful to you. He cares for us like a shepherd cares for his sheep, so the Bible tells us. The sheep don't always understand what the shepherd is doing or why he is leading them through places that seem scary, but a good shepherd always does what is best for the sheep."

In the same way, we learned what we never heard in school, what happened to believers during the Great Patriotic War. This war was the Soviet Union's proudest achievement, its triumph over the treacherous Nazis who attacked our western borders and swept through most of Ukraine in a few months. We all attended the parades on Victory over Germany Day and cheered for the war veterans, who proudly marched down the main street of Zaporozhe, chests covered with rows of medals shining under the spring sun, united in their show of patriotism, proud of the solidarity that helped them vanquish their enemies. We all visited our city's eternal flame, burning forever in memory of those from Zaporozhe who died in the war, a fraction of the almost thirty million who perished in the Soviet Union during those years.

I must have been about fourteen when Grandma told me that many believers thought the Nazi invasion was God's judgment on the Communists for their wanton destruction of human life, His way of liberating the faithful from oppression by the atheists. During the occupation, the Nazis opened some churches, allowing baptisms and church work among the youth, appearing, at first, to be less heavy-handed than the communists.

Then the Germans razed the aeronautical plant, destroyed the factories of Zaporozhe, and demolished the great dam across the Dniepr River, the largest hydro-electrical plant in Europe at that time. They spared nothing, ruining schools, hospitals, and crops, slaughtering herds, confiscating anything of value from people barely able to survive. The Nazis even scooped up some of the fertile black earth that was our pride and the source of much of our wealth, and shoveled it into freight cars to take back to Germany. They killed hundreds of thousands of people, many in mass executions, and took tens of thousands back to Germany to be slave labor in German war factories.

My father's family was poor and didn't have much the Germans wanted, except one cow. As they plundered the village, Nazi soldiers seized the cow and marched further east on their way to invade southern Russia. Papa's family had now lost their major source of food—the milk the cow produced. All they could do was pray to God for help.

A few days later, early one frosty morning, a loud, insistent sound like the engine of a train woke my father and his family, a sound they soon realized was vehement mooing. In the yard stood their cow, which had escaped and found her way home.

"All we could do was praise God," Grandma told me. "During the three years of the German occupation, we thanked God over and over for the miracle of the returned cow. That was how God kept us from starving until the Soviet Army liberated Zaporozhe from the Nazis. Ten million Ukrainians died in that war. Somehow, for some reason, God preserved our family."

"So, Grandma," I said. "The Red Army saved you from the Nazis."

"Yes, Lena, at first we rejoiced, and welcomed our liberation as optimistically as we greet the New Year. But anyone who lived through the occupation was under suspicion. The authorities feared we might be Nazi spies or collaborators. Many people were arrested and sent off to labor camps just for having cooperated with the Nazis in an effort to survive. Your grandfather, as a known Christian, was doubly suspect."

Grandma went on to tell me the whole story. Late one night, Grandpa was arrested. The police confiscated everything the family owned, taking even the children's toys, leaving them only with the clothes they were wearing, and evicted them from the house. Neighbors mocked them for having a traitor in the family. Grandma and her children turned to God and prayed that He would help them survive.

Having nowhere else to go, they crowded into the small houses of others from the church, staying a few days with one family, a few weeks with another. After six months, they decided to return home to their vacant house. None of the officials paid any attention.

Then Grandma discovered a strange bush covered with dark berries growing in the backyard. No one had ever seen a bush like this anywhere. They ate the berries, and my grandmother made all kinds of soups and stews out of the leaves and branches. Often this was the only food they had, the only means they had of avoiding starving to death. A few months later, when their situation was no longer so desperate, the bush died.

Years later, while walking in some woods in America with my father, I noticed that he was looking closely at all of the bushes, examining the leaves and berries. He kept saying, "That's not it, it's not here."

"What are you looking for, Papa?" I asked.

"The bush that saved our lives. I've been looking for it ever since and never found it. So I thought that maybe it grows in America. But it's not here. It must have come straight from God."

Sometimes Papa joined in with his own stories. After the war ended, famine seized the country, not as bad as the great famine in the 1930s, but horrible nevertheless. People spent their days searching for whatever food they could find, prizing each beet as if it were an abundant feast. Every morning my father, who was twelve, would get up early to stand in the bread line. If he arrived late, the store would run out of bread and the family would have nothing to eat. He noticed after a while that if he prayed as he ran down the dark streets he would always come home with bread. "They were childish prayers, of course," he told us, laughing. "But the results did show God's love and concern for my family, and helped my faith grow."

Another time Grandpa told us more. "After my trial, they shipped me in a cattle car across the Soviet Union, through Siberia nearly to the Pacific Ocean. A hundred prisoners were packed in so tightly that most had to stand. If someone fell down, others tumbled on top of him." He rubbed his hands together, remembering the journey made in unheated cars. "It was so cold that frost formed on the bolts near the ceiling. We sucked that frost for a tiny relief from our thirst." Even so, scores died on the way.

God continued to watch over my grandfather by providing him with work in a milk factory, rather than being assigned hard labor in the mines or construction brigades. The prisoners lived on bread, soup, and porridge, barely enough to survive. They slaved all day with only a few minutes' break for meals. "We were like ants, toiling without end, not really knowing what the purpose was. To the guards, we were of no greater value than so many grasshoppers. It was such a miracle that I did not perish. God carried me through," Grandpa told us. The camps in the Far East had higher death rates than the other camps; many had special brigades just to bury those who had died.

After appealing to every agency she could think of in an effort to find her husband, after finally accepting that Grandpa had in fact been killed by the firing squad, Grandma froze in shock one snowy December day when she opened the front door to see Grandpa standing there. He had been released after serving six years of his ten-year sentence. The family's joy at the reunion was as great as if they had all been freed from prison, all feeling as if a great victory had been won; God had preserved them and their house. Many people, their homes destroyed during the war, dug pits in the ground, covering the pits with sod for a roof, living underground for years. My father's family at least had a place to live. No one wanted to hire Grandpa, an ex-prisoner, except for hard labor, but even his meager wages lessened the hardships his family faced.

The released prisoners like my grandfather brought wonderful news back to the believers in Ukraine. "Stalin thought he was hurting our churches, taking away the leaders," they said. "But all he was doing was sending out thousands of missionaries, all over Russia and Siberia." The fruit of their labor was scores of new churches scattered across Siberia, around the prison camps and in towns nearby. What Stalin meant for evil, God used in a mighty way for good.

Hearing the stories, my brothers and I wondered. Would God ever perform miracles like that for us? We found out later that He would, but at great cost to each of us.

CHAPTER 4

PAPA'S SEARCH FOR GOD

Regeneration through labor.
—Slogan in a concentration camp, 1930s[4]

Therefore, if anyone is in Christ, he is a new creation.
—2 Corinthians 5:17a

As told by Lena

EVEN IF I am the only believer in the entire Soviet Union, I will agree to endure whatever punishment you give me for my faith, I will endure it with joy." Pushing his teacup aside, leaning forward with his elbows on his knees, my father fixed his eyes on the face of the speaker. A man from the church was telling the story of his trial and his response to the judge after receiving his sentence. It was 1947, and my fourteen-year-old father had made the acquaintance of some newly returned prisoners. Most of them were incarcerated for their faith during the 1930s, and spent the entire war in prison camps, grateful to God for sparing them from the front lines. Every evening my father sought these men out, drinking in every word. One told of how he took advantage of his position as the fireman for the labor camp, using some of his water supply to secretly baptize new believers.

Others talked of receiving letters from their wives, letters that read: "I am shamed to be married to a traitor to the Soviet Union, a betrayer of the homeland. I am humiliated to have an Anti-Soviet as the father of my children, and no longer want to consider myself married."

"It was difficult to remain joyful in such pain," one man told my father. "We didn't know if those letters were true or if our wives were forced into writing them, threatened with prison and the thought of our children being taken away, to be raised as atheists. But we trusted God, and He was faithful to us."

My father's new friends taught him how to use his faith, how to live it. Before going to prison, these men had accepted that any dreams they had for education or a comfortable life were never going to come true. In the communist state, the best that believers could hope for was the life of a poor laborer or farm worker. After being sent off to the labor camps, these men had to relinquish even their modest desires, such as living quiet lives with their wives and children.

While in prison, their faith was tempered like steel. They overcame their anger at the injustice, and instead did the only thing they could: seek God. He answered, changing their hearts so they could rejoice in their circumstances and learn to forgive their captors and any others who tormented them. By accepting their trials as from God's hand, in trusting Him fully, in surrendering to His will, their faith was strengthened, and they were given peace and joy and a profound sense of God's love. They learned to live wholly for God, to rejoice in fellowship with Him, to be grateful for His love and mercy toward them, and to be channels of Christ's love to everyone around them. It never entered their minds to be angry with God.

"Who am I, that God, the sovereign of the universe, would even notice me? Who am I, that I should tell my Creator how to arrange my life? As God's Word teaches us, that's like the clay telling the potter how to shape the pot!" one man told my father. "God is holy, and just, and what's more, He died to save me from my sins. How can I demand anything more?" During the years they were imprisoned, it probably never entered their minds that one day their stories of faith through trials and the depth of their relationships with God would inspire someone like my father, who would grow up to be used mightily by Him.

Not content with telling my father stories, these men challenged him directly. "Alexei, do you have a relationship with God?"

"I was raised in a believing family," my father answered.

"That's not enough."

"I know the Bible, and I pray to God for things I need, and He answers me."

"No, that's not enough either. You need to be willing to commit your life to God's service, and repent of your sins."

"I haven't committed any great sins. What do I have to repent of?"

"Young man, sin is sin. So what if you've not really committed any big offence? Are you trying to tell us you've never been unkind to your sister or disobedient to your mother? Or have never done anything out of selfish motives? These sins are enough to separate you from God."

Throughout 1949, my father was torn between faith in the God he knew was real, and a desire to just hang out with his friends. Participating in the church youth group intensified his inner struggle. The other five members of the group, single women in their twenties, propelled my father to a deeper understanding of the Bible and how to act on it. The first time they took him to a village to preach, he felt burning shame, knowing he was telling others how to be right with God, and he hadn't made the commitment himself!

Little did he know that thirty years later one of his own sons would feel that same shame, although in more dramatic circumstances. By the end of that year, Papa made his decision and repented publicly in the Upper Khortitsa church.

In the fall of 1949, after finishing the seventh grade, Papa aspired to study metal work in the hydro-energy *teknikum*, or vocational school, where he would receive training in a technical skill and a high school diploma. At first Papa didn't dare hope he'd be able to study anywhere. While tuition was free, he had no money for books or living expenses, and no hope that anyone would help someone whose father was in prison for being a traitor to the Soviet Union. Most likely Papa would be obliged to go to work, to start helping my grandmother support the family. To everyone's surprise, the director of the *teknikum* granted my father a stipend, which would cover his books and living expenses. To this day my father credits God for moving that director to give him exactly the help he needed. Once again, God provided when there was no other hope. Unable to see into the future, my father didn't know how often he would wrestle with his circumstances, forced to rely solely on God and His sometimes dramatic ways of answering prayer.

CHAPTER 5

ADVICE FOR FINDING A WIFE

The whole of life, the entire course of history convincingly confirms the great correctness of Lenin's teaching.
—Mikhail Gorbachev[5]

If any of you lacks wisdom, he should ask God, who gives generously to all without finding fault, and it will be given to him.
—James 1:5

As told by Lena

WHILE OUR PARENTS were occupied with church business, my brothers and I often walked across the yard through the vegetable gardens to visit Grandma and Grandpa. Our brick house faced one street, surrounded by a large yard, and my grandparents' house faced the road behind. Papa and Grandpa built our house for my parent's wedding, and it started as just a bedroom and kitchen. Papa added on to it, one year a bedroom for the children, another year a guest room, another year a larger kitchen. We had no running water, and the kitchen stove, which burned wood or coal, provided the only heat.

"Yakov keeps bossing me around, Grandma. Was Papa like that with his sister?"

"Oh, no, Lena, he took care of her without complaint. There was only one way he was not obedient."

"What was that?"

"He read his books until late at night. If I caught him, I would order him to go to sleep, knowing what he would do. He would turn off the light, wait for me to fall asleep, and then start reading again."

"How did he meet Mama?"

"We were scared he'd never get married," Grandma laughed. "He was so timid, he never even talked to a girl."

Papa was as anxious about finding a wife as if he were taking an examination he had not prepared for, and not only because of his shyness. He knew he needed a wife who was a believer, but none of the girls in the Khortitsa Church seemed appropriate. So he decided to travel across the river to Zaporozhe, to a bigger church with many young people.

In what he now calls his "naiveté," he would dream about traveling somewhere and seeing a woman that he might strike up a conversation with, and then marry her. He prayed to the Lord, that if he did propose to someone, the woman would accept. My father reasoned that if a woman rejected him it would mean that he had acted outside the will of God, a thought that deeply troubled him. He didn't want to fail in his obedience to God.

"Your father also sought advice from older men in the church, mostly from Oleg. What a strict man!" Grandma told us. This Oleg profoundly influenced my father and the formation of his Christian point of view.

"Alexei, you must never use another person in making your choice of a wife," Oleg told my father. "Nor should you rely on circumstances, such as if thus-and-so happens, I will do so-and-so."

"But then what should I do?"

"Be very serious, since God has given us the ability to reason. When you look at a woman, ask yourself 'How will my children perceive her? What will they think if their mother is a salesclerk?'" (This was one of the lowliest jobs in Communist society, almost shamefully capitalistic, so most of the people working in stores were the least educated and had the fewest abilities.)

"If a woman follows a serious lifestyle," Oleg continued, "then she will pass a serious view of the world on to her children." In our country, to say someone is serious is to say that he is a solid, stable person, who is dependable and mature. To say someone is "not serious" is to dismiss him as trifling, insincere, or childish.

Here Grandma would stop her story and gaze at us piercingly. "You children wouldn't marry someone who isn't serious, would you now? And certainly not an unbeliever?"

"Oh, no, of course not, Grandma."

My father's advisor had more advice for him. "It is rare to have one kind of mother and a daughter who follows a completely different path. The apple doesn't fall far from the tree. Look for sincere faith," he said, "and dedication to God, so that the Holy Spirit can work in her."

Papa worried and prayed, and his parents helped him in defining the qualities he wanted in a wife. She should be modest in her behavior and dress, and involved in ministry. In late summer of 1958 his thoughts lingered on one particular girl he'd observed in a large church in Zaporozhe, even though they'd had scant contact. Papa decided to speak to her at the next possible opportunity.

This girl eventually became my mother, Valentina. One Sunday in August of 1958, Valentina and her friend, Nadya, decided to fast and pray, asking God to send them husbands in His time, or to let them know if they were to remain single. They were about twenty-five years old, already considered old maids, and had no prospects of marriage. The next day, a young man proposed to Nadya. Mama had to wait a little longer—until that Thursday.

On August 28 my father proposed to Valentina. They knew each other slightly, but she had never thought much about him. She asked him for two days to pray about his proposal, and accepted him on Saturday. In a way, I don't think Papa's mother ever completely approved of his choice of a wife. At the time she met my father, Mama's clothes were cut a bit more fashionably than my grandmother thought was seemly.

Less than a month later, Papa and Mama officially registered their marriage, and on September 21 they were married in the church. Papa still talks of how his family tried to talk him out of marrying Mama on their wedding day, because her face was so white. "Surely she has TB or pneumonia!" his aunt insisted. Really, Mama was pale from working late the night before preparing food for the wedding guests. Seeing her fatigue, soon after dinner my grandmother sent the newlyweds home, to the house next door my father and grandfather had built. As there were no lights in the yard or in the house, they had to fumble around in the dark to find the bed so they could celebrate their new life together.

Soon after the wedding, the KGB called my father.

"We know your wife," they said. "We know she worked with youth in the church. We haven't bothered her yet. But now you have chosen her. Know we are watching you both."

These threats were no surprise to anyone. Everyone understood the Communist Party's reasoning. Anyone who is religious is not wholeheartedly for the government. If someone is not for the government, they must be an enemy. My grandfather, trying to protect my father, made a large metal chest for my parents as a wedding gift. Having filled it with much of his Christian literature, a large portion of it banned Christian books and magazine articles he had laboriously copied by hand from copies passed from believer to believer, Papa buried the chest in the yard. The rest of his collection of literature was kept in the tool shed, in a concealed space between the ceiling and the attic floor. The KGB never found Papa's forbidden literature, because it was kept hidden, except when he was actually reading a book or magazine. Had any of this literature been found, Papa could have been fined or imprisoned. This is one story my parents never told us until the Gorbachev years brought a little more freedom.

CHAPTER 6

A POWERFUL EARTHQUAKE

All contemporary religions, churches, and all types of religious organizations, Marxism forever looks upon as organs of bourgeoisie reaction serving to defend the exploitation and stultifying of the working class.

—Lenin[6]

Since ancient times no one has heard, no ear has perceived, no eye has seen any God besides you, who acts on behalf of those who wait for him.

—Isaiah 64:4

As told by Lena

"OPEN YOUR BOOKS and let's read Mark chapter four," my brother Yakov said. After he read a few verses, Viktor interrupted. "I am going to recite 1 Thessalonians 5:15. 'Make sure that nobody pays back wrong for wrong, but always try to be kind to each other and to everyone else.'" As soon as he finished, my cousin Zoya spoke up. "Let's sing 'Christ Is Risen.'" Giggles interrupted our singing, and soon there was more laughter than music. Playing church service, imitating our elders, was one of our favorite games when my family visited other believers.

But involvement with the church, for all of the joy it brought to our lives, brought conflict with the government, a struggle both continual and fierce. In the mid-1960s, the authorities attempted to close the Upper Khortitsa church, knowing the church wasn't obeying all the rules. A delegation of six or seven people arrived in two cars, some in a white Volga, some in a black one. The police came to inspect my grandparents' house, where the services were held, checking documents and searching for prohibited literature. My brother, Yakov, who was about six at the time, remembers seeing fear in our parents' eyes, not knowing they were afraid that Grandpa would be arrested again. Before they left, the police sealed up the area used for the church services. With wide eyes and trembling lips, Yakov asked, "Papa, will we still have services?"

"Did you pray, *sinok*?" Papa asked gently.

When the believers gathered to pray that God would keep the church from being closed, Yakov and three-year-old Viktor joined them. "Please, God," they begged. "Give us our church." Soon after, the officials relented and services resumed.

As we grew older, we spent more time in church because our father was a presbyter, which is what the Baptists call pastors. Papa had started preaching in 1956, and began counseling people, writing articles on spiritual topics, and building a reputation as an influential brother. Some years later, my father was appointed a deacon, which involved a great deal of teaching and preaching.

In 1969, the Upper Khortitsa church chose my father to be its presbyter. The government bureaucrats, having wrangled with my father during his service on the regional commission of the Baptist Union, knew he was not going to be easy for them to control, and refused to confirm his new position. Papa and the other brothers countered this opposition, remaining unified in their stand against the authorities. Finally, in 1970, the church leaders received the official documents stating Papa was recognized as presbyter. Only then did they hold the ceremony of laying hands on my father, confirming that he would now assume his full responsibilities, including the right to perform baptisms or weddings. Then he began to travel with Yakov Dukhonchenko, who was senior presbyter for the Zaporozhe *oblast*, visiting churches all around the region. Then Papa was selected to be one of the very few men allowed to study in the one Bible School in the entire Soviet Union. For two years he traveled frequently to Moscow for his studies.

By this time, my parents had four children: my brother Yakov, born in 1959, Viktor in 1962, me in 1966, and Veniamin in 1969. Their dearest hope was that all of their children would grow up as believers. They had no idea how costly a struggle it would be.

For twenty-five years the Upper Khortitsa church worshipped in the small barn attached to my grandparent's house, with only a few interruptions during the Great Patriotic War. Soon the barn, which was no more than about seven feet by ten feet, became too small for the number of believers gathering. They added a veranda, then a second, and a third, and still they didn't have enough space.

Then they decided to rebuild the barn, making it bigger and square in shape, which would be more comfortable for a meeting. My grandfather Gavril prepared all the documents for home renovation, and once they were approved, began the work. Suddenly the authorities notified him that the renovations were considered building a church and that was forbidden.

That decree precipitated the clash my father describes as a "powerful earthquake." The police came and halted further work. The ProKom (Professional Committee) of the Commission for the Affairs of Religious Cults summoned my father and grandfather to their office, and threatened to take the house away and give it to the kindergarten next door. While the whole church labored in prayer, the church leaders started to obtain all kinds of documents granting permission for the work from different government agencies. Since they were having trouble with the local authorities, they worked their way up through the bureaucracy. Some of the brothers traveled to Kiev to get documents from the agencies that had responsibility for all of Ukraine. Others went to Moscow to the national level of the Commission for the Affairs of Religious Cults. Normally submissive members of a small legally registered church battled for months, shaking the system from top to bottom. In the end, the authorities in Moscow intervened, and decided the only way to calm the situation was to allow the renovations to proceed.

Even after the new meeting room was completed, the believers were still cramped for space, so they began to search for a suitable house to buy. Every time they found one, either the fire department or some other agency would interfere, with excuses about fire safety or building codes. For one reason or another, the authorities blocked the acquisition of ten different houses, either forbidding the purchase, or compelling the owners not to sell.

Finally they found a house that belonged to a Pentecostal, recently returned from serving a ten-year prison sentence for his faith. The authorities' usual tactics of persuasion and threats were useless, because the Pentecostal was so opposed to the Soviet powers he didn't listen to anything they said. He told my father he didn't care if they sent him back to prison.

In this way my father and grandfather bought the house at 219 Ulyanova Street. All the renovations were completed by the church members in their spare time. For two years Papa worked his shift at the factory, and then put in a few hours working on the church, in addition to fulfilling his duties as presbyter. Many others, after a full day of work at a factory or office, spent their evenings laboring to renovate the building. The believers officially moved in on Christmas Day, 1976, and dedicated the building on the 9th of

February, 1977. The authorities, appalled that a church was located on a street named after Lenin's family, intensified their scrutiny of the young church leaders in the Zaporozhe *oblast*, who were proving to be highly effective in attracting people to the church.

CHAPTER 7

OUR ILLEGAL SUNDAY SCHOOL

Religion is poison—protect your children.
—Soviet poster, 1930[7]

Jesus said, "Let the little children come to me, and do not hinder them, for the kingdom of heaven belongs to such as these."
—Matthew 19:14

As told by Lena

MAMA SAT IN the front row, Venya and me on her lap, Yasha and Viktor on the floor at her feet. Even when we were small, Mama led us by the hand each week to church services. Many times in the middle of the service, Mama would suddenly lean forward and whisper to Yasha to take us all home. Each time, he escorted us out the back door and across the yard to our house. Within a few minutes one or the other of our grandparents showed up and stayed with us until our parents returned home.

Only years later did we find out what was going on. During every church service, one of the members kept watch, looking for people approaching who were not church members. If a stranger drew near, the lookout passed the word to Mama and she sent us home. Everyone knew that the government sent schoolteachers to visit churches to note which children were present. If any children were caught at church, there would be big fines, or worse.

The government never ceased its efforts to control religious activities. Communism and its promises to create a worker's paradise on earth were to replace any other religion, and all other faiths had to defer to it. During the 1930s they had tried to do this by terror. After easing up a bit during the war years and after, a new wave of persecution started in the early 1960s, and this time the authorities were more subtle and clever.

My father will never forget the day in 1961 when his uncle, Grigorii Ivanovich Utyuzh, who was the presbyter of the Upper Khortitsa church at the time, called him and the other leaders of the church together for a meeting. They gathered together in the long, narrow barn attached to my grandparents' house where church services were held. Grigorii Ivanovich said to them, "Here is a letter that came from our brothers, our Union* leaders, and they say we must obey." Then he read to them from the letter: presbyters no longer have the right to preach in churches other than their own, cannot make an appeal for repentance or preach about the second coming of Jesus, as well as many other restrictions.

My father and most of the other leaders were young then, and wondered what to do. "Should we follow all these rules?" one asked. "Look, they even say children are not allowed to attend services."

"And are we really supposed to follow this rule, limiting the number of baptisms of people aged 18 to 30?"

---

* All registered Baptist churches were required to belong to the Union of Baptist and Evangelical Christian Churches. Those who did not join were considered to be illegal churches, and would be refused registration by the Commission for the Affairs of Religious Cults.

"How could our leaders have agreed to this?" another asked. "That we will no longer have orchestras, pianos, or other musical instruments?"

"It's clear to me," my father said, "that they are aiming a lot of these new rules where they think it will hurt us most. They know that if young people are not brought up in the church, it will be easier for them to be made into atheists."

"So, brothers," said Grigorii Ivanovich. "Shall we follow the lead of the Council of Churches?"

As a result of the Instructional Letter, a new organization formed calling themselves the Council of Churches. This group claimed the Union leaders had compromised with the communist government to the point of betraying the teachings of Christ, and that believers should refuse to accept the Instructional Letter. They did have some truth on their side. There were churches that stopped all children's and youth activities and even presbyters who encouraged parents to not teach their own children anything about God at home. The Council of Churches boldly stood up to the communist authorities and demanded the religious freedom that the Soviet constitution promised, but had never delivered. Many churches left the Union to join the Council of Churches, and that painful division remains to this day.

"In my opinion, no," said one of the deacons. "The Council of Churches is just making a difficult situation more dangerous for everyone. By openly breaking the law, causing all kinds of public uproar, they are giving people the idea that believers are troublemakers and that we deserve the government's punishment. Now the authorities have an excuse to repress us more."

"On the other hand, brothers," Grigorii Ivanovich said, "remember that the new rules will be strictly enforced. See the list? For every violation there is a fine. Or the authorities can take away the church's registration, lock the doors, and forbid us to meet."

"I still don't understand," said the deacon. "How could the Union leaders have agreed to this travesty, this betrayal?"

"I can tell you," Grigorii Ivanovich answered. "Our leaders reasoned that as long as the churches didn't lose their registrations, we could continue to hold services. Maybe this wave of persecution will die down. In the meantime, we do whatever it takes to keep the churches open."

"I don't know. You can walk around a snake, but not get away from it," the deacon answered.

"So what should we do, brothers?" asked another deacon. "Should we openly break the law, and join the Council of Churches? Any church that leaves the Union loses its registration, and church building, and right to hold services."

"You are right," my father put in. "And now they are holding illegal services in the forest, or wherever they can find to meet."

"Maybe it wouldn't be a bad thing to leave the Union," one of the deacons said. "After all, this was something the government forced on us toward the end of the war. Form a union, all you Protestant churches, and you can be legally registered and hold services. That was what they told us. None of the Baptist churches had any objections to forming a Union with the Evangelical Christians, since their doctrines are almost the same as ours. We wanted a union with them for a long time anyway. But to coerce us into a union with the Pentecostals! That was a different story. The authorities just wanted to get us fighting among ourselves."

"They knew that the new All-Union Council of Evangelical Christian and Baptist Churches would be easier for them to control than several different groups. And now we see the results of their plan!"

"There is another thing that troubles me," said Grigorii Ivanovich. "The Union leaders called me and told me that all the other presbyters have already consented to these conditions, so we need to as well. Surely we are not the only ones who haven't determined what to do yet."

"Wait, brothers!" exclaimed another deacon. "That can't be right. I was just talking with one of the presbyters in Zaporozhe. He asked me why we had already agreed to these new rules."

"But we haven't!" several voices cried out.

"I told him that. He said one of the Union leaders in Moscow called him and told him he was the last one to decide. That all the other presbyters have promised to comply with the Instructional Letter."

There was a moment of stunned silence as this news sunk in.

"Has it really come to this?" the first deacon asked, speaking slowly, as if his own words made a rancid taste in his mouth, like he'd been drinking sour milk. "That our Union leaders have compromised themselves so much that they would lie to us? That they would try to pressure us to do what they must know is not pleasing to God?"

"Our leaders have betrayed us, brothers." The deacon held his head in his hands. "What are we to do? There seems to be only two alternatives: to be weak and compromise, or rebel and risk the consequences."

My father slowly leafed through the pages of his Bible, as if to find an answer just by touching the words. "I can think of only one thing: that we ask God for wisdom, for His Word promises that He grants wisdom to anyone who asks for it."

The five of them got on their knees on the worn wooden floor. After over an hour of prayer and discussion, they came to a decision.

"So we are agreed, to take a middle road," Grigorii Ivanovich said. "Our guide will be the Word of God."

"Yes, the Bible says we must obey government authority," my father said. "And that we will do, as long as the government does not command us to do something against God's Word."

"We will continue to teach our children about God at home, and try to have youth meetings and Bible study for the children. We'll find some way to do it."

"If we get caught, we will pay the fines."

"We just might be able to do this," one of the deacons added. "After all, we are not in the capital, in the center, not so noticeable to the authorities."

"And brothers," Grigorii Ivanovich said, "we also agree that we are not going to talk publicly about our disobedience. We will make it clear to the members of the church that the open rebellion of the Council of Churches is not the path we are choosing. We will obey the government in everything that does not contradict God's Word. Otherwise, we will not compromise our faith."

Receiving such wisdom from God for that decision was only the beginning. They knew that God was guiding them, because they all felt peace in their hearts, despite knowing that many trials lay before them. The increased pressure caused by the Instructional Letter and other regulations that came after it called for greater discernment among the church leaders. Letters arrived from the KGB, demanding a list of all the members of the church. Other letters from the Commission for the Affairs of Religious Cults dictated that persons under sixteen were forbidden to attend church services. My father and the other local leaders would read the latest letter and pray. Then they would lay it aside as if it were advice written to someone else and act as they always had done. Knowing they were obeying God's Word, they didn't mind paying big fines when they were caught in violation of the rules.

Because of all of the rules imposed by the Instructional Letter, we didn't attend regular Sunday school. For many years, one of the women in the church, risking fines or imprisonment, organized meetings for children at her house, teaching us songs about Jesus and His love for us. We recited poems about God, vying for the chance to perform. She asked the boys to read from the Scriptures, just like the presbyters or deacons did. And she always served us some kind of sweet treat.

The church found other ways to hold children's programs. If my cousin, Zoya, for example, had a birthday, there would be a big party for all the children in the church. Mama dressed us up and gave us a gift to take. She sent us off to the party in pairs, instructing us to take different routes, so as not to attract attention. Everyone knew that one of the neighbors would report an illegal religious gathering of children. Zoya's parents, or whoever was having the party, made sure their child's birth certificate was on hand. When the police came to break up the meeting, the parents presented the birth certificate to prove it was a legitimate birthday party. Once that interruption was over, we listened to Bible stories and learned about our faith.

Teaching us about God wasn't the end goal; my parents wanted to make sure we loved God and trusted Him. As we would learn later, trusting God was the only way to overcome our trials.

CHAPTER 8

PRAYERS THAT INSULT GOD

Stalin collects dead souls for the lack of living ones.
—Leon Trotsky[8]

Do not be afraid of what you are about to suffer....Be faithful, even to the point of death, and I will give you the crown of life.
—Revelation 2:10

As told by Lena

"PUT THE BAG away, Mama, put it away!" Just one glance at Mama's blue and green patterned shopping bag started the spinning in my head and the churning in my stomach, as if I were seasick. I had horrible pain in my stomach and threw up every time I ate. Mama, trying to keep me warm, fixed me a place to sleep in the kitchen, close to our wood burning stove.

My parents, seeking answers, asked doctor after doctor why I couldn't eat, and even put me in the hospital for six months. No one could determine the cause of my illness; every attempt at a cure was like shooting arrows at a stone. Finally the doctors sent me home to die.

Papa and Mama had wanted a daughter so much, after having two boys. Now, at four years old, I was dying. My parents prayed every day for my healing until they realized their prayers had to change. "Lord, we give our Lena to You. You gave her to us. If You want to take her, then give us the strength to bear the pain." Papa took Mama by the hand. "Valya, you know that nothing can separate us from the love of God. Nothing."

They watched in agony as I wasted away, growing weaker and weaker. Through her tears Mama assured me that God loved me and would always take care of me. One day, one of the brothers in the church told Papa about his father, who was an herbalist. After taking some of the herbs he prescribed, I gradually got better. God didn't answer their prayers right away, but drew my parents closer to Him through the process.

In later years, I wondered how Mama could trust God so much, even when she thought her only daughter would die. All during that time she never questioned God. Only when I was older did I learn how God had demonstrated His never-ending love for her.

Mama was born in 1933, right in the middle of the Great Famine in Ukraine. Stalin was determined to get rid of all private property, especially farmland, so he decided to collectivize all of the farms. The government thought that collective farms would be more efficient requiring fewer people to work on them. This would leave more labor available for factories or grandiose building projects. Stalin didn't have much trouble collectivizing farms in Russia, because many of the villages had used some form of group farming for centuries, usually as part of noblemen's estates. But the Ukrainians farmed independently and didn't want to give their land or livestock to the state.

Each year the government raised the grain quotas the farmers had to turn over to the state. Eventually, the quotas were so high, the farmers didn't have any grain reserves to plant the next year. Stalin's law stated that no grain could be given to the people until the quota was filled. In protest, farmers buried their grain or threw it in the river rather than turn it over. When government agents descended on a village, they seized everything, even the grain the peasants had hidden, leaving the people with nothing to eat. Gleaning ten grains from a field earned a ten year prison sentence.

To try to get the farmers on his side, Stalin announced that a class of rich peasants he called *kulaks* was responsible for all the problems on the farms. This word means "fist" in Russian; this label insinuated that the kulaks used their fists or other force to oppress the poorer peasants. Anyone who owned three or four cows, or two horses, employed more than one worker, or had any kind of status or influence was branded a kulak. Stalin called on the peasants to engage in class struggle against the oppressive kulaks, who were undermining the voluntary movement of collectivizing farms.

The supposed kulaks were rounded up and shot or put in prison. Some were shipped in cattle cars to Siberia, and others sent to work camps. Almost a third of those deported died. The land and livestock of anyone arrested were seized. The remaining farmers slaughtered their cows, pigs, and sheep rather than give in.

During 1932 and 1933, six million people died of starvation in Ukraine, the area once called the breadbasket of Europe. At the peak of the famine, tens of thousands of people died every day, their bodies thrown into huge pits. By the end of 1933, so many farmers of the Zaporozhe region had perished or been shipped away that the authorities had to bring in new people to re-settle the villages and work the collective farms.

My mother, Valentina, was born in the middle of this terrible time. She was the youngest of fourteen children, of whom only four lived to adulthood. Her family subsisted on grass, herbs, whatever they could find. Even the smallest children had to help in the search for food. Valentina survived only because of her older sister, who lived in an area where the famine was not so severe. This sister sent *sukhariki* (pieces of toasted bread), which were saved carefully for

Valentina, as they were the only food she could eat. Many others were not so lucky. People would spend all day looking for food, and when they found nothing, some of them ate those who had already died.

My mother considers her survival an example of how the Lord has cared for her from the day of her birth. There were many believers who starved to death or were taken away, but through all of their ordeals their faith never wavered. They knew that whatever their circumstances, God would be with them. Live or die, they would trust Him, because His Son had died for them. Because she had seen God preserve her life, she wanted to live completely for Him. Whatever her circumstances, whatever pain came to her in life, she would trust Him. She knew that her life, and the lives of all she loved, belonged to God, and He could be trusted to work for good in all circumstances.

Sometimes it wasn't so easy for Mama to trust. In 1951, my mother moved to Zaporozhe to study sewing on the machine. By this time she was already eighteen and had received her internal passport, the standard identification document that listed place of residence, military service, higher education, marriages, and children. Citizens had to register their address with the police, and couldn't move without notifying the authorities.

After she graduated, Mama began working in a tailor's shop in Zaporozhe, sewing men's clothing. Once her co-workers learned of her faith, they harassed her, mocked her, and threatened her with the loss of her job. All my mother could think was that if she were fired for her faith, she'd never be able to find another job. Then what would she do? After having spent the money and time to learn to be a seamstress, it would be so shameful to return to the village and herd cows. Having already made many friends among the youth in the church, she was happy with her life.

One day, the head tailor said to her, "I want to meet with you tomorrow at the consular office. After that meeting, you will no longer work here." As he wrote down why he was firing her, he explained that if she agreed not to attend church, then the company would look at the situation from a completely different perspective. If she was stubborn, then she would be let go and have this all written in her labor book. When she tried to get a new job, a prospective employer would review her labor book, and would discover why she'd been fired.

In later years, Mama described this as one of the scariest times of her life. Even if she had to return to the village as a cowherd, she knew that God would not abandon her. But she didn't want to give up the life she had in Zaporozhe. Preparing for the meeting, she prayed and fasted with her girlfriends.

On March 6, 1953, at ten in the morning, my mother walked into the tailor's shop expecting to be fired. Instead, she found all her coworkers crying. Only then did she learn that Stalin, the Great Leader, the Beloved Comrade, had died.

They never summoned her to the consular office, and the meeting to discuss firing her was never held. During the first few years after Stalin's death the persecution eased a little. A few churches opened, and schools and workplaces were slightly friendlier to believers. Mama was able to keep her job and live quietly for the next few years. She didn't believe that God killed Stalin just to save her job. Instead, she knew that He caused the tailor to put off taking any action just long enough. "You see, my children," she would say to us, "God knows your struggles. He loves you and will help you through them."

When I was about six, Mama's faith was severely tested again. Pain burned in her left breast. Swelling to twice its normal size, it turned green and black and smelled like rotting garbage. Our normally energetic mother was tired all the time and losing weight. Venya, my youngest brother, was only three, and it was getting harder and harder for Mama to care for her four children, to cook and clean and work in the garden. The doctors told her a tumor was growing, and that a mastectomy was her only chance to save her life.

Mama dreaded the thought of surgery. For the next year we tried every treatment people suggested. Rub the breast with garlic. Rub the breast with urine. The whole house smelled of urine for a month. We tried different herbs and the skin of a beet. No matter how strange the remedy, Mama tried them all, without success.

Constantly worrying about her children, about leaving her little ones, she barely considered her own health. The whole church was praying; all the churches in the *oblast* were praying; many people were fasting for Mama's recovery. We knew that without God, there really was no hope. Mama prayed and prayed to God to save her, thinking that without a mother, her children would certainly be lost.

One day she realized that such prayers were insulting to God. Did she really believe that God couldn't take care of her children without her? This thought penetrated her doubts like a searchlight pierces the fog. Mama repented, and started asking for strength to face the surgery. God answered by giving her comfort and peace, right to her very core. Even if she were taken now, she could still leave her children with memories of the mother who deeply loved them. Her weak, shriveled hand stroking my hair, with a wan smile on her sunken face, she gently said, "You can see that I am going to die. The pain is not leaving me. Papa and Grandma are here to take care of you, and God will be always with you."

As the pain intensified, Mama finally agreed to surgery. The night before the operation, many of our friends came over to pray for Mama. They gave her into the Lord's hands, asking Him to preserve her life. We four children stood behind, holding up our hands in prayer, praying in unison, like a choir, "Lord, leave us our Mama!" We were so scared we couldn't say anything else.

When Mama came home a week or so later, we heard what had happened. The oncologist told Mama they were prepared to remove the whole breast. First they performed a biopsy, to see what they were dealing with. All they could find was pus, just some kind of infection contained in a sac. No tumor. They were completely perplexed by the outcome. "You are a happy woman," the doctor said. "Already the infection is gone. We don't understand where it came from, but it is gone. What is different about you? Who are you?"

"Yes, I am happy," Mama told her. "God took care of everything."

There was great rejoicing in the church, not just because Mama's life had been spared. There was gratitude for how God used her illness to strengthen her faith, and to show the doctors in the hospital who didn't know Him just what He can do to save those who place their faith in Him. While my brothers and I envied the strong faith of our parents, we didn't know then that God would give us the same kind of faith in the same way, by taking us through suffering into joy.

CHAPTER 9

GIVE US THIS DAY OUR DAILY BREAD

Religion is the enemy of industrialization.
—Soviet poster, 1930s[9]

Whatever you do, work at it with all your heart, as working for the Lord, not for men.
—Colossians 3:23

As told by Lena

"IF YOU WANT chicken for dinner tonight," she shouted, "go kill that chicken yourself!" Our next door neighbor was tired of always having to be the one to kill the chickens. All the kids within earshot came running to watch. Her husband slowly walked into his backyard, hanging his head. He caught a chicken, and stood with one foot on each wing, holding it to the ground. Closing his eyes, pausing to put off the distasteful task, wincing, he sliced off the chicken's head, jumping backwards to avoid being sprayed by its blood. The headless chicken flapped its wings and flew around the yard in an erratic circle. For us kids that was so funny, such wonderful entertainment, watching the neighbor who was too scared to kill the chicken properly, yet he let it fly around without a head.

It may seem heartless to laugh at the headless chicken, but we all understood that the animals we kept weren't just pets; they were a source of food. In one back corner of our yard stood wooden pens where we kept ducks, pigs, and rabbits, and our outhouse. In front of these were the chicken coop and summer kitchen, where Mama cooked in hot weather when she didn't want to heat up the house. Apple trees grew nearby, providing some shade on hot days. In the front corner was our well, and next to it, the place we kept coal. On either side of the driveway that ran from the street to my grandparents' house sprawled two large vegetable gardens where we grew potatoes, cabbages, tomatoes, cucumbers, onions, and carrots. In the middle of the other half of the yard, across the driveway from the summer kitchen, stood our house. A boisterous profusion of gooseberry and raspberry bushes took over most of the rest of that side of the yard, with a few apple and apricot trees lining the front, along the street. There was always plenty for my brothers and me to do, hauling water or coal into the house, caring for the animals, or tending the gardens.

These activities weren't necessary just because Mama and Papa thought gardening would be a good hobby for us. While we never went hungry, our family was poor, as we all knew, because of Papa's faith. After graduating from the *teknikum* in 1953, my father went from place to place looking for a job, but no one was hiring young metalworkers. He tried everywhere he could think of, and finally appealed to his cousin Shura. Some years earlier, she had turned her back on Christianity and joined the Communist party, and was now the assistant personnel director of a large factory.

Through Shura, my father was hired as a master, or lead technician. When another worker, the secretary of the Communist Youth League, found out that a Baptist had been given such a responsible job, he complained and forged letters full of accusations against my father. He charged Papa with crimes like trying to sabotage the factory, or worse, proselytizing the other workers. Knowing the accusations were completely false, my father tried to stay out of the conflict. Then another person in the department spoke up, saying that as a member of the Communist Party, he could not possibly work under a Baptist.

By this time, persecution had eased up a little. While some people were still put in prison or labor camps for their faith, the government was mostly using other means to intimidate believers such as making sure they were only given menial jobs, never got promoted, or were fired.

And so it was with my father. After only six months on the job, he was let go. His cousin was reprimanded for putting a Baptist in a position of responsibility. From that time on, my father would find a job only to get fired a short while later for being a Baptist. He would then start somewhere else, and again lose his job. In one year he was fired five times for his faith.

Finally, he approached a transformer factory where the boss was a secret church member. He gave this man a signed statement saying he wouldn't ask for any kind of technical responsibilities, even though he was well-qualified. Under these terms he was hired to be a metal worker, and they let him work there from 1956 to 1977. Since he was working at a low level, he received low wages as well. When he was hired, Papa was grateful to have a job, but along with his family grew his frustration with the unjust system that condemned believers to the most menial jobs. Trusting God to provide day by day strengthened his faith and taught him to surrender to God's will; the pain of these experiences helped him years later to help my brothers through similar trials.

CHAPTER 10

RECEIVE ALL FROM GOD'S HAND

[T]he Communist Party, which relies on the only true concept of the world, the scientific concept, cannot with regard to religion adopt a neutral and indifferent attitude concerning an ideology having nothing in common with science.
—Nikita Khrushchev[10]

The eyes of the Lord keep watch over knowledge, but he frustrates the words of the unfaithful.
—Proverbs 22:12

As told by Lena

WAVING PAPA OFF to work, Mama fastened the gate to the yard every day so that when her four children woke up they couldn't run into the street. She and Papa agreed that we should have as little contact as possible with unbelieving kids. We played the same games as the other kids; the only difference was we could only play with the children of other believers, which offended some of the neighbors. Knowing this, the authorities tried to use us to influence Papa, to pressure him into adapting his ministry to be more acceptable to the Party officials. Isolating children from too much contact with other kids, from society, was considered to be unhealthy, harmful to children, and anti-Soviet, and when coupled with dangerous religious teaching, was almost as bad as child abuse. At one point the neighbors lodged a complaint, citing a time when Veniamin cried out while being spanked, saying that the Brynzas were overly strict with their children and punished them too harshly. My parents knew that these complaints were raised by people who had been bribed to do it, as some other neighbors came and asked if there was some kind of "compromise" that could be reached, maybe letting us play with the non-believing kids once in awhile. My parents just couldn't agree. They knew that by limiting our contact with non-believing kids, they were protecting us from influences that might undermine our faith. As we got older, we would have to face the pressure to conform to the world on our own. As long as they were able, Mama and Papa protected us as much as they could.

When asked in later years to explain why they were so adamant about keeping outside influences to a minimum for as long as they could, Papa often responded, "To understand those times, and how we responded, you have to understand the history of the Baptist Churches in Ukraine." Then he would explain.

Soon after the German Mennonites came to Ukraine and started handing out Bibles to their Ukrainian neighbors, it wasn't long before the Ukrainians started to compare what they read with the Orthodox teaching. They found many examples where the Gospels state one thing, and the Orthodox Church teaches something completely different. One debate arose over the question of baptism. In Scripture, it seemed, only adults who had come to faith were baptized. But the Orthodox Church baptized infants. Many of the Ukrainians who were meeting to study the Bible decided to break away from the Orthodox Church and start their own churches, adopting much of the Mennonite teaching. Others wanted to remain within the Orthodox Church, but when they were discouraged from reading the Bible, they also left. Considering infant baptism to be against God's Word, these new churches only baptized adults, so the name "Baptists" came into use.

Another Bible-reading movement in the Russian Empire started among the aristocracy of St. Petersburg. Many foreigners living there in the capital of the Empire did not attend Catholic or Lutheran churches, which intrigued the Russian elites, who wanted to know what this other form of religious belief was all about. From this grew a movement of seeking God, of seeking a more personal faith in Jesus Christ. The seekers invited foreign preachers to come and teach. Meetings were held in the homes of aristocrats, and in keeping with Jesus' teaching, these were open to all, regardless of social position. So gathering in palaces were government ministers, counts and princesses, dishwashers and street cleaners, listening to the Word of God and worshipping together.

This northern movement faced its own persecution, and even some of the aristocrats were fined, imprisoned, or sent into exile for teaching differently than the Orthodox Church. Still, it spread and grew into what became the Evangelical Christian Church. These two groups of Protestant churches survived much persecution under the tsars and the communist regime, and even managed to have some legal recognition. But there were very few years from the time Protestants came to the Russian Empire in the late 1700s that believers were allowed to worship as they pleased or to bring their children up in their own faith. For nearly two hundred years, believers in the Soviet Union had experienced living with persecution, and my parents knew the tidal wave of atheistic propaganda that was waiting for us once we started school. All school children were under constant pressure to conform to the religion of the day, whether Orthodoxy or Communism. My parents, knowing what lay ahead for us, wanted to have a few years to allow the roots of our faith to grow, without anyone trying to talk us out of it.

The government also used other means to discourage young people from staying in the church. The laws varied over the years: at times no one under the age of twenty-five could be baptized, at others the cutoff was thirty. This meant a young person had to wait many years to become an official church member and be able to receive communion. If someone did persevere in their faith until they could be legally baptized, they had to write a letter to the church requesting baptism. Presbyters were required to submit a list of people who were baptized to the *oblast*, or Regional, Professional Committee (ProKom) of the Department of Affairs of Religious Cults, which would immediately give a copy to the Communist Party, which would in turn notify employers, schools, universities, and places where people lived. People would be made to wait two or three years to be baptized, so employers and coworkers or professors and fellow students had plenty of time to try to convince the person to give up the idea of baptism.

My parents had been through these trials themselves. At the time Mama was baptized in her youth, it was illegal to baptize someone of her age. Because the presbyter saw how desperately Mama wanted to be baptized, he agreed to baptize her and five others secretly, one night down by the river. Somehow the authorities found out, and removed him from his post.

Papa was baptized a few years later, in 1954. The presbyter agreed to baptize him, but only if it could be done officially, publicly announced in the church. Once someone was baptized, they would never again be fully accepted as part of the group at work or school, or advance at their job. As a result, those who were shallow believers left the church, while others were baptized illegally in secret. Every time Papa told us of his baptism, he emphasized that he had waited five years, praying and trusting God, and was prepared for the repercussions.

Legal baptisms were usually performed secretly, in an effort to evade the KGB's thugs, who were sometimes sent to interrupt the service, violent thugs who administered threats or beatings. During the years of communism, nearly all baptisms were done in remote areas in the middle of the night or before dawn.

Early one Sunday morning, my father walked to a deserted spot on the Dniepr River with just the presbyter and one witness. Finally he would be baptized, his deepest longing fulfilled! His joy was so great he barely noticed the chill in the early morning air, or the icy waters of the river, still cold in early June. Because he was baptized officially, all the factories knew of his faith. It was no surprise to him that he had so much trouble finding a job.

While there was much of my parents' and grandparents' lives we didn't know until we were older, they openly shared with us their love for God and each other. At first, when we heard the stories of believers who had endured terrible difficulties, who God saved miraculously when they were starving or in prison, we thought of these people as heroes. We focused on the drama, the ways God saved people. Reflecting on what we learned in school—about the Red Army that saved our people from the Nazis, and Lenin, who saved us from the oppression of the tsar, and even the pig that saved Ukraine—we realized that many others put their faith in someone or something other than God, and because of that, we were different.

As we grew older, we began to see that God didn't help everyone in the same way. Some were saved by miracles; others endured, trusting God for the next day, the next step, the next breath. During the famine and the terror, some were saved from arrest, or found food when they needed it—while others did not. Yet, even those dying of starvation or tortured in a prison camp, received a peace that couldn't be explained in human terms. For those who had faith, God gave the comfort of knowing that even if they didn't survive the current crisis, they would have eternity with Him in heaven. They understood that all things come to them through God's hands, so that they could know Him and His love for them in a much deeper way, to help them become more like Christ, and so that many would see His glory. If their suffering brought others to God, they rejoiced that God used them. And they trusted God's promise that whatever they lost in this life for the sake of their faith, God would restore many times over in heaven. That we would learn these lessons for ourselves, at the cost of much pain, never occurred to us when we were children.

CHAPTER 11

I MEET THE BONE EATER

The most important phase of eliminating religion lies in the education of children.
—Banner in Museum of the History of Atheism and Religion, Leningrad[11]

Train a child in the way he should go, and when he is old he will not turn from it.
—Proverbs 22:6

As told by Lena

MAMA CAREFULLY PULLED my long hair back and pinned it with a white bow almost half the size of my head. At last I was old enough to go to school. For years I'd watched Yakov and Viktor set off, dressed in their school uniforms: dark brown pants, white or blue shirts, envious as if they'd been given a gift I was denied. Now it was finally my turn. Mama and Papa didn't wholeheartedly share my eagerness, knowing they could no longer shield me completely from the outside world. Mama gripped my hand as she walked me to school on the first day. September 1st was a holiday in Soviet schools, celebrating the beginning of another year. Mama's expression as we walked along the dirt road looked more like she was escorting me to a battle. Which, of course, she was.

As we approached Elementary School Number 81, a tall, two-story red brick schoolhouse constructed by Germans over half a century earlier, fear weakened my knees as my shyness muffled my excitement. I clenched Mama's hand tighter, relieved that she would be the one to find my new teacher and do all the talking.

In Soviet schools, children had the same teachers for the first three years. To my relief, I was assigned to Valentina Feodorovna, who was not a complete stranger, as she had taught both my older brothers. Over the years, Valentina managed to find a common language with our parents. Her husband's grandmother was an Orthodox believer, so she had some sympathy for believers.

Like the other girls, I wore the standard uniform: a dark brown dress, with a white collar and cuffs. Over it went a black apron for everyday, white for holidays. Starting in third grade there was a required addition to the uniform: the red scarf of the Young Pioneers, the Communist version of Boy or Girl Scouts. Some years earlier, my parents prayed with other believers to decide whether to allow their children to join or not, eventually concluding that this was a choice for each family to make. My parents felt it was better for their children to join the Pioneers, wear the red scarf, and participate in the activities, since we were already seen as dangerously different from other kids. My brothers and I learned to take our Pioneer scarves out of our pockets and put them on when needed. We understood that all the Pioneer teachings about atheism and communism were meaningless, and we simply conformed outwardly.

Those first three years of my education passed peacefully enough, largely due to Valentina Feodorovna's benevolence. In fourth grade the routine changed. We had different teachers for each subject, with a main teacher who would oversee all of our work. This main teacher was the one who was most important to please.

When Yakov started fourth grade, he was assigned to a teacher who was equally strict with everybody, believers and non-believers alike. Viktor's teacher was a third cousin of ours; not a believer, but sympathetic. I ended up with a martinet named Olga Kostorezova. Olga had short iron gray permed hair, was a little heavy with a thin sharp face, and usually wore drab brown clothes. She moved in nervous jerks, like a chicken pecking at the ground. By the middle of the first day I found out that she yelled at the kids in her class all the time. The next day I learned that she loathed Christians. Often during lessons, whether it was history or mathematics, Olga asked "Where is God?" I slithered down into my chair to shield myself from the smirks of my classmates as she answered her own question saying, "He's not here." If I did my lessons badly, she would rake my face with her eyes and ask, "Is that how your church teaches you to study? Is that how your parents teach you? Is that how God teaches you?" It was humiliating to be the target of her caustic inquiries.

If something disappointing happened, like our class lost a game to another one, Olga was as quick to assign blame as a dog is to bark at a squirrel. "It's because Lena was lazy and only wanted to pray a little."

She would make me stand while she mocked me, saying "Lena, have you thought about when you will be in heaven? You will look down on us frying in hell. Will you put salt and pepper on us?"

Illness stimulated no sympathy. "Did you pray? You must not have made your offering to God."

"What if my son fell in love with you? What would you say to him?" This was a hard one. I knew her son was in prison, and thought maybe that was why she was so angry. But how to answer her question?

If I didn't answer, she pressed me. "Why are you quiet? I am talking to you."

Or, "Show us your knees; we want to see how many hours you have been praying."

I was a good target for her because I was too shy to answer back; I would just stand quietly, feeling beaten in my spirit. "She's got the right name," I often thought. Her last name means "bone eater." I could feel her words cracking and crushing my bones. No matter what she did, I tried to be kind and polite, but she never warmed up to me. Years later when I invited all my former teachers to my wedding, she was one of the few who didn't come.

One day after Olga had given me a particularly hard time, I went home in tears. Mama was busy remaking a coat for Viktor, a used coat she bought since we couldn't afford to buy new. Because of her tailoring experience, she could remake old clothes to fit beautifully. She looked up at me when I slunk into the kitchen, head hanging. "Lena, what's wrong?"

I let my tears answer for me. "Is it your teacher again?" I nodded wordlessly.

"Oh, Lena, I am sorry. I know how you feel. Did I ever tell you how when I was working for the tailor my coworkers forced me to go to the movies with them, even when I said I didn't want to? It was so shocking for me, because I knew that Christians never went to the movies. Even though my boss ordered me to watch the film, I sat there with my eyes closed!" She laughed a little at the memory.

"Mama, I don't want to go back there ever again."

Mama stood up and gave me a hug. "Come into the kitchen with me, Lena. I made some *pirog* this morning. Do you want some?"

We went into the kitchen and I ate some of Mama's *pirog*, comforted by the dense cake and hot tea. "Lena, I know this is hard for you. But you are not the only person to have this problem. This is just part of growing up in a Christian home. This is something we cannot change, something we don't have a choice about."

Then she spoke about others who had suffered. "Your father had it worse in school than you do. Remember? He started first grade twice because the war disrupted the school. At least you have books and papers to use, and don't have to try to memorize what the teacher reads to you. Be grateful that all you have to put up with is a little teasing."

"But, Mama, I am going to have to put up with her for the next five years!"

"Yes, Lena, I know. But the time will pass. God will help you."

Easy for you to say, I thought. *You don't have to face the bone eater every day.*

Years later Mama was proved to be right. When I was in the seventh grade, I repented publicly in the church. Suddenly the situation changed. I was able to meet Olga's sarcasm with confidence instead of succumbing to tears and shame. Once I was no longer a weak target, she backed off. While I had been asking God to change Olga, He was waiting for me to be ready for Him to do some work in me. Once I had fully placed my trust in Him, He changed me so I could have victory over my circumstances.

I didn't know all this, that drab November day. All I knew was that while my parents were sympathetic, they never allowed me to wallow in self-pity. Mama asked me, "Do you think you can just swim through life like a fish, diving in the ocean while the storm rages above? You have to go to school, or the government will take you away from us and send you to an orphanage." She prayed with me, then said, "Think, Lena, about those who've gone on before you. How did Moses feel, hemmed in against the Red Sea? He didn't know how God would save them; he just knew he could trust God. And what did God do? He made a way out." I would think about my grandparents and others whose faith in God had saved them, and was inspired to be brave and faithful like they had been, trusting that God would help me too.

CHAPTER 12

PERSECUTION AT HOME AND WORK

It is impossible for us to give responsible positions to men whose philosophical convictions are diametrically opposed to ours and could not, therefore, sincerely cooperate with us in pushing our program forward.[12]

The fear of the Lord teaches a man wisdom, and humility comes before honor.
—Proverbs 15:33

As told by Lena

ONE OF MY favorite times of the day was when Papa came home from work. My brothers and I waited eagerly, watching the street, looking for him riding toward us on his bicycle. Then we ran to meet him, the one who reached him first would ride back home on the handlebars. And that person was the first to see what Papa was bringing home. If he'd been paid, there would be cookies, or cheese, the Hollandski cheese that Mama loved.

Wherever Papa was, we were sure to find something interesting happening. He wasn't home much when I was growing up because he kept his job at the factory even after he'd been made presbyter of the Upper Khortitsa church when I was three. When he was home, my brothers and I followed him around the yard, watching him work. Whether he was digging potatoes in the garden or making beautiful things out of metal, we just wanted to be near him.

Every day started with prayer, even when we were so small we needed to be set on our knees. No matter how busy he was, every evening he found time to read the Bible to us and teach us about God's love for us. Sometimes Mama got out the seven-string guitar that Papa had bought her, and we sang, praising God together. Our parents tried to create an atmosphere of warmth and love, a haven from the pressures and persecution around us. Looking back, my brothers and I appreciate what our parents did for us, and are grateful for the example they set for us of how to live in a way pleasing to God.

For the most part, my parents tried to keep us at home after school, busy with chores. Any request to go off somewhere in the neighborhood was always refused. And we consistently got the same answer to our question of "why not?" Papa or Mama's reply: "Because we are bringing you up, not the street."

As we grew older, we all got involved with sports at school. Yakov and Viktor were shot putters, I played basketball and volleyball, and all the boys played soccer. But our parents were against it. Fearful of anything that competed for our attention and commitment to the Lord, they prayed that their children wouldn't get involved in sports, that they would remain focused on the Word of God.

My father's travels and Mama's labor around the house did not go unnoticed by the neighbors. Many of the pickets of the green fence that bordered our yard were loose or missing. From time to time Mama picked up a hammer to fix it. The neighbor would say to her, "Valya, you shouldn't repair that fence yourself. Are you really without a husband?"

Another neighbor asked Mama to marry him. "I'm already married," she replied. He retorted, "No, you're not, you're here alone with these children." The neighbors never noticed that when Papa came home at night he dug in the garden or did other work that was too heavy for Mama. She can laugh now at what the neighbors thought, but for a long time she felt the sting of the neighbors' words as if they had hit her with a lash.

Papa paid a higher price. His immediate supervisor at the factory treated him well, but those higher up continually tried to "re-educate" him.

Sometimes they were subtle in the re-education process, sometimes not. Once some photos were taken of the best workers, and my father was among them. The boss hung all the photos of the other workers up in a large display, but not Papa's. "It would be inappropriate to publicly honor a believer," they told him. "Take your photo home and hang it up there if you want to."

Over and over Papa was nominated for awards by his coworkers, only to be disqualified by the political officer of the factory. How could a believer, one opposed to the Soviet system, be awarded a medal? How shameful it would be for the factory to include the name of a Baptist in its list of best workers!

Once, another worker, a man of German descent who was bolder than the rest, came to Papa's defense, protesting the injustice. "You know he is the best worker," he told the political officer.

"We can't possibly honor a Baptist," he replied. "How can we give him a red medal, red for the color of the blood shed in the revolution?" The German worker continued to argue, taking his complaint to the boss.

Finally, the boss appealed to my father. "You know, Brynza, we just can't give you a prize, and you know why."

"I understand," my father answered.

"But we have a problem with some of the others, and they refuse to let this matter drop."

"What do you want me to do about it?" Papa asked.

"Would you accept some extra pay in place of the medal?" the man asked.

My father paused before answering thoughtfully, "Yes, that would be a good solution." Inwardly he was laughing. While he wished for acknowledgment of his work, with four growing children at home some extra money was of greater value to him than any communist medal. The bosses never understood that Papa was striving to live his life for approval from God, willing to lose the favor of the bosses or forgo some public recognition if it meant pleasing God.

Sometimes the situation turned ugly. My father's job included cleaning and calibrating expensive Swiss measuring equipment. Once a month, the supervisor dispensed for him the exact amount of alcohol needed to clean the spindles. To avoid interruptions, Papa preformed this task on Saturdays or Sundays when no one else was around.

One Monday morning when Papa arrived at work a crowd was waiting for him: the boss, several supervisors, the chief mechanic, the political officer. "Brynza, what have you done?"

"Untrustworthy Baptist!"

"Are you trying to sabotage the factory?"

"What are you talking about?" my father replied. It took him awhile to understand what was going on, because they were all yelling at once.

"Come and see for yourself," they told him. They marched Papa over to the Swiss equipment. Instead of shiny metal, the calibrating rods were covered with yellow crystals, like hard frost. "What did you clean the equipment with?" they asked.

"Alcohol, as usual."

"And did you check the amount you used?"

"Yes, I did it just as I always do."

"Maybe you walked away for a moment; maybe someone put something in the alcohol."

"No," said Papa. "I know not to leave in the middle of cleaning the spindles."

"How could you do this? We trusted you. Why have you done this? You know we didn't have to let a Baptist work here." Papa's mind was reeling. What charge would they bring against him? What punishment would they give him? Carelessness on the job would be fined; sabotage could mean a prison sentence.

The supervisor added, "We saw that you had a little alcohol left over. We tested it and it was only 30% alcohol. Where did you get it?"

Papa said, "The mechanic gave it to me."

They all looked at each other, thinking, knowing immediately that the mechanic had probably drunk some of the alcohol and diluted the rest with water. None of them wanted to make any more fuss, now that it was clear that the Baptist wasn't the guilty party. "Well, we knew all along that Brynza wouldn't drink the alcohol!" After a few more jokes about Baptists, they all went back to work. No one was going to be accused of carelessness or sabotage. Papa praised God that he had the opportunity to prove that believers could be trusted. Years later, the boss talked to Papa about his long years of service, and the many attempts to re-educate Papa to accept Communist teaching. "It would have been better if you had re-educated all the others, Brynza, to make them as honest as you are."

CHAPTER 13

JOY IN SPITE OF TERROR

We must execute not only the guilty. Execution of the innocent will impress the masses even more.
—Nikolai Krylenko, Lenin's Commissar for Justice[13]

God is just: He will pay back trouble to those who trouble you.
—2 Thessalonians 1:6

As told by Lena

WHEN I WAS ten or eleven, I found a new interest: spying on my older brothers. By accident I had discovered that when they were out with "friends" this often meant girls. Trailing them silently along twisted paths though the woods and fields, lying flat in the grass so they wouldn't see me, I wondered: Is he going to kiss her? Any time either of my brothers kissed a girl, I raced home to tell my parents what an awful thing Yakov or Viktor had done, certain I was helping my parents to keep my brothers from anything that might lure them away from God.

My brothers' reaction? Various threats. "Lena, you tell on us again and we'll tell Mama what you did. We saw you at school, with your skirt hiked up way above your knees, short like the other girls."

Spying, which was a game to me, was a deadly serious business for the KGB, one of its major tools as the persecution of Christians shifted to a more subtle form, veiled under the pretense of enforcing laws and protecting society from dangerous cults.

One autumn day a new face appeared in the church, a young man about thirty years old named Sergei who drove a red Zaparozhets car. After a few visits, Sergei publicly repented in the church, and started to read the Bible, ask questions, and even attend the youth meeting. (At that time the youth meeting was open to people up to age thirty and could be held openly).

By the following July Sergei was preparing to be baptized. Mama and Papa discussed Sergei several times. "There is something strange about Sergei. He is a new believer, but he knows a lot about the Bible," Papa observed.

"He is also unusually active in the church. Normally people don't grow spiritually that fast."

"How can such a young man own a car? Most people wait ten years or more to get one."

"Looks like sheep, smells like wolf," was Mama's opinion.

Before anyone was baptized, the brothers met to decide if the person was ready to become a formal member of the church. After praying about Sergei, asking God for wisdom, they decided not to baptize him. One of them took Sergei aside to tell him that there seemed to be something not right about his faith. Sergei left and never came back.

Not long after, Papa came home saying, "God is great, God is great! Surely the One we serve is greater than any power in the world." He explained that he found out that Sergei had been sent to the church as a KGB spy. "Sergei already 'repented' in a church in a different *oblast* after winning the confidence of the members there, and then fed information about the church to the authorities."

This was one of the ways Satan used to try to infiltrate the church, but God gave wisdom to His servants when they asked for it, and gave them the victory. God's blessing was evident to all, even to us children.

This victory was significant because when people expressed interest in the church, believers didn't automatically assume their desire to participate was prompted by the KGB. People came to the church for many reasons. Some had read atheistic books and wanted to verify what these books said about the Bible. Others felt emptiness in their souls, an emptiness that could only be filled by God. Others saw a difference in the believers and wanted to know why. Some came to faith listening to Christian radio programs, especially one from Quito, Ecuador. All these people sought and found God, despite the relentless pressure to reject Christianity.

Back in the 1930s, spies and informers were routinely used to repress the church, not just to gain information. During those years, Stalin grew increasingly alarmed about people who he feared opposed his regime. He purged these supposed resisters from the ranks of the Communist party, and then turned his attention to anyone else who had "anti-Soviet thoughts" or "counter-revolutionary tendencies." He also needed slaves to build all of the factories and to meet all of the production norms described in his Five-Year Plan. He got them by arresting people, torturing them into confessing all kinds of political crimes, and then shipping those who had survived to labor camps. People were instructed that they had a duty to denounce anyone who was not a zealous worker for the state and completely loyal to communist ideals.

Those who were accused were usually arrested at night. To this day, my father can hear in his ears the sound of the car they called the Black Raven, swooping down at night like a carrion bird to take people away. During much of the 1930s, the Black Ravens flew every night, seeking their prey. People were encouraged to denounce their neighbors, which led to many false accusations just to avoid being the one arrested. If someone couldn't think of any "enemies of the people," they would be harshly rebuked or even arrested themselves for "lacking in revolutionary vigilance."

Believers were automatically suspect. My grandfather's faith was well known, so my grandmother kept a sack by the door with dry biscuits and a change of clothing, just in case the car stopped one night to take my grandfather. Papa remembers lying in bed, night after night, watching his parents, silhouetted in the dim light, peering from the window as the Black Raven passed by. Then they would get down on their knees, thanking God that one more day had been given to them. Little did Papa know then that years later the car would come for him.

Millions of people in the Soviet Union were swallowed up in the Terror; almost everyone had a family member who'd been imprisoned or killed. The authorities gave extra attention to Ukraine. Ukraine had resisted joining the Soviet Union, and now the government wanted to make sure that all Ukrainian nationalistic feeling was stamped out. We Ukrainians had a history of loving liberty and equality and didn't submit easily. Stalin's men hunted down scientists, scholars, and those with political influence. Once they destroyed all of the elite in Ukrainian society, they could rule the rest of the people like slaves.

Persecution forced most of the believers to cling more tightly to God as they trusted God to help them in all circumstances, no matter how difficult. They drew strength from each other, supporting and encouraging each other to press on.

By the time my father was born in 1933, most of the churches, or houses of prayer, as the Baptists called them, had been closed. There was no place to gather for worship. Somehow my grandmother preserved her Bible, her big family Bible with black and white pictures in it. Just owning a Bible was enough of a crime to merit time in the labor camps.

Once, when he was four or five, my father's parents woke him and his sister up in the middle of the night.

"Wake up, Sara." Papa could hear his mother lifting his sister out of bed. "Put your clothes on."

"But Mama, I can't see in the dark."

"Hush. I'll help you after I get Lyonya dressed." My father stood silently as my grandmother hastily dressed him, feeling her tension but not understanding it.

Just before he opened the door, my grandfather paused and said, "Children, you must be very quiet. You cannot talk once we are outside. Understand?"

No one asked any questions. They silently walked through the sleeping streets of the village, my grandmother gripping my father's small hand tightly. They walked past the last house in the village, past empty fields, and into the dark forest. To my father's surprise, there was another family there. My grandfather walked right up to them and sat down, motioning for the others to do the same. Another family arrived soon after. Ilya Romanovich, the local presbyter, served communion. Then, allowing some time between each family's departure, they all left, taking different routes home. My father's overwhelming memory of this midnight communion was how much he wanted to go back to sleep. He had no idea about the risks they were taking. Had they been caught, prison and death were the certain consequences.

Years later, my brothers and I sat spell-bound at our grandparents' kitchen table as they told stories of those times, and of those who had stayed faithful, wondering if we could be like them. Would we ever have that kind of courage? How did their faith grow so strong? Did God love us that much, that He would do such things for us?

By the end of the 1930s, the Terror started to wane, but the Black Ravens still haunted the streets at night and people still lived in fear. People avoided their neighbors, afraid to say anything that would give someone a reason to turn them in. Stalin had found a way to intimidate and control the whole country.

Mama also had stories from those years to tell. Her mother came to faith in 1932, the year before Mama was born. Mama's mother, Maria, lived in the small village of Orlyanka. As in most rural areas, the majority of people were Russian Orthodox, and Maria was a devout Orthodox believer. Around the time of my mother's birth, there weren't any Baptists in the village; only some traveling evangelists who would come through now and again. Then some believers settled in Orlyanka, and Maria noticed what she called "light in their souls."

Not everyone felt that way. People regarded the Baptists with suspicion, and rumors scuttled through the village like rats in a barn. It was whispered that all kinds of things went on at the Baptist meetings including eating babies and having wild orgies. Maria didn't understand how these polite, modest people could be involved in such wickedness. Curious, she convinced her best friend Dasha to accompany her to the church meeting.

At the meeting, the believers read from the Bible, explaining the meaning of the verse John 3:16, "For God so loved the world that he gave his one and only Son, that whoever believes in him shall not perish but have eternal life." Dasha quickly wrote it down so they could compare it to the Orthodox literature, determined to find out if the gossip was true—that the Baptists used different gospels. Sure enough, when they went home and checked, the Baptist gospels and Orthodox literature said the same thing. "What can this mean?" they wondered. "It is written the same in their gospels and in ours." Maria, who was virtually illiterate, had such a thirst to discover the truth that she learned how to read, using the Bible and what help Dasha could give her.

One day when they came to the service, they sensed anticipation in the air. An elderly evangelist named Nikita Tkachenko preached powerfully about salvation, explaining how Jesus came for all sinners, how He suffered, and how, when the time comes, God will judge. At the end of his preaching, he said, "Those who want to reconcile with God, know you can do it and you will have eternal life. Whoever wants this raise your hand."

Maria raised her hand and said, "I want to. Who should I pay?" She asked this because the Orthodox priests charged for services such as baptisms.

"What do you mean?" Nikita answered. "It's free. Just stand and repent."

Dasha grabbed Maria's arm. "Wait, what will your husband say?"

Maria answered, "My husband is for now, but God is for eternity."

Dasha said, "In that case, I want to be baptized, too." The two of them stood and repented, and came to Christ.

Returning home that day, Maria was met with complete devastation in her yard. A calf had gotten loose and trampled all the baby chickens. My grandfather was furious; his wife had been off at some religious cult meeting and the chicks were dead. During those days, having private livestock was enough to get someone shot or sent off to Siberia, and now all the neighbors had seen the calf running around the yard. He threatened Maria and told her never to go back to the Baptist services again. She answered, "Grisha, you can beat me all you want today or every day, but I won't care. I now know that all this is temporary. I can't walk away from the Lord."

This marked the beginning of a completely changed life for Maria. Throwing away all of her fortune telling cards, she trusted God for her future. Within a year, her husband, seeing a profound change in her, repented as well.

The year was 1933, and repression was fierce, Stalin's fist choking the country, the Black Ravens flying every night. My grandfather, as director of the sunflower oil factory in the village, was a target, and even more so after he'd become a believer. One night, having heard the authorities were coming for him, he fled to another village. He was only able to return home after the monthly quota of arrests had been made.

Raised during these years of terror by those whose daily reliance on God for the next crust of bread, or the next morning of freedom, taught them to trust Him continually. Their daily repentance of sin made them more like Christ. My parents' own faith matured so they could look beyond their own daily trials to God's promise of eternal life. This ability to rely on God proved its worth as they tried to help their own children withstand persecution.

CHAPTER 14

PAPA'S PROMOTION

Lenin's slogans are better than anything else for children.
—Banner in Museum of the History of Atheism
and Religion, Leningrad[14]

You have made known to me the path of life; you will fill me with joy in your presence, with eternal pleasures at your right hand.
—Psalm 16:11

As told by Lena

TO MAKE UP for his many absences, Papa often took us with him when he visited other churches. Accompanying Papa to a church in Zaporozhe when I was six years old, I was thrilled to learn they were dedicating babies to the Lord during the service, because I loved to look at the babies. However, this time there was a twelve-year-old boy among them. His mother wasn't a believer, but she brought her son, Igor, to be dedicated at the suggestion of one of her friends. I never thought I would ever see this boy again, or that he'd ever have a place in my life.

Another time Papa took the whole family to visit another village on some church business. We rode the train out into the country, through fields of sunflowers nodding their golden heads sagely in the August heat. When we arrived, Papa and Mama sent us out to play while they conferred with local church leaders. Feeling hungry, we children rambled into the nearby fields, gathered some corn and made a campfire to cook it. When Papa and Mama found us, they asked where we had gotten the corn.

"We picked it in the fields of the *kolkhoz* (collective farm)," we replied.

"What have you done? This isn't ours. What if Papa had planted it, and raised it, and then someone else took it? Take it back to where you got it, and put it back exactly where you got it." They were so ashamed that their children had stolen food.

We didn't really understand what we'd done at first, because when believers got together, everyone shared food freely. Papa read to us from the Word of God that it is forbidden to steal and that thieves won't have a part in the Kingdom of Heaven. He said, "It is much better to eat what Mama has made than to eat something that is stolen. If they catch you, I can go to prison." Papa's strong sense of honor was offended by our seemingly small theft. But his unyielding integrity saved him many times over the years, as his ministry became more and more dangerous.

When I was eight, Yakov Dukhonchenko, who had been the senior presbyter of the Zaparozhye *oblast*, was selected to be the senior presbyter of all Ukraine. Papa was chosen to replace him. As senior presbyter for the *oblast*, he'd have to give up his job in the factory; there would be no time for it. We'd always been poor; now things were about to get worse. The church provided a small salary (in later years, Mama described it as "miserly"), about half what Papa earned at the factory. Since the government considered presbyters to be parasites feeding off the work of real laborers, not contributing any benefit to society, they charged Papa about one-third of his income in taxes. People who labored in the cause of building communism paid about twelve or thirteen percent.

For a long time we lived with uncertainty, like people waiting for a delayed train. The authorities refused to approve Papa's selection. Many church members wrote letters to the leadership of the Union in Kiev, saying that if Papa didn't become the senior presbyter of the *oblast*, they would leave the Union and join the unregistered Council of Churches. The persecution of this group was publicized in the West, embarrassing the communist government, which claimed there was religious freedom in the Soviet Union. The authorities didn't want an entire *oblast* of thirty churches to suddenly join this vocal opposition. They also didn't want a strong leader in a visible position of authority. After working with Papa for the five years that he'd been the local presbyter, they knew that they couldn't control him and hadn't succeeded in compromising him.

The government wasn't the only opposition to Papa's new role; also objecting was my long-suffering mother. As it was, she rarely saw Papa, and thought it would only get worse with his new responsibilities. Not only would he still be leading the Upper Khortitsa church, but he'd be traveling around the *oblast*, supporting thirty other churches. And travel wasn't easy in those days. Sometimes Papa might be able to find someone to take him in their car, but usually he rode the bus or the train.

Under the Union rules, the wife and parents of the candidate had to give a testimony regarding his character, and give their consent to him taking on the new position. At first my mother and grandparents balked. They freely provided excellent testimonies about Papa, but fearing for his safety and even his life, were not eager to consent to his taking on such a difficult and dangerous role. While the government no longer relied on terror to stamp out the church, it hadn't given up. The new method was to imprison or kill just enough people so no one forgot the terror of earlier times and what could happen to those who refused to embrace communist teachings. For the rest, they used petty rules, constant harassment and interference, fines, and social pressure from neighbors or coworkers to drip on people like drops of water on a rock, until all resistance has worn away. Papa, as the leader of an entire *oblast*, would be a prime target and under constant scrutiny.

After Papa took the position, Mama told him that while he was the *oblast* presbyter, at home she was the local presbyter. By this she meant she would take care of everything at home: digging in the garden, laying bricks for a new wall, or dealing with the school on behalf of any of her four children. She knew the neighbors would have even more reason to make jokes at her expense, but she was ready to do whatever God required of her. For years she did most of the heavy work around the house without complaint, considering this to be her contribution to God's work, to free Papa up for other responsibilities.

Aside from that, it's hard to blame Mama for being reluctant to allow Papa to become the *oblast* presbyter. From time to time we heard about the martyrdom of another pastor or evangelist, usually from an unregistered church. Others were put in prison or labor camps. And in the 1970s, the government added a new threat. The Communist Party decided that anyone who couldn't believe in communism must be insane, and therefore belonged in a psychiatric hospital. Many dissidents, not just believers, were put in these hospitals and treated with drugs, often until their minds were destroyed.

As if that wasn't enough to worry her, Mama knew what a daunting task Papa was facing. Part of Papa's job would be dealing with all the government bureaucracies and their parallel overlapping structures of ministries, departments, and administrators. Not only did he have to contend with the Union and its leadership, but also the Commission for the Affairs of Religious Cults and its various committees and councils. Sometimes the Communist Party, local administrators such as mayors or city officials, or the KGB would try to interfere with the church or its members. At other times he battled with higher level bureaucrats in Kiev or even Moscow. Mama knew just how time-consuming and fatiguing this would be.

Even considering the risks, Papa felt certain God was calling him. He didn't know why he had been chosen, why out of the other brothers he was the one for the job; all he knew was that he needed to faithfully carry out the work God gave him to do. For over two years Papa served as the senior presbyter, but the authorities didn't give him the documents that granted him the post until February of 1977. Only then did he quit his job at the factory.

For the seventeen years Papa served as *oblast* presbyter, he was the shield for the members and the church. If one of the church members somehow landed a good job, nonbelievers complained that it was unfair for believers to have a better job than them. To resolve these complaints Papa met with the labor union leaders. If one of the believers was fired, Papa complained to the authorities: sometimes the labor union, sometimes the factory manager, sometimes the KGB. With all of the parallel structures of authority, there were numerous people Papa could appeal to. Sometimes he worked his way up the bureaucracy, culminating in writing letters to officials in Moscow. Papa knew that the factory managers had to produce to norms set by Moscow, and that it was preferable for that manager to not have any public trouble or any complaints going to the higher-ups. No one wanted the bureaucrats in Kiev or Moscow looking into how they did their jobs; no one wanted extra attention from the KGB. By working through these different bureaucracies, Papa was sometimes, but not always, able to get people their jobs back, or reduce some of the persecution they were facing.

As it turned out, many of Mama's fears were justified. Usually Papa set aside a day each week to spend at the church receiving people who had spiritual questions, wanted his advice, or were having problems at work. Inevitably, if he told a person to come on Tuesday, they would say they couldn't make it, so he'd let them come on Monday, which was supposed to be his day off. Papa wasn't able to preserve this time for prayer or study, because he was constantly meeting with people. At first, my parents fought against this, but then humbled themselves. They decided that God had called them to live in service to other people so they couldn't complain. The door of our house was always open, and rarely a day went by without a guest. Papa often called home to say, "Valya, I will come in an hour with five of the brothers." Mama knew that in that hour she needed to prepare something to eat. Somehow she always managed to feed whoever came, despite our family's limited budget. We children hardly knew what it was to have dinner without any guests; in fact, we thought it was boring without them. By watching our parents, we learned what it means to be available for God, for His service.

During this time, in the middle of the dreary Brezhnev years when Soviet society itself was stagnating, Vladimir Antonovich Tseona arrived from Chernivitski *oblast* to organize a youth orchestra in our church. The Instructional Letter was no longer in force, and the youth orchestra became a wonderful force in the life of the church. Vladimir Antonovich, not wanting any child to be left out, barely gave Papa time to finish the service before he jumped to his feet and started to talk with parents. He went from house to house, convincing families to allow their children to be in the orchestra. His enthusiasm was contagious, and soon we had a woodwind/brass orchestra, a string orchestra of Ukrainian folk instruments, and a choir. All of this, of course, was strongly discouraged by the government. Youth meetings were forbidden, and the authorities knew that these musical groups were used as a cover for religious activities, but they couldn't shut them down without proof. As long as we performed at our local church, we were within the law and the authorities couldn't stop us.

The director of the local music school came to the church to persuade the parents to send their children there for a course of study. He even promised that if there were enough children from the church, they could all be in one group together. "And give us your music," he offered, "and we will teach the children from the music you give us." So that's how the oldest three Brynza children graduated from the musical school, even though we didn't have any special talent.

Soon we became as enthusiastic as Vladimir was. All three of us were in the string orchestra: Yakov played bass mandolin, Viktor tenor mandolin, and I, soprano mandolin. Yakov and Viktor were also in the brass orchestra as well, Yakov on drums and Viktor on trombone. I sang in the choir. We assumed Vladimir Antonovich's zeal because he poured himself out for us.

As a leader, Vladimir Antonovich combined a mixture of love and strictness. If any of us forgot our music, we'd have to walk home to get it, even if it meant we missed the whole rehearsal. Not many kids forgot their music more than once! The youth orchestras and choir performed on holidays, at weddings, funerals, and baptisms, and traveled all over Ukraine. Just for some fun along the road, Vladimir Antonovich organized picnics for us and brought a soccer ball along. This was all very exciting for us, knitting us closely together, cementing relationships between us. In a way, our shared adventures made up for the taunting and teasing we endured at school, and helped us to stay strong in our faith. Sometimes we were too daring, singing in other churches or even public places like the train station. But Papa didn't want to stop us. He knew that if we were caught, he and the pastor of the church where we performed would be fined, and the fines were higher than their monthly salaries. For Papa, being summoned for interrogation or having to pay fines because we had not followed the instructions of the *ispolkom* exactly were small irritants, a small price to pay in exchange for watching a generation of new believers grow and mature.

Papa was right to take the risks he did; the fruit of Vladimir Antonovich's work is obvious to us now. Vladimir Antonovich came when Yakov was sixteen, and very few of his peers got involved with the youth orchestra. All but three of the kids Yakov's age ended up leaving the church; Vladimir Antonovich came too late for them. The children who were the same age as Viktor and I and had the benefit of several years in the youth orchestra, remained faithful and stayed in the church. Venya was ten when Vladimir Antonovich left due to pressure from the authorities, and most of the kids Venya's age also left the church. Such was the influence that one person was able to have, and it was enough to counteract all the pressure the government could muster.

CHAPTER 15

THE SOVIETS' HAMMER AND GOD'S HAMMER

... [M]oral is everything that strengthens the dictatorship of the proletariat, promotes victory over capitalism, advances and promotes the construction of socialism....All that assists in the victory of socialism, all that helps the work of the Party and the working class in socialist construction—all of this is good, moral, and all that hinders the construction of socialism—all of that is immoral and deserves contempt.
—Soviet Antireligious Propagandist[15]

Woe to him who builds his palace by unrighteousness.
—Jeremiah 22:13a

As told by Lena

IN 1974, THE same year my father was chosen to be senior presbyter, the Commission for the Affairs of Religious Cults appointed a new director of its Zaporozhe *oblast* branch. His superiors commanded him to rigorously control the activities of the churches. This man, named Anton Markov, an ambitious former

KGB agent, immediately vowed to put believers on their knees before the Soviet power.

Every Monday at nine Papa met with Markov and the members of the *oblast ispolkom* (executive committee) of the Commission for the Affairs of Religious Cults. The *ispolkom* interrogated Papa about minute details of every church activity, often fining him large sums for not following all their instructions precisely. Usually the fines were for offenses such as the youth musical group had met more often than was allowed, or a church member had been caught at work with Christian literature. Markov regularly threatened to remove Papa from his position or send him to prison.

Papa understood Markov's zeal very well. If he managed to reduce the number of Christians in the Zaporozhe *oblast*, he would be rewarded with bonuses and awards, and maybe even get promoted to a prestigious position in Moscow. So every Monday, Papa came home completely drained, limp like a cardboard box left out in the rain. All he ever said in front of us children was, "He never changes." Some days he and Mama would go in their bedroom and shut the door. Only later did Mama tell me why. Sometimes Markov would have a policeman or KGB agent get a little physically rough with Papa, grabbing him by the collar and throwing him up against the wall. Papa would never let on to us kids that they had hurt him in any way, because he didn't want us to worry.

Spurred on by Markov, the authorities constantly sought ways to undermine Papa's ministry. They found several brothers and sisters in different churches who would give him money when he would go there on his regular visits. "This is for you," they'd say. Papa understood that these were bribes, because he was not legally allowed to accept money from church members. On his return to Zaparozhye he would go straight to the captain of the police, who always feigned surprise. Then the captain would send Papa to the Commission for the Affairs of Religious Cults, and Papa would ask, "This comrade brought me money. Did you send it to me? But there is no receipt from you with it." By inquiring, Papa let Markov and his minions know that he knew the money came from them. Of course they wouldn't admit to trying to bribe him, and would insist they knew nothing about it. Had Papa ever taken the money he could have been fined, imprisoned, or removed from his position.

They used other means to try to compromise Papa as well. Churches were forbidden to make any expenditures to extend help to someone, to buy food or clothing for the poor. The church could do so only if someone from the Commission for the Affairs of Religious Cults came and checked the books and approved the transaction. Charges were brought against Papa that he was asking for donations and then stealing the money.

For months, sixteen people searched the church's books, investigating everything. But they never found anything out of order. Papa would announce in the service, "Brothers and sisters, we cannot use money from the church funds to meet needs. But there are those among us who are poor. If you want to contribute, put your donation in the plate with a note that the money is for the deacon's ministry, not the church." Then the deacons would count the money, not my father, and they decided how to use it.

Even when there weren't specific charges, Papa was constantly called to the *oblast ispolkom* to answer questions, often on Sunday evenings. They knew that he led a service Saturday night, and then two or three on Sunday, all in different churches. After all that, they thought he'd be tired and more likely to confess to some crime or agree to compromise and work with them. God helped Papa to stand firm.

Papa never thought what he was doing was so unusual. After all, the Bible tells us to be honest and to not steal what does not belong to us. Years later, a brother came through Zaparozhye who was a missionary traveling all through Russia, even to Kamchatka on the Pacific coast. When he heard Papa's name he said, "I've heard the name. Brynza was one of the only ones left that they couldn't buy."

Markov used other means to free the *oblast* of the parasites of religion, as he called us. In the front window of the main department store he displayed pictures of Baptist pastors, my father among them, all with ugly expressions on their faces. He organized a monthly debate between an atheistic philosopher and a pastor. These debates were held at the Palace of Culture and were attended by students and teachers. After a while, Papa refused to participate, since these gatherings were more like forums for spreading communist propaganda and not serious debates. Markov's zeal turned Zaporozhe into one of the most repressive *oblast*s.

Markov, like his predecessors, avidly searched for prohibited literature, such as Bibles, songbooks, and religious writings, destroying all that he found. After decades of strict bans on religious literature, many churches had only one Bible. Papa was determined that more people in our church would have access to Bibles and songbooks. At that time, very few people came into the USSR from other countries, so that was not a possible source of materials. Papa regularly traveled to Kiev where he could buy illegally printed New Testaments and songbooks. He also bought a typewriter, but didn't register it. In those days all typewriters had to be registered with the authorities so they could monitor what was being typed. Papa wasn't about to let the authorities know he was producing Christian literature! For years, one of the sisters from the church came regularly to our house and sat in Papa's office with the door closed for hours. We didn't know until many years later that she was typing copies of religious pamphlets, even though such an act could be punished with a prison sentence.

Markov, determined to triumph over my father, over the church, and over God, resolved to smash all remnants of the Christian faith like grain under a hammer and often turned his threats into action. Several times he abruptly summoned Papa to a meeting. We waited at home, wondering where Papa was. Each time Mama borrowed the neighbor's telephone to call different government offices, only to be told that Papa had been called away. Once or twice she even sent Yakov to look for our father at Markov's office, but Yakov never found out anything. Papa would come home very late from these meetings, long after we'd gone to bed.

I still remember the times the police car picked Papa up at home, the black car everyone called the *Bobik*, the one they used to take away criminals. Even before Papa became the *oblast* presbyter, he'd been taken away by the police a few times.

I was only eight the first time this happened. On a warm summer afternoon Mama left to go to the store. My brothers were working in the garden; I was inside washing dishes. We heard a car drive into the yard, and all four of us ran to see who it was. Our curiosity turned to chilly fear when we saw the *Bobik*. As the police officers got out of the car, we all ran to tell Papa. He came back outside with us and walked over to the car. My brothers and I huddled together near the house, understanding this was some adult kind of talk we shouldn't have any part of.

The officers showed Papa a handful of documents and read the charges off one by one. "Last week you preached in another city in the *oblast*. This is not allowed. Last month you allowed a preacher from another *oblast* to speak in your church. This is not allowed. We have five reasons to arrest you; you must come with us." Papa said something to them that we couldn't hear. One of the policemen nodded his head. "All right, but hurry up."

Papa walked slowly toward us. "Children, I have to go with the police now. Tell your mother where I have gone." He prayed with us for a moment, asking God to protect us, hugging us one by one. As he turned to go he said, "Listen to your mother, and pray." Returning to the waiting police car, he climbed in.

As the *Bobik* drove away with Papa in the back seat, we were consumed with the feeling that we had just said good-bye to our father forever. We scurried like frightened squirrels to our grandparents' house. Struggling with our tears, trying to catch our breath, we told our grandparents what had happened. Grandma started to cry, but quickly rallied enough to get on her knees. Grandpa, my brothers, and I joined her and begged God to protect our father.

When Mama returned from her shopping, she found all of us at home, in a complete panic. We had a hundred questions for her. "Mama, what do you think they are doing to our papa right now? Mama, when will we see Papa again?"

Mama wiped her eyes every time she gave us the only answer she had. "Children, trust God. Papa is in God's hands."

A few people from the church came by, saying they had heard what had happened. "Valya, we want to pray with you, to support you," they told Mama.

Night came, but no Papa. All night we slept on and off, waking up several times and wondering. Tears still form in my eyes when I recall the dread we had in our hearts, wondering if Papa would ever come home.

In the morning we had more questions for Mama. She tried to keep us busy, and we spent much time in prayer.

Around ten that night the door opened and Papa walked in. Tears pooled in his eyes as he hugged and kissed each one of us. Then we all knelt in prayer to thank God for returning him to us.

Each time Papa was taken away, we had the same fears. Sometimes after the *Bobik* drove away with Papa, the neighbors congregated in the street and asked us what crime Papa had committed. This always made Yakov angry. "Why are they asking that? They know exactly why Papa was taken away!" he fumed, angry at the injustice. Each time Mama led us in the house and we prayed together, beseeching God to protect Papa, to bring him home to us.

One time, as the *Bobik* drove off with Papa in the back seat, we wondered why the second police car didn't leave. Our ignorance didn't last long. Three or four policemen entered the house and searched for illegal Christian literature. They never found it, because it was in the trunk buried in the yard or in the false ceiling in the shed. They didn't find the illegal typewriter, either. My brothers and I huddled together with Mama, watching wide-eyed, praying silently. Finally they left us, their clumping footsteps loud as they walked across the yard to their car. We stood, frozen in silence, watching them drive away.

"Children, we must pray. First we must thank God that they didn't find anything," Mama said to us. "And then we must pray for Papa."

The five of us knelt on the floor and prayed and cried for hours. At first we thought it would be like the other times, when they kept Papa for a few hours, yelled at him a bit, and threatened him with prison.

As the hours continued to pass, our fear grew. It was 1984, and we were all old enough to know about Grandpa and the firing squad, about Yakov Dukhonchenko sitting in prison for six years, and another close friend of my parents' in prison for fifteen years, about torture and psychiatric hospitals. Pastors and other believers were still dying for their faith. All night long we cried and prayed, wondering if they were beating Papa, if they'd already killed him, if we'd ever see him again. Anything could happen. Even though they sent him home the next morning, it seemed as though that fear lasted like he was gone for days.

When Papa came home, he could see joy in our faces through our exhaustion. His biggest worry through that long night was not for himself and what they might do to him. Instead, he thought of his family, and how they would survive without him. This time he consoled himself by thinking that Yakov and Viktor were already grown men, and even Venya was fifteen. Not like the first time he'd been taken away when I was eight and Venya was only five. Then he was really scared for us, and for Mama, who'd be left with four children to support.

With no other hope, he prayed, offering fragments of petitions, in between the questions shouted at him, with pieces of Bible verses memorized long ago. "Strengthen me, O God. Have mercy on me. Let them be confounded that seek my soul." All night a portrait of Lenin glared at him.

As he hugged us and listened to our fears for him, he made light of the whole experience. "My children, don't you see? They are only trying to scare us."

What he told Mama about that long night of interrogation is a different story. He never complained of any pain in front of us children, so we never knew he'd been beaten. Through that long night he had been pushed around, thrown against the wall, and yelled at for hours. "One more time, and we'll throw you in prison. Don't you know the rules? You can't bring any other pastors to preach in your church. Will you obey, or not? Why are you so stubborn? Why do you have so many youth meetings? Do you want to see your children again?"

Far worse than that, though, was what they had done two years earlier. Markov, obsessed with the idea of removing Papa from his position as *oblast* presbyter, was searching for any grounds, however flimsy. The authorities knew that a presbyter is supposed to have good control of his household, and the Baptist leadership would consider it disgraceful for the son of a presbyter to end up in prison. My youngest brother Venya's rebellious behavior was giving them just the excuse they were looking for to act against Papa. If Venya got into worse trouble, the Baptist leadership might well pressure Papa to step down. The authorities would be rid of him, without having to act themselves.

In 1982, the school began looking closely at Venya in response to pressure from Markov and the Commission for the Affairs of Religious Cults. Venya's teacher, Nina, brought up his terrible behavior in all the parents' meetings. Young and wanting to impress the bosses, Nina was looking for any reason to make a formal complaint about Venya. She accused my parents of isolating Venya from all aspects of Soviet society and exposing him to dangerous religious teaching, causing his delinquent behavior. The school had all kinds of studies showing that religious teaching leads to nervous disturbances and psychological disorders. Veniamin's behavior, they said, only confirmed these studies.

The school formed a special parents' committee to discuss the fact that the Brynzas couldn't control their youngest child. They knew we older children had been well-behaved in school, but even so, they decided to recommend that the government legally deprive Papa and Mama of their parental rights regarding Veniamin. Had they been ordinary people, the authorities wouldn't have done anything. They took aggressive action against Papa because he was a senior presbyter they could not bend to their will.

Right around this time, Papa's mother died. As was our custom, her funeral, complete with open casket heaped with gladiolas, was held outside in the yard. Since evangelism outside a registered church building was forbidden, major events such as weddings and funerals were our only opportunity to witness to unbelievers. An inspector from Kiev came, and presented Papa with thirty-two violations of the law, including the use of the church orchestra for a funeral, and the fact that we had the service in the yard. They didn't want anyone hearing the Word of God preached! Recommendations came from the Communist Party, and then from the ProKom (the committee that actually had power to act in situations like this) that Papa should be taken from his posts as both *oblast* presbyter and local presbyter. Not only was his son out of control, but he himself was a law-breaker. By taking Veniamin away, they would establish that Papa could not control his son, the first part of their charge.

Papa knew the only solution was to transfer Venya to a different school. The petition to remove parental rights had to come from the school the child was currently attending, and the director of that school had to provide all the documentation; documents from a former school wouldn't count. Knowing this, Papa went to a school where the director accepted believers' children if they had problems at other schools. He was acquainted with her because her grandmother had been a member of the church, and he knew that while she herself was a Communist, she was sympathetic to believers.

When Papa arrived in her office, she knew immediately why he had come. "Alexei Gavrilovich, what's going on with Veniamin that has caused such uproar?"

Papa explained the situation, and finished his story by saying, "So you see, it is impossible to keep Venya with that teacher. She is openly searching for reasons to complain."

The director, Nina Afanasievna, answered, "Let's do this, but do it quickly. I've been director of this school for twenty-five years, and this isn't anything big." She warned Papa that the commission for the removing of their parental rights was getting ready to act. "No one really wants to deprive you of any of your children, but simply to limit your religious activities. This is just a way to put pressure on you. So let Veniamin come to my school," she said. In the space of one day, she completed all the paperwork so Venya could switch schools.

In the next Party meeting, after the secretary of the Regional Commission reported on Nina Afanasievna's work, the bosses yelled at her and cursed her, and they wrote a document requesting the Communist Party to remove Brynza from his position. But Nina Afanasievna, who was an old Communist, knew just what to say to them. She addressed the meeting and said, "You don't have the right to take this child away. There isn't sufficient reason to do this. If a child studies under me, I will make sure he is brought up properly." She knew all the rules and said they needed to give specific reasons for taking children away from their parents: concrete reasons, not slippery ones. She was just, and demanded that they also be just. When all of her family and neighbors asked her why she accepted Venya and refused to back down, she kept giving the same answers.

To most people's surprise, Nina Afanasievna prevailed and the case against my parents was dropped. The all-powerful government had simply given up. Papa and Mama always said that their children belong to God and to them, not the Communist Party. Once again God heard our prayers and rescued us when there was no other hope.

I knew my father suffered greatly during the fight to keep Veniamin, because soon after he developed diabetes from the stress. But I didn't really understand how deeply he agonized over that situation until years later when he came to America. He was invited to speak in a church, and as I translated for him, he told the story of how God rescued Veniamin from being taken away.

"Of all they did to me during those years," my father said, "that was the worst. To live under constant scrutiny, to be harassed and fined; threatened with church closures, beatings, or prison, all those things were directed at me. I had made my choice to follow God, whatever the consequences. This time they chose to strike me through my son, to cause me pain because he had to suffer because of me. I would have gladly gone to prison instead of having him taken away."

Papa has said many times that the first thing he is going to do when he gets to heaven is kneel before Jesus and thank Him for Markov, the KGB, and other bureaucrats who made his life so difficult during those years. Without them, he never would have had such a close relationship with God.

My father tells a story about Michelangelo, the famous artist and sculptor. Once he was asked what he was making. Michelangelo answered, "It's an angel."

His questioner replied, "I don't see the form of an angel."

Michelangelo said, I see the angel in the marble, and will carve until I set him free.

In the same way, God, using his hammer and chisel, takes away what is unnecessary in the life of the believer. Sometimes it causes pain. There are no random people or events in the life of the believer; all of them are God's tools that He uses to make us more like Christ. Cooperation with this process was the focus of my father's life, and he tried to make it the aspiration of all the believers in his church. By letting God have His way in our lives, we can truly be set free and know the great love He has for us. Meanwhile, the communist government, using its hammer and sickle, was trying to take all freedom out of our lives, wanting to retain all power for themselves. For standing up to this, my grandfather had suffered for his faith, and my father suffered for his, because of their great love for God. The knowledge of the never-ending love of Christ, and the victory over circumstances that He brings was what Papa wanted to pass down to his own children, and what the government was doing all it could to prevent.

PART II
SEEKING AND FINDING

Yakov and Viktor, Lena's older brothers, share how they were tempted by the choice of career and wealth over faith in Christ, and how they learned to trust God for the future. Igor, who Lena eventually married, tells his own story of growing up in an unbelieving household and finding faith despite the obstacles and opposition put in his way by the communist system.

CHAPTER 16

CAN FROG'S SKIN CURE CANCER?

Every Soviet citizen can study, increase his professional aptitude or train in a specialty without any cost to himself.[16]

O Lord my God, I called to you for help and you healed me.
—Psalm 30:2

As told by Yakov

VITYA RAN AHEAD, chasing a bird. Lena dawdled behind, picking pink and lavender wildflowers, stopping to marvel at the changing colors of the high grasses of the fields as they turned from bright green to shades of pale yellow and brown.

"Hurry up, Lena," I chided my six-year-old sister. "Mama's waiting for us."

We hiked through the fields until we reached a small pond where Vitya was already standing at the edge, studying the water. Lena and I joined him in an anxious search for frogs. Female frogs. Lena dashed over to me, with a tiny frog clenched in her small fist. "Is this a good one, Yasha?" she asked.

"Let's look at its hands," I said.

Vitya chimed in. "See, Lena, its hands are too fat under the part that looks like a thumb. And it's too small, anyway. Remember, the girl frogs are the big ones."

We continued our frantic hunt for just the right frog. I heard a splash and saw Vitya grab at something in the muddy water. He raised his hand, clutching a brownish-green frog, mouth smiling in triumph, eyes battling hope and fear.

"Let me see it, Vitya," I said.

We gathered around and intently examined that frog as if the fate of the world depended on it. And in many ways, for us, it did.

Some months earlier, Mama fell ill with severe pain in her left breast. The doctors informed her that she had cancer and needed an operation. Alarmed by the idea of surgery, she decided to try prayer and any kind of home treatment she could come up with. Neighbors and people from the church offered suggestions of things to try, but nothing helped. At times, any kind of noise intensified the agonizing pain, especially noises that mimicked the throbbing heat in her breast, like the sound of a ball Vitya bounced in the yard outside her bedroom window one afternoon, a sound that reduced her to tears.

One day Vitya and I overheard a neighbor tell Mama the skin of a female frog could cure her. We decided that we would find the frogs. Lena begged to come, and we allowed her to, but left three-year-old Venya behind.

Vitya went and caught another frog, and we compared their hands. Yes, the first frog definitely had thinner hands under the thumb, and was bigger. It must be a female. Vitya put it in a bag and we started home. A fragile hope, faint as the soft smells of the wildflowers in Lena's hands, drifted around us. Maybe we had found something to help Mama. Maybe our world would not be destroyed.

Once in the backyard, Vitya and I went to work, carefully skinning the frog while Lena watched, fascinated. Then we carried our prize into Mama's bedroom.

As always, the room smelled of rotting illness. Mama smiled at us weakly and reached out to stroke Lena's hair. "Mama," I said. "Look what we've brought you! It's the skin of a female frog!"

"So you heard what Nina told me? Thank you, children. Let's try it."

I handed the frog skin to Mama and she placed it on her swollen, black breast. Looking into her face anxiously, I asked, "Does that help?"

"There is some relief," Mama said. She let out a long sigh. "It takes the heat out. Thank you, *sinok*. Thank you, all of you."

I felt such relief to be able to help Mama, such a sense of achievement. This must be how doctors feel when they cure their patients, when they have figured out how to make people feel better. Maybe, I should study to become a doctor.

The rest of that summer, Vitya, Lena, and I went on frog hunts nearly every day. While the cool frog skin took away some of Mama's pain, she grew sicker every day. Finally she gave in and decided to have the operation.

The night before the surgery, I huddled with my brothers and sister, praying aimless, terrified prayers, pleading with God to leave us our mother. Mama attempted to reassure us that Papa would be with us, our grandparents would be with us, God would take care of us, but her efforts were as futile as trying to soothe pain with a snowflake.

The next day we paced between the house and the street, waiting for Papa to come and tell us the results of the surgery. When he opened the gate to the yard, we besieged him with questions. Before he could say anything, a twelve-foot long branch fell from the tree by the front door of the house.

Grandma began to wail. "Oh, my son, that means there has been a death! It must mean that Valya is no more!"

I jumped onto my bike and rode to the hospital, my grandmother's words and the cries of Lena and Viktor in my ears. No, it can't be! My mama can't be dead.

Arriving at the hospital, I threw my bike down on the ground and leaned against the wall, trying to get my breath, struggling for control, my panting turning into sobs as the thought of Mama's death overwhelmed me.

A doctor smoking a cigarette nearby approached me. "What's the matter? Why are you howling?" she asked.

"It's because my mama has died," I told her.

"What's your mother's name?"

"Brynza."

The doctor smiled. "No, she's alive. Why do you think she is dead?"

"My grandmother said so. She must be dead."

"Come in and see for yourself," the doctor said. Tossing her cigarette aside, she ushered me inside and had me put on a white lab coat like doctors wear. We went up to the ward and the doctor led me to a bed by the window. "Now, tell me, who is this?"

"It's Mama," I answered.

"Valentina Grigorievna, open your eyes. You have company."

Mama slowly opened her eyes and gazed at me. I took a deep breath, barely able to believe it. "Mama, are you alive?" I asked.

"Yes, Yasha, I am," she answered, reaching for my hand.

"Now go home and let your mother rest," the doctor told me.

Riding home on my bike I thought of how happy I was that Mama was alive, and how much I enjoyed wearing the white coat of a doctor. I had always wanted to be a doctor; now I was sure of it. What I didn't know was this desire would cause me great pain in the years to come.

CHAPTER 17

AMBITION AND FAITH COLLIDE

We do not conceal our attitude to the religious outlook as being non-materialistic and unscientific.
—Mikhail Gorbachev[17]

Do not be wise in your own eyes; fear the Lord and shun evil.
—Proverbs 3:7

As told by Yakov

THE ONLY PROBLEM with my aspiration was that everyone, including my father, told me it was impossible.

"Yasha, I don't understand why you are so determined to get a higher education."

"Papa, you always say that education is a good thing."

"That is true. But you know that to get into the university, you must first join the *Komsomol*. And that is impossible, because they demand pledges of atheism. They will never allow believers into their universities."

"If God gave me these abilities and talents, shouldn't I use them?"

"If we lived in a just society you would be right. But we live in a sinful world. I don't want you to be disappointed, that you would work so hard to get into a university, and then never get in. Or if you did get in by some miracle, they would make it so hard for you that you would quit. They could even manufacture some reason to throw you out! And if you did finish, you could end up like I did in a job beneath your abilities because no one would trust you with responsibility. Wouldn't it be better to accept the situation and avoid all that pain? Why try to jump higher than your own head?"

I knew Papa was trying to protect me, but I was determined to try to succeed against all odds by working hard and proving myself. Knowing that the teachers routinely gave me lower grades than I deserved, knowing that they were penalizing me for my parents' faith, I resolved to use my love for studying to show them all, to earn such high grades that they would have to let me into the university.

As it turned out, my hard work did improve my grades, but it wasn't the long hours I spent memorizing the exploits of key figures in the struggle to create a classless society or calculating square roots. Instead, it was the endless drills on the sports field that led to the pivotal moment. Cradling the metal ball into my neck, keeping my elbow parallel to the ground, leaping back on my left leg, twisting in a tight spin, I punched the shot put into the air, straining to keep my balance within the white circle, listening to the cheers of the crowd, cheers for me, the winner of the competition. I was in the ninth grade, a champion shot putter, the best athlete in the school. Kids I went to school with my whole life, who taunted me, who called me "Baptist," were cheering me on, using not just my name, Yakov, but the affectionate nickname "Yasha," all because I'd won high honors for our school. With every successful throw of the shot put, my popularity soared higher.

Suddenly, my grades improved and my coaches and teachers were concerned for my future. "Yakov, you know you could have a bright future ahead of you," they told me. "Star athlete. Top student. All you have to do is join the *Komsomol*." The message was clear: success would be mine, if I would just give up my faith.

So gradually that I didn't notice what was happening, I began to live the life of a double-minded man, like the one James describes in his epistle, tossed about by every wave of the sea. I enjoyed playing the drums in the youth orchestra; I knew God existed. But I wanted to live like others of my generation, to have the same choices and opportunities they did. I knew that God's Word was a light for my path, the surest guide, but more and more, I was following the blinding white light of my ambitions.

Only Papa's eyes changed, doubt flickering through them like a ripple in a pond, the first time I told him I didn't want to go to church. The rest of his face remained set like flint. Gently he asked, "Why not?"

"I don't know," I answered. "I just don't want to."

"Oh, *sinok*," Papa said. "God is waiting for you there. And the brothers and sisters will miss you."

Mama cried and stroked my arm. "You know, Yasha, we are worried about you. Why won't you go to the youth meeting? It would be better."

As my attendance at church events grew sporadic, Papa had serious conversations with me about choosing my path in life. All through our childhood, our parents had told us we have to choose. If we choose one behavior, we will get one result, choose another, the result will be different. Always a black and white choice: choosing God's way led to blessing, they told us, and choosing the world's way led to bad consequences. Now it seemed to me that choosing the world would get me what I wanted; choosing faith would mean giving up my dreams, a higher price than I was willing to pay.

Papa just didn't understand the temptation I was facing. He wasn't plagued by ambition; he accepted his place in the world as God's will and didn't fight it. Once, after I'd skipped church for about a month, Papa asked me if he had offended me in some way that was keeping me from the church. Puzzled, I answered, "Me? Offend you? I'm not in church because I'm not worthy to be there." While I was inwardly pleased that Papa talked to me on an adult level, his question showed how little he understood my sense of being in a cage, and my answer showed how little I could explain it to him. All I wanted was to live like everyone else, but I was trapped between the label "Baptist" the Communist Party put on me, a label which doomed me to a life of menial, low-paying jobs, and the limits the church put on me, which taught me to submit to such a life, and to not covet an interesting job, western clothing, or any of the comforts that money can buy. All I could see were the gray metal bars of the restraining and shrinking cage.

Most of my time during the next several months was spent studying or on the sports field. Punching the shot put into the air was a release for me, and the gliding arc of the ball reflected my desires to be free. As the shot putter, I had to stay in the limits of the circle, but the ball could fly high. *That's all I want,* I thought. *The chance to break free of the limits imposed on me by the repression of the state and the rules of my parents.*

CHAPTER 18

I CHALLENGE GOD

Communist education presupposes emancipation from religious prejudices and superstitions, which hinder individual Soviet people from fully developing their creative powers.[18]

May the God of peace...equip you with everything good for doing his will, and may he work in us what is pleasing to him, through Jesus Christ.
—Hebrews 13:20-21

As told by Yakov

EVENTUALLY, I DECIDED that if God wanted me to waste my life as an impoverished outcast, then He and I had a big problem. Maybe my parents were wrong to subject themselves to a life of misery, I thought. How could God want His servants to be oppressed? What could be so terrible about desiring a happy, decent life?

For the first time in my life, I even considered joining the *Komsomol*. The only problem was the public profession of atheism required for membership; deep down, I still believed in God. But if I did join, none of the teachers would question my decision. In their minds, I would be embracing the truth and renouncing a lie.

Finally, I told my parents I would no longer go to church. Nothing was going to get in the way of my ambition for education and a career.

"How can we change your mind?" My mother asked me, weeping. Her grief barely registered, or maybe it did, but I punched it away. I was in the shotputter's circle and she was outside.

"I don't want to discuss this," I told her.

"At least stay with the youth orchestra."

I shook my head.

"Please!" she grabbed onto my arm and sobbed harder. "There must be a way to bring you back! What can I do?"

"Blue jeans," I said.

My mother let go of my arm and took a step back. "What? Blue jeans?"

"I don't have anything to wear to the youth meeting. Give me a pair of jeans, and then I'll go." A dirty trick, since we both knew buying a pair of jeans was impossible, but I didn't care. Jeans cost about 150 rubles. That was more than my father's salary for a month. Even if you had the money to pay for them, jeans were almost impossible to find.

My mother looked at me with a mixture of sadness and pity. "What you're doing is very disrespectful," she said quietly. "You know we can't give you jeans."

My parents stayed up late many nights praying about my demand for blue jeans, asking God to soften my heart on this matter, and to give them wisdom about what to do. I lay in bed letting their words move right past me like water slipping over mossy stone.

A few days went by, then a week. One night at dinner my father told us he received a notice from the post office that a package addressed to him had arrived from America. From time to time people from the West sent books or religious literature to my father.

Of course, Bibles and Christian magazines were always confiscated; sometimes the books slipped past the censors. But a package? We couldn't imagine what it could possibly contain.

"I'm not sure if I should pick it up," my father said, scooping some *pelmeni* onto his plate. "According to the notice we owe thirty rubles in customs duty and whatever's inside may not be worth that much." There was another difficulty as well. People who had contacts in the West were automatically regarded with suspicion. The last thing my father needed was to be under even more scrutiny; as a pastor, he was already suspect in the eyes of the State. Receiving personal items from the capitalist West might cause even more problems for him.

"Maybe it's a box of toys," Veniamin said.

"Or candy," Viktor suggested.

"Really, Vitya? What kind of candy do you think it is?" Lena asked.

Our dinner conversation was punctuated with laughter that night, as we all tried to guess what was in the package. Papa decided that since we were so curious, there was nothing else to be done but to pay the thirty rubles and find out.

The brown paper package was about the size of a large loaf of bread. Someone had written my father's name, Alexei Brynza, and our address in magic marker. There was no return address.

We watched eagerly as Papa took a pair of scissors and cut the edge of the box, each of us, no doubt, wishing it would contain our deepest desires.

Inside the box, rolled up like a sausage, lay a brand new pair of Lee blue jeans. No note, just the jeans. Viktor, Lena, and Veniamin stared in total astonishment, and then began talking at once, reaching out to stroke the fabric. I was numb. My parents exchanged a long look of amazement and regret. I knew that they wanted no compromise with the world and stood firmly against any chasing after fashion or anything else that might lead us away from God.

But they knew that God was using a pair of miracle jeans to draw me to Himself. Despite their reservations, they accepted God's provision of jeans as His will.

"Yasha," Papa said softly. "Here are your jeans, *sinok*." His voice was gentler toward me than I had heard it sound for a long time. "Go put them on, and then we will pray together." My father placed the jeans in my arms.

As I took the jeans from my father, I felt a bit nervous. How can these be normal pants? I wondered. By all accounts they shouldn't even be here. I was almost afraid to put them on. But as soon as the Lees were in my hands, I knew they were exactly as they seemed. Men's, bell bottoms, prewashed, the tags still in place. I went into my room and put on a pair of jeans for the first time in my life, noticing the denim felt stiffer and more substantial than the cotton pants I was used to. They fit me well. I sat down on the bed. God had performed a huge miracle so that I would continue to serve Him, so that I would not deny my faith. I was still plagued with questions. Why was I sentenced to remaining uneducated and poor for being a Christian? And why were the atheists the only ones who could be educated and successful, enjoying material comforts I could only dream of? Were the blue jeans the only consolation I was to have for the drab existence I was certain lay before me?

CHAPTER 19

AN ENEMY OF THE ESTABLISHED ORDER

In order to cleanse the universities of politically unreliable and generally undesirable elements, the university council shall appoint a screening commission... [which] will conduct a political verification of students at the time of admission.[19]

Let their lying lips be silenced, for with pride and contempt they speak arrogantly against the righteous.
—Psalm 31:18

As told by Yakov

WHATEVER HAPPINESS MY renewed attendance at church brought my parents didn't last long. After graduating high school, I decided to try to enter the University and study medicine. I yearned for an education so that I could live in a higher class than my parents, so that I could indulge in Western quality clothing and restaurant meals.

Papa, sincerely puzzled over why I could not accept the inevitable, asked "Yasha, why spend so much effort on something that's not going to work out? Why try to catch the wind in your hands? Get a technical education, learn a trade, and get a job. Then serve God in the church the way I did." What Papa didn't understand was that I was convinced I could serve God and fulfill my ambitions as well. Taking a job involving the mindless repetition of factory labor would be like being locked in a cage; I wanted to spread my wings and fly.

I signed up to take exams at a university in Kiev, and brought my transcripts in for an interview with the registrar. Reporting to the registrar's office on a stifling hot summer day, the sky darkening with the approach of storm clouds, I was trying not to feel nervous, hoping this man might somehow overlook the word "Baptist" written large in red pencil across my records. I really needed another miracle from God this time.

We shook hands. The registrar was very fat and smelled of cigarettes, his round eyes with too much lid giving him a face that would always appear tired even when he was not. His office was bare except for the obligatory framed portrait of Lenin hung on the back wall. Lenin lived, Lenin lives, Lenin will live forever, was the slogan. How could they not see that they had replaced the living God for one that was only a man?

"Oh, Lord, please hear my prayer," I thought as I sat down on the wooden chair in front of his desk. "I ask you for another miracle Lord, another miracle in Jesus' name."

The man, opening my folder, started to read, smoothing back his dark hair, hair that was receding on both sides, the stripe left on the top of his head shaped like the tongue of a large animal.

"Young man, where do you think you are going?" the registrar abruptly asked. "Don't you know there is something in your documents that is a problem?" He tapped one finger where the word "Baptist" was written across my forms as if testing to see if the letters were hot.

"Yes."

"Your grades are very good, Brynza." He sounded surprised.

"Yes," I said again, telling myself not to get angry. I was one of the few Christians that I knew with good grades. I looked at the portrait behind him for distraction. Lenin stared blankly over my head. It was dark enough now that the registrar was partly in shadow, which exaggerated the lines of his face. Although he was still fairly young, his features sagged downward as if the flesh itself no longer wanted to be joined to the bone that held it.

"It's very hard for a Baptist to succeed in school." My voice was respectful, kind even, and I wished my mother were there to hear me talk this way. "I performed well in my classes, but I still would have received bad marks if it weren't for a coach who wanted me on the shot putting team. He made sure my teachers were fair; otherwise I would have been near the bottom of the class." This could make him angry, but I had nothing to lose. "I believe if you think about it, you'll know I'm telling the truth."

Instead of answering, the registrar just raised his eyebrows, and went back to reading my records. "Will you turn on the light, please?" he asked after a moment. "It's by the door."

While the man studied my documents, I waited immobile, as if any motion on my part would ruin my chances. I began to pray again. The registrar was still interested enough to keep me here; maybe there was a chance. After a few more minutes, he closed my file.

"This may not be a university in Moscow," the registrar said, "but we pride ourselves in training our students to be solely at the disposal of Communist ideals. Our nation is still in the transition from capitalism to the creation of a classless society and the withering away of the state. To deviate from the socialist ideology in the slightest degree means strengthening the opposition to our cause of freeing all workers from oppression and exploitation."

He sounded a bit rehearsed to me, but I nodded eagerly, leaning forward, praying with one part of my mind and listening with another.

"I'll be honest. You are intelligent and full of potential. But allowing a Baptist to attend classes here isn't a risk the university can accept."

His words pounded me like a sledgehammer breaking up concrete. Always it came to this moment where people in power crush those without it. I knew I didn't have the strength to stand up and leave his office. I didn't have the strength to live the rest of my life.

"You must understand that if I admitted you and you proselytized the other students it wouldn't be good for them or the university. Or what if you became a doctor and talked about God to your patients? That's not acceptable." He was glancing quickly around the room as he talked, looking everywhere but at me, which made the situation worse. A real man will meet your eye. It was like being killed in battle by a cowardly soldier.

"We've built a great nation," the registrar continued. "And we are struggling to build world communism, starting right here in the Soviet Union. If everyone believed like you, then where would we be? Giving higher education to religious people, to enemies of the established order, could impede the progress of socialism."

I didn't answer. It was finished, and there was nothing to say.

The man began putting my papers back in the file folder. "If you don't mind my asking," he said. "Why are you a Baptist? Oh, I know who your father is. But there is no need for that medieval mildew, now that the Party has eradicated the yoke of economic oppression and all citizens can strive for a better life on earth." It was time to go now, but I didn't have enough left in me to even rise out of that chair. It was like that moment when the school bully finally leaves you lying in the snow, and you can't think of any good reason to ever get up again.

CHAPTER 20

TRAPPED IN A CAGE

One of the most important tasks of Communist education is to overcome religious prejudices in people's mentality.[20]

The fear of the LORD *is the beginning of knowledge.*
—Proverbs 1:7a

As told by Yakov

NO MATTER, I thought. *So I won't be a doctor.* But I will not give up my desire for higher education. The white light of my ambition blinded me to every other possibility. Even though my father thought I was wasting my time, I decided to try again. I knew my chances of getting in to a university were about the same as if I had put on a glittery leotard and tried to beat out Olga Korbut for Olympic Gold, but I decided to apply to an engineering university.

At least this university allowed me to take their entrance exams. The tests were oral and each student was given a grade ranging from one to five. As soon as I sat down, the professors showed me how the word "Baptist" was written on my paperwork in big red letters. The first exam was physics. The professor gave me a three. He kept saying, "You don't know this, you don't know that," when I was sure I had given the correct answers. The next exam was mathematics. Again a three. After that, I knew there was no point in taking any more exams.

Riding home on the bus, my chest tightened with rage, rage that consumed my soul, fueled by a sense of injustice. The authorities had shut me in a cage with no way out. I looked out the window as we drove onto the bridge, the bridge built on top of the huge dam across the Dniepr River, the dam that created the reservoir that buried the famous Zaporozhe rapids. The powers had subdued the river to their will, and that's what they were doing to me. The sunlight glinted white off the hard concrete. I just wanted to live, to breathe, and I couldn't, because of the label "Baptist."

Arriving home, I told Papa what had happened. My anger at the thwarting of my ambition built up like steam in an engine, and finally burst forth.

"Papa, all of your ministries and services are ruining my life! How will I be able to live? What am I supposed to do now?"

As soon as the words were out of my mouth, I could see the pain in my father's face. His eyes were framed with abruptly tapering eyebrows above and dark circles underneath and the lids drooped slightly at the corners. Deep lines ran from his nose to the corners of his mouth, a wide, generous mouth that loved to laugh, savoring the few opportunities for mirth he had. His chin and jaw were still firm; they had to be to withstand the constant pressure he was under. As I looked at him I could see lines appearing in his wide forehead and that the edge of his thick dark hair was receding. He had sacrificed so much, had given his whole life, and now his firstborn son tells him he has ruined all.

"Papa, do you understand? I just want to have some room to breathe, to live, and not feel that I am trapped in a cage. How can you stand it?"

My father put his hand on my arm. "You're my son," he said, "and I love you. Even when things are difficult between us, I love you. You are my treasure here on this earth. If necessary, I'd lay my own life down for you without even hesitating." Holding my hands now in both of his, my father looked right into my eyes and spoke very clearly. "However, if I had to send you, willingly, to a horrible, painful death because I knew that act would save others, oh, Yakov, it would be so terrible. Can you imagine? I would feel as if my heart were cut from my body. But that's what God did for humankind, do you understand? He loves us so much that He gave his only son so that we may be saved. You ask how I can draw breath. I do it every day with huge gratitude because I am loved so much by God, sinner that I am. Yasha, listen. His yoke is easy, and His burden light. Take up His yoke, and you will find the freedom you crave."

I knew now the real struggle before me. God calls us to give our lives over to Him, because Jesus died for us that we might live. Submitting to His will was what all believers are called to do, no matter how unpleasant or inconvenient. I had watched some women in the church grow up, grow old, and never get married. They came to church with bowed, uncovered heads, yearning to be able to wear the head scarf that married women wore to services. It never occurred to me that they might have sacrificed some dreams as well. And I knew my father had always wanted a more challenging job at the factory. How many millions of believers were denied the opportunity for rewarding work, or even to be allowed to live their lives outside of a prison, because of their faith? But it felt like killing a part of me to let my dreams go. Anger alternated with despair.

I prayed long and hard over this question, but received no guidance from God. It was as if He had already provided all the information I needed, and the rest was up to me. My choice came slowly, carefully reasoned over a period of months. What would I gain and what would I lose by going in a given direction? I weighed worldly success against the approval of my family. I compared jeans bought by a doctor with jeans that came straight from God. I imagined walking with the Socialist government and I imagined walking with Christ. I contrasted my parents' lives with the lives of my friends' parents, people who didn't know God. So many broken lives, broken families. Living God's way did bring rewards in this life. In that way, my rational mind decided God was the better choice; I wanted to live the way my parents did.

However, knowing in my mind and submitting my will were two different things. The words my father said to me on that day we had that fight began to hit home. God sacrificed His only son for me, and I was sulking about giving up a career. I considered the believers of my parents' and grandparents' generation. How did they survive? During the Great Terror, the choice was believe, and be punished with death or labor camp, or not believe, and be punished with death or labor camp. Believers could only survive by clinging to God, by trusting in Him that whatever happened in this life, they would have eternal life in the next. They looked beyond the rapids of the present struggle to the safe harbor of the peace and joy that only comes from Jesus that will be ours for eternity. The Lord kept my family safe in an incredibly hostile world, but instead of responding with gratitude I had wanted to bend Him to my will. Still, I struggled. I wanted to serve God, but not in some obscure drudgery. God calls us to be living sacrifices, to sacrifice our lives and ambitions for Him. There really was only one choice, and although I still wished for a better life, I also remembered God's response to Paul when he asked to be healed of some affliction. "My grace is sufficient for thee." The New Year was approaching, and I knew there would be an altar call at the end of the service on December 31. Many of the people who grew up in the church made their public repentance on New Year's Eve. I decided to be one of them this year.

CHAPTER 21

REFINING LIKE SILVER

Labor in the Soviet Union has become a source of joy, creativity and material well-being.[20]

When anxiety was great within me, your consolation brought joy to my soul.
—Psalm 94:19

As told by Yakov

I DON'T FEEL the cold like other men. Many times, I have stood outside comfortably while people nearby are blue-lipped and shivering. This was a blessing for me. If the Communists were in fact building heaven here on earth, they certainly didn't heat their paradise very well. Apartments stayed chilly all winter, and public buildings were worse. I remember sitting in school with the class completely bundled up in hats and scarves, the teacher's gloves white with chalk dust.

It was New Year's Eve, 1977. The service always lasted from eight until midnight. As usual, all of the preachers spoke about the New Year as a good time to begin a new life, and that all people need a personal relationship with Jesus. The youth orchestra played, the choir sang hymns, many written in minor keys reflecting the sadness of our lives, including one sung every New Year, "The years are flying by; we are one more year closer to God." One of the deacons reported how many people had joined the church in the last year and how many had gone to be with the Lord.

Papa, the last to preach, started about 11:15. "How many of you, brothers and sisters, will be with us when Christ returns?" he asked. "And how many of you will have heard His Word but not done anything about it?"

That was me; I knew it. I knew God's Word, but had not submitted to it, convinced I knew better than God what should happen. When Papa made the call, I was among the first to go forward to repent, to give my life to God, to enter the New Year on my knees.

A few months earlier, I began a job in a metal factory. On the first day, the foreman showed me my tools and trained me how to fix the conveyer belt. The whole process took about thirty minutes. When he finished, I asked, "Is that all?"

Something must have showed on my face because the foreman glanced at me curiously. "That's all. Why, is there a problem?"

"No, no problem." What could I say? I was eighteen years old, had just received training for the job I would probably have for the rest of my life, training that had taken less than an hour. A monkey could have carried out my tasks if he had thumbs to hold the wrench. I was hungry for so much more. My ambition was too intense, I knew that. My desires were partly of the flesh rather than the spirit, and they were consuming me.

While I was waiting to be summoned to make a repair, I watched some of the other workers. Their task was to pick up a piece of metal, bring it to a table, drill four perfectly spaced holes in each corner, and then carry the sheet to the next station. The job took two people. There was an almost hypnotic rhythm in their routine:

carry, drill, carry, stack. As I was waiting, a man came over to me. He retracted the muscles of his face, revealing the double row of steel caps running across all of his front teeth, top and bottom. Most of the hair on his head was gone, but he had plenty growing out of his ears and nose.

"Hello," he said enthusiastically shaking my hand. "I'm Timoshenko. Ivan Borisovich Timoshenko. It's wonderful to have someone new here. The man before you was so lazy that we fell way behind on production. I swear to you, I've never seen someone move so slowly. I used to tell him, 'Sergei, you've got to go faster,' but he never listened."

"I'm a hard worker," I said.

He smiled, and his silver teeth glinted in the dim light from the bulb above us. I glanced from the metal tool in my hands to the metal in his mouth, thinking for a crazy second that this factory was slowly eating him, starting with his teeth. "So, what's your name, comrade?" he asked.

"Brynza. Yakov Brynza."

Suddenly the heat of the factory turned to ice. "Brynza? You're from that Baptist family. I heard a Baptist was coming to work here."

Instantly I knew who Ivan Borisovich was: the political officer. Every factory and organization employed one, to ensure the workers had the proper socialist spirit.

"I intend to do my job well," I told him.

"And what does that mean?" he snarled at me. "I know what job you mean to do, you Christian! Sabotage the labor effort and undermine communist ideals. I'll be watching you."

From then on, Ivan Borisovich made a point of watching me work, all the while spitting comments about believers. "Do you really believe God is everywhere? Well, He's not here."

"We have liberated mankind from exploitation, but you believers would rather cling to lies and fairy tales."

"I'm watching you, enemy of Marxist philosophy."

He would slither up behind me, hoping to catch me in some act of sabotage. Every tiny deviation from perfection gave him a chance to criticize. Or else he'd join in conversations I was having with coworkers.

"Did you fellows know that Brynza is a Baptist?" he'd say. "Tell us, Brynza, is it true? Do you really drink blood in your services?"

"It's not real blood...."

"That's enough, Brynza. You know you could be fired for proselytizing."

Anger consumed me like acid, and I took my struggle to my father. Papa was sitting at his desk, his open Bible illuminated by a single lamp. Was it the dim lights, or were the lines etched more deeply in his face? Were the circles under his eyes darker because I was adding to his pain? I wondered.

"Papa," I said, "I'm with Christ now, so why do I still get so angry even when I don't want to? Why is it so hard for me to act the way I know I should?"

My father patted me on the shoulder. "Let's take a look," he said ruffling through the finger-worn pages of his small black Bible, the gold letters "*BIBLIA*" on the cover slightly faded. That Bible was a living member of our family. It had a voice that was every bit as distinctive as the gentle authority of my father's.

"This isn't working out," I said. "I've accepted Christ and I truly want to serve God. So why am I so angry? I thought everything would get easier."

My father found Romans 7 and began to read. "For what I am doing, I do not understand. For what I will to do, that I do not practice; but what I hate, that I do" (7:15 NKJV). He read slowly, emphasizing each phrase with deliberate care. "For I know that in me (that is, in my flesh) nothing good dwells; for to will is present with me, but *how* to perform what is good I do not find" (7:18 NKJV).

Listening to him, I could feel the perfect, pointed journey of those words from God to Paul, reaching me two thousand years later in our small house.

"For the good that I will *to do,* I do not do; but the evil I will not *to do,* that I practice. Now if I do what I will not *to do,* it is no longer I who do it, but sin that dwells in me" (7:19-20 NKJV).

My father continued to read, and I felt a turning deep inside, a hidden clock being reset to the correct time. Repentance doesn't happen once, I thought, it happens every day.

He closed the Bible, and looked up. My father's skin was tinged with pink as if he'd gone for a walk outdoors. "So, you see, Paul struggled, I struggle, and so will you. Yasha, I don't have your ambitions, but my road is no easier. It's just different. I sin. You know I struggle with keeping my temper."

"Yes," I said. "I understand."

"All of these trials are God's way of purifying us, removing the sin from us. He is refining us like silver, so that we are more like Jesus. It's not easy, nor is it quick."

While my father's words brought me some comfort, I still had no idea how I would get through the next day at that factory, let alone the rest of my life.

CHAPTER 22

SURRENDER BRINGS VICTORY

Religion will not last because it is an ideological construct which will find less and less correlation to current economic and political relations.
—Soviet Antireligious Journal[22]

For the eyes of the LORD range throughout the earth to strengthen those whose hearts are fully committed to him.
—2 Chronicles 16:9

As told by Yakov

I WORKED HARD that day, and the next, and the next. Ivan Borisovich never let up his harassment of me. I accepted that this was God's way of making me more like His Son, but even so, there were plenty of days when, despite all my prayers, my anger welled up just at the sight of Ivan.

On the surface, my days were uneventful; underneath, I wrestled with resentment and bitterness. Every day I prayed for a submissive heart. I asked God to give me the strength to accept my life, but I still yearned to be more than a factory worker.

Winter ended, and then it was spring. I'd been toiling in the factory for about a year. One day at work, I read a notice posted on the bulletin board from the Moscow State Institute of Steel and Alloys, announcing the start of the new academic year. Although I didn't know anyone who had gone to that university, it had a good reputation. In 1970 it won the Best Technical Institute of Higher Education in the USSR prize from the World Universities Congress.

The program lasted six years, and students who completed it earned a degree in Metallurgical Engineering. The instant I saw that flier I desperately wanted to go. True, it wasn't medical school, but I didn't care. I would have gone for a degree in oriental art if it meant getting out of that factory and into a university.

I wrote to the university, requesting an application, but as soon as I received it, I knew it was useless to even try. In order to be considered, workers needed a signature from their direct supervisor as well as the chief of the labor union. My supervisor would sign; I was sure of that. He was the foreman of our section, and even though the man didn't like Baptists, I knew he would sign my application, understanding that it would never get past the head of the labor union. That way, later on he could say, "I did my best for you, Brynza."

But the labor boss, Marchenko, was out of the question. The one time I'd met him, he said, "Brynza, hmmm. Are you part of that Baptist family?" When I replied that yes, I was a Christian, he answered, "People like you are bad for the Socialist system. We have a single, unified vision that keeps us healthy and strong, and your ideas are not a part of it." He turned to the foreman who was standing next to him. "Make sure this man doesn't cause any problems."

I tried and tried to think of a way to get Marchenko to sign my forms, but no solution came to me. I filled out all the forms, and took them to work with me every day knowing that it was futile, but I was unwilling to completely give up. I begged God to intervene, and prayed equally as hard for patience and humility if He did not.

Finally I could wait no longer. I asked the foreman for permission to leave a few minutes early to go to the labor boss' office, and he said, "Of course, Brynza. Good luck." We both knew I had no chance.

The labor union office was in a dirty yellow building with a tin roof. I walked inside, blinking in the sudden dimness. The door to the chief's office was closed. I stood there for a moment, praying. *"We know that all things work together for the good of those who love God: those who are called according to His purpose."* I knocked. There was no answer, so after a few seconds, I knocked again.

"Yes," said a voice from inside the room. I opened the door, but instead of the labor boss, there was a very young woman. "May I help you?" she asked. She had a large, complicated blond hairdo completely surrounding her face, and she peered at me from inside of it like an alley cat peeking from the bushes. She seemed more frightened than I.

"I'm looking for Marchenko," I said.

"He's on vacation sunbathing. I'm filling in for him, so what is it you need?"

For a moment I was stunned into absolute silence. The whole time I angrily fought God, He was slowly preparing all the pieces of this great miracle.

"I have some documents to be signed," I said. My voice sounded too tense for someone with simple paperwork, and the woman looked at me curiously.

"What kind of documents? I don't know if I'm allowed to sign documents."

"Really? How long have you worked here?"

"Two weeks. So I don't know…"

"I wondered why I had never seen you before. Did you grow up in the city?"

In desperation I kept her chatting, thinking as long as she continued to talk, she at least hadn't said no. After a few minutes of small talk, she asked to see my papers.

Handing over the application, I forced my expression to be neutral, almost bored.

The woman started leafing through the pages. "Moscow, eh? I suppose it would be all right. It seems routine enough to me." As she took out the stamp from the Labor Union, all the breath suddenly left my lungs like I'd taken a hard hit playing hockey. I prayed to calm myself, *Lord, please let this miracle be real.* I could hear my own attempts to breathe, quick and jagged.

Even though I was literally falling to pieces in front of her, the woman remained oblivious. Whap! She thunked down the stamp, asking, "Have you ever been to Moscow? I haven't. Twenty-six hours on the train is a long way to go." Whap, whap, two more stamps. Her hand moved quickly, making the nail polish on the tips of her fingers blur into a single, bright line. It formed a red stripe in the air in front of me. Whap. "Here you go," she said. "All the best to you."

I walked outside and leaned against the building, clutching my forms and trying to collect myself. What had I done to deserve this miracle? Nothing. It was pure grace.

At that moment I had no idea that a few weeks later, when a representative from the university came to the factory to interview me, and Marchenko learned that his substitute had stamped my forms, that a scandal would erupt in the factory. I also didn't know that my education would be delayed again while I served my two years of mandatory military service. And it was only years later, when I was partway through my studies in Moscow, that I realized the perfection of God's timing, that He had more reasons for making me wait, not just to learn to trust Him. During my years in the university, Brezhnev died, and the government began what it called a dismantling of communism. I was freer to question, to have fellowship with the thirty or forty other believers also studying in Moscow, none of which would have been possible had I attended the university even a few years earlier. Farther into the future, I would realize that God gave back to me everything I thought I had lost during the years of persecution. But all that was ahead of me; all I knew now was the miracle of God's love for me, His grace freely given, and how He moves in all circumstances.

I decided to walk home rather than crowding onto a trolley. Tucking the stamped application under my arm, I began to amble down the street, caught up in the swirling of my thoughts, smiling at the whiff of sweetness from the red and yellow flowers an old woman was selling. No longer was I trying to row the boat of my ambition upstream, trying to get ahead of God. Instead, God had unfurled a blazing white sail and had provided the wind to fuel my dreams, a white sail vivid against the blue sky and golden afternoon.

CHAPTER 23

FIGHTING TO AVOID CONFLICT

Glory to Labor!
—Sign on Factory[23]

Glory in his holy name; let the hearts of those who seek the Lord *rejoice.*
—1 Chronicles 16:10

As told by Viktor

"GLORY TO THE heroes of Soviet Labor!" proclaimed the red letters on the rippling banner the auto factory workers waved as they marched in the Labor Day parade. The people in the front of the crowd cheered. My friends and I loitering in the back were too busy to bother. Labor Day, May 1, is by far my favorite holiday, I thought. We get the day off. More time for fun. I washed down some sweet rolls with lemonade, ignoring the parade. The air was gently hot that day, warm like bread fresh from the oven. Another group marched by, the slogans on their banner encouraging us all to produce more for the workers' paradise we lived in. One banner urged "Let's catch up with and surpass America." Once the festivities wound down, my friends and I raced off to the fields outside of town for the real pleasure of the day—soccer.

After a few hours, I told my friends I had to leave. "Come on, Vitya, just play a little more."

"You know I can't. You know I have to feed my rabbits."

"Play a bit longer," they coaxed me. "We'll help you pick grass later."

Later I sped home, a big sack stuffed with grass for my herd of fifty or so rabbits slung over my shoulders. My family always tended animals: goats, pigs, chickens, or ducks. But the rabbits were mine. My parents recognized my love of animals, and decided to foster this interest by entrusting me with some that would be my very own.

So when a neighbor gave me two rabbits, Papa and Mama encouraged me in my desire to raise more. Papa and I labored an entire afternoon constructing a wooden cage. Soon I had thirty rabbits, then fifty.

At first I didn't question why my parents were so supportive of this new hobby. A few months earlier, when I turned twelve, I stopped obeying my parents' rules about coming home early. Why come home to chores or homework when I could be playing soccer or just loafing with my friends? It took me a few years to realize tending rabbits was intended to keep me busy at home and not playing soccer.

Breeding rabbits was not just a pastime or strategy to keep me out of trouble. Without the rabbits we would have rarely eaten meat. While I knew from the start the rabbits would one day appear on our dinner table, the first time I had to kill one of them was traumatic. Cradling the bunny in my arms, stroking its soft, warm fur, crying, mourning as if I was attending the funeral of someone I dearly loved, I carried it to the backyard to slaughter it.

When I wasn't in school or busy with chores, I pursued happiness in the form of having a good time, often accompanying my friends to the movies or the circus, even though these really weren't activities Baptists approved of. Every time, it was the same story. I'd have fun with my buddies, then on the way home the uneasy feeling would begin to grow. I would look around—were there any other believers in sight? What if Jesus came back while I was at the movies, and didn't take me? Christians didn't go to the movies. We were to be separated from the world. I walked faster, hoping to see someone from the church. Soon I was running for home, bursting through the front door. No one was home. Frantically I grabbed the Bible and opened it. Relief flooded me as I saw the words still on the pages. I knew that the church would remain on earth as long as the Word of God did. If the Word was still here, then so were the other believers. I hadn't been left behind. Looking back, I laugh at my mangled theology. My understanding was limited but somehow my parents had managed to impress some of their values on me.

As I grew older, I developed a taste for other hobbies. Fighting was one of them. Kids at school who enjoyed picking on me for being a Baptist paid for their taunts in bloody noses or black eyes. All I wanted was to get along with everyone. If necessary, I would gain peace by using my physical strength.

Some of this aggression spilled over at home. Mama and Papa were often away on church business, and Yakov was put in charge. One day, when he was almost seventeen, he was particularly bossy, savoring his power and authority over the rest of us. I came in from feeding my rabbits and our other animals. Yasha was seated at the kitchen table, school books and papers spread around, issuing orders like some kind of medieval tsar.

"Lena, when you are done peeling the potatoes, you need to clean the floors. Venya, did you pick the berries yet? And go weed the tomatoes."

Then he looked up and saw me. "What took you so long? Papa wants more coal brought in. Get started."

What gives him the right to talk to me, or any of us, that way? I thought. *Just because he's the oldest? I don't think so.* At that moment I decided I was going to teach him a lesson. Yakov was three years older and smarter, but I was bigger and stronger.

"I'm not going to give in to you anymore," I told him. I'm not sure who started it, but pretty soon I was beating him and he had picked up a chair to hit me with. I could feel a surge of power each time I struck him, and a wild joy in proving I was stronger. Lena, who was watching the whole affair, started to sob. "Stop it! You'll kill each other!" she cried. We stopped, ashamed, and never fought at home anymore.

As I grew older, I wanted to try forbidden activities, like smoking and drinking. I also wanted to know what it was like to be drunk, and found out when I was fifteen. What my friends and I were doing and what we drank that day I have long forgotten. What I do remember is that soaring pride I felt. Now that I'd been drunk, I was my own man, really grown up.

Even though my parents were powerless to stop me from smoking or drinking, I couldn't deceive them. Every time I'd been out with my buddies, up to no good, Papa or Mama met me at the door. "Viktor, why were you and your friends smoking on the way home from school?"

I'd eaten some candy when I started for home, which I was sure covered up the smell on my breath. "No, I was standing near some people smoking." My parents never fell for that.

"And who were you fighting with?" they would ask.

"How did you know that?" I would reply in surprise.

"God told us, through some of our kind friends. You know that your footprints will always get home before you do."

In our house, punishment fell quickly on the child who came home late, forgot to finish chores, or neglected homework, falling swifter for smoking, drinking, or fighting. Skipping church activities was never punished. Devotion to God had to be our own choice.

At that time in my life, going to church appealed to me as much as eating potatoes without salt. I was present at the services and youth meetings just to escape arguing with my parents. As much as I enjoyed fistfights, I hated conflict and tried to avoid it like cats shun water. Mama's tears and Papa's quiet disappointment were mightier than the belt we were whipped with for other transgressions. I worked hard to avoid them at all costs. *Why create a scandal*, I thought. *If I can please my parents by going to the youth meeting, I'll go. If it pleases my friends to go to the movies with them afterward, I'll go.*

While our parents gladly sent us off to evening youth meetings, they expected us to return home by ten. After the meetings, Yasha and I often walked some of the girls home or went to a small café to drink tea. Then we'd play soccer or hockey, depending on the season, till well after midnight. We knew we could get away with it when Papa and Mama had been called away on some church business—a funeral at this church, a pastor sick at another needing Papa to fill in, or some kind of problem in one of the thirty-two churches under Papa's oversight that demanded his attention. Because of the distance involved and the difficulty in travel, my parents often didn't return home until two in the morning. If we were caught out late, we'd get a whipping from Papa. "Don't you know we are worried about you? There could have been a car accident. Or you could have been attacked by some drunks," Papa would say as he readied the belt.

CHAPTER 24

FOOLISH AND WISE CHOICES

It's clear to everyone that a young man with religious inclinations cannot possibly make a career. If he is not on our side spiritually and politically, there is no place for him.
—Comrade Mironov, Communist Party Official[24]

L<small>ORD</small>, you have assigned me my portion and my cup; you have made my lot secure.
—Psalm 16:5

As told by Viktor

STUMBLING HOME AT one in the morning after an evening drinking with my buddies, I opened the locked front door with a thin knife. Freezing like a startled animal sensing danger, one hand still grasping the doorknob, in the moonlight I saw my parents waiting for me in the kitchen. "Sit down, Vitya," Papa said.

I sat down at the table, across from Mama. The full moon shone through the kitchen window, glaring at me like an accusing eye. Papa fixed his gaze on me and said, "We are not going to whip you anymore. You must choose the path of your life. Now that you have finished school, you are old enough to decide for yourself. At your age I was already preaching, and had decided these eternal questions for myself."

I hadn't rejected the faith, and didn't plan on it. The pleasures of the world attracted me, and I wanted to have both. Papa pushed his empty tea cup away from himself and continued. "Let's look at our neighbors on the street and see how they have decided for themselves. Who do you want to be like? What about our poor Jewish neighbors? Their daughter abandoned their traditions, went out on the street, and came home pregnant. Do you want that kind of life?" He looked straight at me, his eyes demanding an answer.

"No, Papa, I don't."

"And what about the two guys across the street, who were a few years older than you in school? The ones who fought continuously. I heard that at a wedding they beat each other so badly an ambulance was called. Do you want that kind of life?"

"No, I don't like that kind of life."

"How about the guy down the street who fought so much that he ended up in prison? Is that what you want?"

"No, I don't want that either."

Papa brought up at least twenty examples. In the case of every neighbor, Papa showed me that they all had chosen the life they wanted. None of their choices held any appeal for me. This one was in prison; that one a slave to alcohol. Others were drifting aimlessly. My parents made it clear to me that I needed to consider the neighbors and our own family, and consider the results of the lives they were leading. Then I would need to choose. "Look around you, look at our family, and decide."

But I wasn't ready to choose. I had some other ideas about my life. It still irked me how my teachers and classmates had laughed at me for being from a Christian, believing family. A scene from a few years earlier flashed into my mind. Along with some of the other boys from school, I participated in a shooting competition using AK-47s. The Minister of the Military for the *oblast* observed the competition. After I won, he congratulated me. "Brynza, you can do more than pray; you can shoot!" Even he knew about my faith and felt obligated to comment on it. All anyone could see when they looked at me was the label "Baptist." I desired salvation, but I didn't want to suffer for it. The world offered some pleasures that I wanted to taste and was willing to live a double life to get them both.

Fed up with the baggy, shapeless clothes of faded gray, mass produced by Soviet factories, the only clothes we could afford to buy, I wanted money. I bought some khaki pants and dyed them to make them look like fashionably worn blue jeans. Then I began to sell them on the black market, standing with others who were trying out capitalism on a small scale, all of us in a row behind the main food market. I stood there, holding up a pair of my fake jeans for people to see. If I saw any police coming, I stuffed the jeans into the bag at my feet, just like everyone else was doing. When the police left, business resumed.

I peddled my fake jeans on the black market and in the dormitories of the *uchilishe*, the technical school I attended after finishing eighth grade. At that time, there was such a shortage of jeans that I had no trouble selling them. In that way I could earn a few rubles of my own. While we had never gone hungry or lacked clothes to wear, I thirsted for more—western clothes, gourmet food, money for ice cream or cigarettes.

One day one of the older guys from the market struck up a conversation with me. "How did you get started in the jeans business?" he asked me.

"I wanted some money and thought this was a good way to get it," I answered.

"So it was all your idea?" the man said thoughtfully. "You appear to have a talent for making money, young man."

"I like selling things," I told him. "And I like making money even more."

He smiled at me, crinkling the corners of his eyes. "That's not the sentiment of someone striving to build world communism," he joked.

"I'm not really thinking about that," I answered quickly. "I just wanted to be able to buy some new clothes."

"No matter," he said, waving his hand in the air as if to brush away an unwanted fly. "A clever man will always have a hat for his head. And you seem like a clever fellow. How would you like to make even more money?"

"How?"

"All you need to do is take a suitcase of clothes to Dnipropetrovsk," he told me.

This seemed easy enough to me. Just ride the bus for two hours, deliver a suitcase and come back. I readily agreed, once he told me how much he was going to pay me. It was more money than I could make in a month. He gave me a full suitcase, as well as a bag of pants and sports shoes, and the address where I was to take the luggage.

When Yakov found out, he called me a speculator.

"What are you talking about? This isn't speculation in clothing sales."

"Then what is it?" Yakov demanded. "They pay you a lot of money just to carry a suitcase."

"Yasha, it's just business."

"Vitya, how do you know it's not narcotics?" I laughed at that idea, but I knew Yakov would tell my parents about my new business venture. They didn't understand my desire for excitement, for fun, and this new job was just what I thought I was looking for.

Papa strove to reason with me. "You don't need to be doing this. Do you understand the consequences? Do you want to go to prison?"

"Papa, it's all right. Nothing is going to happen."

"Have you forgotten that the authorities are just looking for a reason to remove me from my post as senior presbyter? Do you want me to be fined? Or perhaps put in prison?"

"Of course I don't. But what could go wrong? I'm just riding the bus to deliver a suitcase. Besides, if anything happens, I can take care of it."

My parents were horrified by what I was doing, and shamed that one of their sons would be so lawless. "We should be examples for good, not evil," Mama pointed out to me. She started to pray, "God, go with him and protect him, if nothing can be done to convince him to do what is right." The words of Mama's prayer lingered in my memory like unwanted guests.

Every time I took one of these trips to Dnipropetrovsk and Mama sent me off with prayers, I missed the bus. Or else it would break down, or arrive late so I'd miss the person I was to meet on the other end. It wasn't many weeks before I realized I was not going to be a success at being a carrier of clothes or drugs or whatever they had in the suitcase. It was as pointless to fight against Mama's prayers as trying to empty the river with a bucket. The power behind Mama's prayers was God Himself.

During this time, my whole purpose in life was to have fun and to avoid problems. While I enjoyed my jeans business and smoking with my friends, I didn't want any friction with my parents. Attending church and youth activities was a small price to pay for preserving a good relationship with Papa and Mama. Besides, the youth orchestra was thrilling; traveling to perform in other churches was strictly forbidden by the government. Of course, if the authorities discovered that we had played for another church, my father, as the *oblast* presbyter, would pay large fines. Allowing such trips was like stealing meat from a sleeping bear, but Papa was willing to pay a high price to keep the youth involved in the church. Most of the children who were the same age as Lena and me stayed in the church and believed. We might have had our struggles, but we never completely lost faith. After Vladimir Antonovich left our church, many of the children of Veniamin's age started to drift away. While the youth orchestra and choir continued, the kids of that age group no longer had a zealous leader who understood them with his soul and inspired them to stay true to their faith.

So many adventures we had, traveling all over Ukraine with the youth orchestra. Every time we planned a trip, we waited in anticipation like small children before a holiday, because that's what Vladimir Antonovich made of each and every excursion. He planned picnics and soccer games to amuse us as we traveled, creating a joyous atmosphere and memories we would treasure forever.

One such outing took us to Berdyansk, a small city on the Azov Sea. Twenty or so of us gathered in one corner of the train station's drab waiting hall, piling our instruments and coats high on the wooden benches. A few of the girls handed out cookies and other treats. We were laughing and eating, singing Christian songs accompanied by Sergei's guitar. The echoes of our voices off the bare concrete walls strengthened our harmonies, enhancing the beauty of the music. Some people waiting for their trains gathered around and listened to us sing, glad to have some entertainment. Others started to talk with us, intrigued that young people were involved with the church. Soviet propaganda taught that only old, illiterate people believed in God.

Then I felt a slow chill creeping through the room, like a slowly rising fog. The waiting hall seemed darker, as if the sun had been covered by a cloud. There was a stillness about the people in the hall, and most of my friends stopped singing. They were all looking at something behind me. I turned around and saw two police officers approaching. One was young, not much older than most of us and skinny like a chicken. "Hey, guys, stop singing, o.k.? You know you're not allowed to do this!" he said.

The second, older one was not so polite. He was a large man, with the red face of an angry man. He glared at us with bloodshot eyes and said, "What are you thinking? This is illegal propaganda! Do you think you are in a church? Why are you creating this disturbance?"

Vladimir Antonovich quietly answered, "There's no harm in our singing. I don't think we are disturbing anyone."

"You know that in the Soviet Union there is separation of church and state. You can sing your songs about fairy tales in your church if you want to, but not on government property. If you don't stop, we'll have to take you to the police station."

Some of the girls glanced nervously at each other. I knew what they were thinking. Would we really have to go to the station? What would they do to us there? Would there be fines, or worse? We'd all heard the stories of believers being beaten by the KGB. It still happened sometimes. I tried to not look worried.

"Young man, why do you tell them to stop?" a grandmotherly woman who had been listening to us said to them. "I'd rather hear them singing than for them to be drunk." She set down the bucket of potatoes she was carrying with a thump. "I'd much rather listen to them sing."

A few people in the crowd made some noises like they agreed. "It doesn't matter what you think, *babushka*," the older officer said. "Those songs are illegal and must not be sung here. We have the right to take you all in."

"Fine, fine," Vladimir Antonovich told him. "We don't want to cause any trouble." The police officers watched as we collected our instruments and other belongings and went outside to the benches on the platform. Then we started to sing again.

Experiences like this welded us together, giving us a sense of belonging that we never felt in school where we were always the outsiders. The bonds between us helped strengthen our faith in God. Each time the police questioned us, we could have been arrested.

Yet over and over we witnessed how Vladimir Antonovich used the wisdom God gave him by always speaking softly to the police, never being confrontational, and God always protected us. Serving God became an adventure, and trusting God was a daily reality.

On New Year's Day of 1980, when I was 17, I sat in the church service with my three friends Vova, Sasha, and Zhurik. My father was preaching on his usual New Year's theme of the new and abundant life that can be found in God. The four of us were so moved by the service we declared to each other, "Let's start a new, good life, and turn to God." We left church that day with the intention of repenting during the evening service. On the way home I bought a bottle of beer. Regret washed over me faster than the beer flowed down my throat. "How can I repent when I've just drunk beer?" I truly wanted to start a new life, to repent, but thought that it wasn't going to work out. My weaknesses and love of pleasure were too strong for me to overcome in my own strength. All day I was fighting with myself, wondering what to do. None of us four repented that night.

A few days later, on the evening of January 6, which was the Orthodox Christmas Eve, about twenty-five of the youth went Christmas caroling. This was illegal, but as usual my father was willing to risk the fine. When we went caroling, we traveled by train to nearby villages or settlements, singing for non-believers and leaving tracts. On our return, we gathered in our kitchen, sitting up practically until morning, drinking tea, eating some of the napoleons Mama baked in preparation for Lena's birthday on the seventh, and talking about what had happened while we were caroling.

This particular time, my friend Zhurik bought a bottle of wine while we were waiting for the train. "That's funny, Zhurik, taking wine along when we are going to preach," I told him. After an hour's ride on the local train to the village of Novoe Zaporozhye, the rest of the group went from door to door singing and reading from the

Bible. Zhurik, Vova, Sasha, and I snuck off to the graveyard and drank a little wine. Soon the four of us were feeling good. Around eleven we rejoined the rest of the group.

We walked past a store where some local youths were loafing. Tonight there was something interesting for them to look at—the girls who'd come from the city. "She looks nice," I heard one say about one of the girls from our church. "Let's invite her to the café."

"Hey, girls! Why do you want to hang around with these guys? It's more fun with us."

The group from the church moved on. "Leave the girls alone," Vova told the locals.

They argued with us. We had to hit two of them to end the argument. Then we went on and caught up with the rest of the group.

About midnight we decided to go home. On the way to the train station we ran into about thirty local youths in long leather coats, out to avenge themselves for the two that we had hit. They insulted some of the girls in the group and a fight broke out. Vova was beaten badly in the face before it was over. Zhurik had a broken arm, and Sasha, a broken leg. I escaped with just a few bruises.

Of course, the parents of the others who were in the fight came to our house the next day to ask how it started. Naturally, none of us culprits admitted what really happened for at least the next ten years. Privately we asked Vova, who was hurt the worst, for forgiveness. But I started to feel uncomfortable in my spirit, wrestling with my shame. The words of Job, "I am a worm, not a man" kept running through my head. We had made so many people worry, and had taken a big risk that could have had bad consequences for many others, not to mention what could have happened to my father. All because we wanted to drink some wine and pick some fights. *This is no way to live,* I thought.

During the Christmas service next morning, Papa gave an altar call inviting people to repent. I felt my heart pounding. God was calling me, but I resisted, even though I understood that if I didn't repent, tomorrow the guilt would be even worse. I kept thinking about the night before and how it turned out badly and that Vova wouldn't be able to come to the service for a few days because of his injuries. I writhed with shame, realizing I was like a wild animal, unable to control myself. I wanted to repent, but couldn't. There was so much to give up—the fun of drinking and smoking and fighting—but I knew I couldn't live like that anymore. As strong as I was physically, I knew I was too weak to change my own heart or my own behavior. God would have to change me, and provide the courage and boldness to be able to stand and publicly repent in the church. After ten days of struggle, with God's help I repented on a cold January Sunday. Joy replacing shame was only one change in my life that was visible to all. From that time on I clearly understood why several parents had said, "God forbid that Vitya would come after my daughter!" This was a reflection of the kind of life I had been leading.

I knew my repentance was real because making money or smoking didn't seem so important any more. Papa told me that God had entered my heart and that I needed to cling to that thought. It wasn't long before I could see other changes. I had never been much of a reader. After I repented, I'd sit down to read two chapters in my Bible and before I knew it, I'd read three or more. Suddenly I had all kinds of time to read the Bible, when before I never could seem to fit it in. And I don't know where all the words came from, that enabled me to pray for as long as ten minutes. Earlier I never understood how my parents could pray for hours. Now that my heart belonged to the Lord, I understood what it meant to live for Jesus, and to be changed by Him, and to have a relationship with Him. Now I had a purpose in life. All the things I couldn't change on my own, Jesus was able to change, and He changed me from a person leading a double life into a single-minded servant.

A few months later I graduated from the *uchilishe*. Many of my classmates decided to attend chauffeurs' school because there was no tuition. All that was necessary was to obtain a reference from the *uchilishe* stating that the person had studied well and had graduated. The *uchilishe* readily gave me a reference, so I confidently presented it and my other documents to the registrar at the chauffeurs' school. Seeing that all of my documents were marked in red letters "Baptist," he laughed rudely. Sneering insolently he said, "Do you really think, Baptist, you are going to study? You're not going to."

I argued a little with him. "But I got good grades in the *uchilishe*, and I have a good reference."

"Just get out of here and stop wasting my time. Parasites like you don't deserve any education."

The following Monday Papa went to the Commission for the Affairs of Religious Cults. The authorities said that there will never be that kind of freedom for believers, to receive whatever education they wanted. Papa called around to all the powers and the communists and the authorities over religion at that time, everyone that he knew. No one could help in any way. Disappointment weighed on my soul. Papa calmed me down, saying, "Satan has succeeded this time, but not forever." I understood that nothing happens accidentally in the life of a believer, that what others mean for evil in my life, God will use for good. But what now?

Fulfilling my mandatory service in the army was my only choice. Fighting against it, not wanting to submit, I understood this was the will of God. In the end it was easier for me to accept the thwarting of my plans than it had been for my ambitious older brother.

Soon after Yakov was accepted into the university, he found he had to go into the army. At least for him, he knew that when his two years were up, he could still pursue his dream. The army sent him to Gorkii (now Nizhny Novgorod), and at first none of the officers wanted him under their command. It was the same old story; all his papers had "Baptist" written in big red letters at the top.

After two months or so, they put Yakov in charge of the food warehouse. There had been several thefts, and they sternly told Yakov they expected no more. Yakov never gave in when people tried to bribe him to let them steal food, even when they tried to threaten him or intimidate him, because God showed him how to handle them. When Yakov completed his time in the army, the officer told Yakov that he gave that job to him because "everyone knows Baptists don't steal."

Maybe that's how it will be for me, I thought. *I'll get a good job, stay out of trouble, serve quietly, and avoid conflict.*

There was another reason I did not want to join the army. By this time the war in Afghanistan had begun. Terrible stories circulated of the enemy's practice of torturing our captured soldiers to death. My family prayed long about this, but in the end, we found we didn't really have to worry. Christians were not considered trustworthy, so the army never sent believers to a war zone. Yet again God protected His own!

Instead of Afghanistan, the army sent me to Volgograd, where I thought I'd learn how to build rockets. Since I was one of those undependable Christians who might be spies or saboteurs, I was put to work sweeping the floors. After I'd been there about a month, I met a Pentecostal, and then another Baptist, then more. Papa promised me that wherever the army sent me, there would be other believers. I was expecting to find one or two, so it was a thrill to meet fifty from all over the USSR. On one of the army holidays, we held a worship service in a corner of the stadium. After that, whoever was able met in the stadium every evening. Although the army kept us busy almost every minute of the day, there were never less than ten at our evening meetings. We even took a picture of our gathering to send home. It was our way of fighting back against the system that tried to take away our faith.

But our activities didn't go unnoticed. The political officer called me, as one of the organizers, to his office, and said, "Religious activities are prohibited. You need to stop meeting." We continued to gather for worship anyway. The KGB men ground their teeth, called some of us in, and asked, "What's going on?"

"You know what's going on," we answered. "What did you call us in for?"

"Because you haven't stopped your religious meetings. Don't you know it's forbidden to meet?"

Another officer added, "You have more than twenty people. That's already a church. It's forbidden to have a church in the army!"

The other believers and I looked at each other. "Why not? Let's have a church in the army."

At that, they sent us away with stern warnings and threats about hard labor and punishment cells if we didn't give up gathering together. For me, there was no question in my mind what I was going to do. The Bible tells us to not give up meeting together, and we had to obey the Bible over what the army said. Those meetings gave us such strength, encouragement, and a sense of God's love for us, that we could stand firm and endure all the atheistic lectures and teasing from the officers and other soldiers. I have to admit, I enjoyed the battle. This was better than any fistfight; a much better way to resist the atheists' efforts to take away our faith.

There were informers everywhere, and in our group of believers it was no different. The other leaders and I kept getting called in to the military police. They talked and talked like the endless droning of insects and then let me go. One day a high-ranking officer challenged me, "Tomorrow you must decide. If you don't do as we want, then tomorrow you will go work with cement."

"I don't need until tomorrow to decide," I answered. "Hard work doesn't scare me."

"Believe me, Brynza," he said. "You very much do not want to be sent to hard labor."

The hard labor turned out to be cleaning the nearby nuclear weapons plant. I swept the floors and hauled trash, having no idea whether the trash was radioactive or not. After two months I caught a severe sore throat. They sent me to the army hospital. About a week later there was an accident on the base and scores of injured soldiers were brought in. The hospital staff put me to work to help out. Because the doctors noticed I was a hard and trustworthy worker, they kept me for the remaining fourteen or fifteen months of my army service. I worked in several departments, taking the history of illness and helping to bathe and feed the patients. From time to time the commander of my old unit came to take me back. The doctors always told him, "This man is sick. He can't go back to hard labor."

I was beginning to understand how God works in our lives. He sends small trials and helps us to pass through them, then puts us in a good place, like my job in the hospital. I had much more free time than I had before and was able to freely go to church services or youth meetings off the base. God gave me the victory in that fight with the army.

CHAPTER 25

GOD PROTECTS AND PROVIDES

*Nobody trusted anyone else, and every acquaintance
was a suspected police informer.*
—Nadezhda Mandelstan[25]

*Trust in the L*ORD *with all your heart and lean not on your own
understanding; in all your ways acknowledge him,
and he will make your paths straight.*
—Proverbs 3:5-6

As told by Viktor

WHEN I RETURNED home from the army, my parents weren't sure if I'd completely turned my back on my old loves: fighting, smoking, and money. To keep me busy, Papa helped me get a job at the factory.

Soon after I'd started working, a guy named Pasha sidled up to me at the beginning of the shift. We started chatting, Pasha asking me a few questions about the church. I wasn't surprised by this, because I'd heard Papa's stories of when he worked in the factory and people asked him questions. Of course, they were usually questions meant to try to "re-educate him." Yakov had his own stories of how people would ask him questions during work, questions about the Bible or the church. Yakov, trying to be careful not to break any rules, would offer to talk to the person during a break or after work. Then these people's interest melted like ice cream under a hot sun.

Pasha was different. He seemed genuinely interested in what we did at church, what my parents were like, and everything about me. We became good friends, even though he was about ten years older. I often rode my motorcycle out to the country to eat dinner with Pasha and his wife Valya at their *dacha*.

One evening while we feasted on fried fish and potatoes, tomatoes and cucumbers, pirog and a lot of tea, Valya avoided looking at me. She followed me outside as I was leaving. She clearly wanted to say something. I couldn't imagine what.

"It's been pleasant, Vitya…" her voice trailed off uncertainly.

I waited for Valya to go on. She struggled for a minute and then said, "Don't be afraid of Pasha. But you need to know, he is working for the KGB."

Shocked, I went back in the house and asked Pasha, "Are we really friends, or are you working for someone?"

Pasha's face turned the color of a beet. "No, it's nothing like that. You know, I agreed to work for them for a price. Now that we have become friends, it's not comfortable for me, and I am torturing myself. I told Valya I don't know how I can do this anymore."

From then on, Pasha would show me his notebook with all the questions he was supposed to ask. The KGB wanted to know what was talked about at work, what was said about God, how pastors and leaders were chosen, where leaders worked, what money was received—all they needed to know to try to interfere with God's church. Pasha and I came up with answers that didn't tell them anything, or else I'd just say I didn't know. God protected me by turning a spy into my loyal friend.

Over the next three years, I assisted my father in his ministry and traveled with him around the *oblast*. In the summer of 1985, Papa and I needed to go to a village called Novova Selevka, about 130 kilometers from Zaporozhe. There we would lead the Saturday night service, stay overnight, then help the church with some questions related to the election of deacons.

However, there was a severe shortage of gasoline. Papa got on the telephone, seeking someone who could take us there in a car. Several men in the church owned cars and drove Papa around the *oblast*, freely donating their time. No one had any gas. There weren't any trains or buses that would get us there on time. As he always did when there was a problem, Papa got on his knees and prayed. "Lord, give favor to your servants so that someone would come and give the gasoline."

While Papa was praying, the telephone rang. Papa answered, and soon after, Yakov Vassilievich drove up in his tiny green Moskvich. "I've got about fifteen liters of gasoline," he said. "Enough for us to get to Novova Selevka, but not back."

Papa said, "Viktor, get ready, we're going. God will see about the gasoline."

When we arrived in Novova Selevka, the pastor remarked, "It's so good that you came. Last week my son was here, and he brought a canister of gasoline in case there would be a need for it, even though I don't have a car. I thought that if you came, I would give it to you to get home."

Tears filled my eyes. God heard my father's simple prayer, "God, You see our need; please send gasoline." We didn't even have time to say any more, but God had already responded. So many times God answered us, but when hard times came I struggled with doubts. Papa's eyes glistened with tears. Even my father, who had seen God's power so many times, had moments of wavering, wondering if God was really so powerful that He could help us in all things. The trials we faced every day were like unrelenting storms that threatened to drown us. Sometimes we'd even feel that we were sinking into a pit, and that God could help us, but didn't want to. But every time He showed how faithful He was, and that He would provide or help in just the right time. His time, not ours. I didn't need to look for my own adventures or to supply my own needs; God had proved He could provide for me and make my life exciting while He was at it.

Later that year, God provided for me in another way. I got married. My choice was Luba, who played mandolin in the string orchestra and sang in the youth choir. Like me, she savored the thrill of doing things the government said were forbidden, like singing Christian songs in the train station. She had organized some of the other girls in the church to send care packages of canned food or treats to the guys from the church who had gone into the army, and one of them was me.

Other than that, quiet Luba hadn't stood out among the youth and I never paid her any attention. I did pay attention to other girls. Maybe I acted like I was thinking about a future life with some of them, but not with Luba.

Then I started to think that I needed to get married, to have a family. I said to the Lord, "It's time for me to get married. Send me my wife, the companion of my life." My parents and I prayed to know God's will and discussed who would be suitable. Like my brothers and sister, I respected Papa's wisdom and valued his advice. Papa asked, "What about Luba? The best qualities are there: she is a believer, has a kind heart, loves to serve." My mother already knew Luba quite well, as they had often worked together preparing for weddings at the church. At that point I didn't believe Luba was the one for me.

I thought that God would answer my prayer quickly. I was wrong. After about six months of continuing to pray for a wife, I began to think about Luba. Such a warm person, with a close relationship with God. Whenever the youth would get together, and there was the need to prepare something or clean up, Luba was always the first one to help.

Suddenly I realized that it would be very hard for me to live without her. No matter what I said, she supported me. We had common thoughts and we could always come to a decision together. After two months of spending more and more time together, our relationship deepened. At the youth meeting, no one noticed anything, because I behaved very properly with all the girls, addressing them all using the affectionate form of their names, like Tanyachka in place of Tanya, or Nadyachka instead of Nadya, as if I were flirting equally with every one of them. But after the meetings, I'd go to Luba's house and spend time with her and her family.

Luba's parents weren't against our relationship. They gave me a blessing and even prayed with me before I went to Luba to propose. Like every girl, Luba dreamed of a man coming with flowers, getting on his knees and asking for her hand.

In the middle of a conversation about ministry in the church, I abruptly asked Luba, "When will we have a wedding?"

She was wide-eyed with shock. What kind of a proposal was that! She said, "Are we going to get married?"

"Yes. Yasha is getting married in the summer, and after that we can." Seeing her hesitation, I asked, "Do I have to make a proposal?"

"No," she said slowly. "Everyone makes proposals."

We got married in September of 1985, just a few months after Yakov and Olya.

I sometimes think my parents were relieved when Yakov and I got married. We had struggled with making choices in life, wanting careers or money, excitement or adventure. But then we found our way to faith, choosing our wives among the girls at the church, not dating, but following the usual Baptist way of courting. We got to know Olya and Luba through church activities, spending time with them and their families, praying for God's guidance. This isn't exactly how Lena did it.

CHAPTER 26

A SKEPTICAL SCIENTIST

Religion is nothing, a deception....Destroying religion, we say: study science. Science instead of religion. You need to know how nature and human society function. Only in these conditions is it possible to give meaning to your existence.
—Soviet Newspaper[26]

The fool says in his heart, "There is no God."
—Psalm 14:1a

As told by Igor

AT THE TIME of my birth in 1960 almost no one in the country was a practicing Christian. And who can blame them? If you owned a Bible, the government would take it away and burn it. And sometimes they would take you away as well, off to prison for wanting to read that subversive book.

So, of course, my family didn't go to church. They were also superstitious; my grandmother had me baptized as a baby, not because she believed in God, but to stay on His good side — just in case He was real.

When I was about five, my grandmother told me that I had a guardian angel who protected me. I have no idea why she said that, but I'm sure she regretted it. As soon as the words were out of her mouth I had questions. "What does my angel look like, Grandma? Is he taller than Papa? What color is his hair?" After I pestered her for a while, she finally said, "Stop asking me, I don't know. Ask God."

So that evening, I asked God to show me my angel. For some reason I asked very loudly, thinking God was a long way away and you had to yell if you wanted Him to hear you. My mother and grandmother just laughed at me.

That night I dreamed I was walking down a village street. Suddenly a huge black bull sped toward me. There was no time to get away; I knew the bull would trample me to death in one second. Then a boy appeared, a normal-looking boy, a little older than me and about a head taller. What he did was not normal at all. He took hold of one of the bull's horns, lifted him up, and walked away. Just like that, I was saved! I woke up, my heart pounding, and raced to tell my mother and grandmother about my dream.

As I told them the story, they looked at each other with fear in their eyes. Then they made me sit down and tell them the whole dream again. They listened intently, their stunned, shock-widened eyes never leaving my face. What I had dreamed had actually taken place years earlier when I was a small baby. I was too little, of course, to remember anything about it.

At that time, my grandma lived in a tiny village in Russia, and my mother took me to visit her. One day while they were in the backyard talking, I managed to crawl out on to the road. My mother looked up and saw me there, and she also saw a large bull that had gone crazy. He stampeded down the road straight at me, snorting with savage anger. My mother stood watching, her hand clutching at her throat, knowing the distance between us was too great for her to rescue me, certain that in one moment her firstborn child would be killed.

Instead the bull's body flew over me in an abrupt bound and he continued galloping down the road. Now, you might expect a horse to jump over an obstacle on the road, but not a mad bull. They are famous for trampling on people. It was a miracle.

Five years later when I told them my dream, my mother and grandmother realized that it was an angel who picked up the bull and made it pass over me. Yet this revelation had little effect on their lives.

At the time, it didn't change my life either, but now I realize this dream was the beginning of my relationship with God, the first glimmer of His light into my heart. I didn't know it, but God wouldn't be content just showing me miracles. He was out for much more.

Carefully I checked my math. Nine times nine is eighty-one. That's right. So 329 times 794 equals 261,226. Perfectly correct. I liked mathematics because there were verifiable answers—you were right or you were wrong. Absolutely. Not like some subjects where it was hard to know what was true and what wasn't. My pencil rolled off the table and hit the kitchen floor. Our kitchen was so small that there was no room for a regular table, so my father made one that folded up into the wall when we weren't using it. Just big enough for my books, papers, and homework, it was too small for our whole family to sit around; my parents ate after my sister and I finished.

In the early 1970s in the Soviet Union, this was how most people lived. Our apartment building was a five-story Khrushchovy, named after the leader who'd been in power during the time it was built in the 1950s. It reflected the times: small rooms, low ceilings, cramped existence. We lived on the top floor, and like most Khrushchovys, there was no elevator. Still, people were grateful for these apartments. Many older apartments didn't have hot running water, and the people living in communal apartments shared a bathroom and kitchen with other families. Besides the kitchen, we had two other rooms: a bedroom for my parents, and a living room where I slept. My mother hung brightly-colored patterned carpets on the walls to create some warmth in the sterile, utilitarian rooms. We lived like most everyone else I knew, and I never thought my life would turn out any differently.

For years I prayed for a younger sister, instinctively reaching out to a power stronger than myself, thinking it costs nothing to ask. When I was eight, Angela was born. Then I wasn't so sure I wanted her around! Much of my time was spent as her nanny while my mother worked as a clerk in a store. And now there was someone sleeping in the living room with me.

At the local elementary school, my grades didn't make me stand out one way or another. What really interested me was learning how things work. I often got in trouble for taking things, like the iron, the radio, or the vacuum cleaner apart just to see how they worked. Sometimes I couldn't put them back together. My father sternly ordered me not to tinker with our household goods anymore. One day I was watching television and got curious. *Just how does this work?* I thought. *If I just pull on this knob, will I be able to take this apart and get a look inside?* Less than a minute later, I was standing with the knob in my hand, unable to return it to its proper place. Panic seized me as I thought about what my father would say and I started to cry.

Just then my father came home. "Igor, why are you crying?"

"I don't want to tell you."

"Why not?"

"You'll beat me."

"I know what you've done — you've broken something again! Tell me what you broke."

I steadfastly refused to tell my father what I had done. He searched the apartment, looking at everything we owned, trying to discover what it was I had broken. In exasperation he commanded me to confess. "And I won't beat you if you tell me."

Silently I held the knob from the television out to him. Startled, he looked at it, his eyes narrowing. Then he beat me anyway.

It was a great day for my parents when I discovered the model airplane club run by the Young Pioneers, the organization sponsored by the Communist Party for kids aged seven to fourteen. Everyone I knew joined the Pioneers, and proudly wore the uniform red kerchief, red for the blood shed during the glorious October Revolution. Sometimes the Pioneers held meetings at school or went on outings to the circus. No one wanted to be left out of those outings! What was most interesting to me were the Pioneer clubs that met at the Palace of Culture. On most days after school, we could go to our club meetings: the boys to activities like radio, carpentry, or metal work, the girls to sewing. Some kids painted or learned to play musical instruments.

For me it was model airplanes. There were no kits for us to assemble — all we had were plans and diagrams. Each piece had to be cut from wood and shaped to the specifications on the plans. There was a teacher who occasionally answered questions; mostly he worked on constructing his own model airplane. So we just figured it out by ourselves. I sat in the same room with that guy three or four days a week for years, and I can barely remember what he looked like, so little interaction did I have with him.

I still remember the thrill the first time I flew the model plane I built: I can date my love for aviation from that moment. We took our planes to a competition against other Pioneers clubs. I never won a competition, but it didn't matter to me. What was important was the process of building — getting it right so the plane would fly.

In high school, I transformed from being an average student to one of the best. Science absorbed me completely, igniting my intellect. I continually questioned. What is the natural world made of? How does it work? Lab experiments in chemistry and physics held an unending fascination for me. At sixteen, I decided to devote my life to science. After finishing high school with a red diploma (highest honors), I enrolled in the technical aviation *technikum*, or technical college.

The years in the technical college were a joy for me. With advancing knowledge and sophistication, I was able to explore the physical world in ever-greater depth. I was increasingly awed by the beauty and harmony of the natural world, its complex structures, the intricacy of its order, and perfect workings.

Then I realized that all my classmates seemed to accept without question what we had been taught from the time that we were small children; namely, that the entire world, all that we see, is the result of some random accident. It struck me as ludicrous to believe that all of this beauty and order could have come about by chance.

I considered the alternative—that God had created everything. This was a bit of a problem for me, because I had never heard anyone speak positively about God. I knew some people believed in a God who lived far away, above the sky, and that He had made the world. But these were the uneducated people, illiterate, backward. Our first cosmonaut, Yuri Gagarin, returned from space saying he didn't see God out there, and the Communist Party declared that the matter was settled — there is no God. I wasn't so sure. To me, that was like looking inside a machine to find its inventor.

In the back of my head was the nagging thought that for nearly 2000 years many believed the theory of Spontaneous Generation— that life spontaneously sprung into being, based on observations of flies suddenly generating out of rotting meat. The wise men of the day scoffed at any criticism of this theory until it was replaced with Darwinism. Could Darwinism also be wrong? How could I find out the truth?

My skepticism lingered. How could such a complicated universe come into being by chance? I didn't talk much about my doubts concerning Soviet materialism. Questioning the accepted Communist dogma was not tolerated; few dared even raise the obvious questions. I knew that my growing belief in a Creator could get me expelled from the *Komsomol* (Young Communist League). After all, I had made the required pledge to support atheism when I joined. Expulsion from the *Komsomol* would mean I would forfeit my access to higher education and would never be given a chance to work at a professional level. Only lowly, menial jobs would be open to me.

Because I knew no one who was questioning the way I was, I began to think that there was something wrong with me. *Surely the problem is that I just do not understand the atheists' arguments properly*, I reasoned. So to improve myself, to compensate for what was lacking in my mental abilities, I began to study logic. The result of that study was I realized that the atheists were not only aligned against science, but against logic as well. No matter how I tried to escape the conclusion, it was apparent that Darwinism was really just a more sophisticated version of Spontaneous Generation. After all, the atheists explained that life sprang out of the primordial slime, activated by a bolt of lightning. To me, it was still the same theory — life originates out of something that is not alive. But why couldn't all these scientists see the major contradictions in their theories? Or were they just ignoring them? There was no evidence to prove their theory; there was no way to verify their conclusions. This wasn't like mathematics, where you could check the calculation, or physics, where you could run an experiment to prove or disprove the theory. No one could go back in time to observe the process. And the answers they gave were shallow, never enough.

One of my friends, Misha, was asking the same questions. Together we pondered creation, looking for answers in science, in logic, in philosophy, in eastern and Hindu thought. Our research even led us into Yoga. I soon lost interest in it, but Misha became an avid practitioner.

One frosty day Misha and I were walking in the forest, discussing the mysteries of creation. "Now we know that no one in science argues with the First and Second Laws of Thermodynamics, right?"

"That's right," Misha said. "We all know that the amount of energy in the universe is constant; it can neither be created nor destroyed."

"And we know that the form of energy is constantly changing, so that less and less of it is available. The result is that everything is naturally wearing down."

"And left to itself, everything is becoming more disordered. Maybe the next time Mama tells me to straighten up my books I should tell her it's just the Second Law of Thermodynamics at work!"

"Seriously, Misha! Every system in nature moves from the complex to the simple, wearing down, becoming more random and less complex. The only exception is when there is an introduction of energy into the system."

"So our friends the atheists would have us believe that life starts very simply out of nothing, and all by itself gets more and more complex!"

"Which is completely opposite to all the laws of nature! Laws that have been verified in the lab over and over by many scientists!"

"So they take their theory of evolution, don't bother to explain how it can be in violation of the laws of thermodynamics, and tell us to believe it on the strength of a tooth or a bone they dig up somewhere. With no more evidence than that."

"See that log hut? Logically, we must assume that someone built it."

"That's right. We have no data from our experience to suggest that a hut can come into being by accident."

"And living things, fish and animals and people, are much more complicated than a hut."

"People used to think the cells in our bodies were just bits of matter. Now they know they are not so simple. First they said cells were like factories, then like computers. Now there is nothing they can compare with them; they are just too complicated, more like a miniature universe. And we are to accept the idea that the first one-celled living things just mutated out of some chemicals in the sea that were struck by lightning?"

"Would they also have us believe that lightning hitting a garbage dump would produce a television set?"

"I read in a probability textbook that the chances of a live cell appearing from nothing are less than for a monkey to accidentally type a word-perfect copy of Hamlet."

As we walked, our feet scrunched the soft snow, our steps making a sound like shli, shli, shli, a sound much like the Russian word for "they were going," and we found a tiny six-inch snowman perched on a fence post. I asked Misha "Where did this come from?"

He grinned before replying, "Of course, it evolved."

"Yes, some storm winds must have accidentally created it!" Our laughter echoed through the snowy forest. It was well none of our *Komsomol* leaders were around to hear us mocking their materialistic creed. By this time I had concluded that creation must have a creator; I still had no idea of His identity.

CHAPTER 27

ON A HELICOPTER IN AFGHANISTAN

The dispatch of limited Soviet forces to Afghanistan serves one purpose—to render aid and assistance in repelling acts of external aggression.
—Brezhnev's answer to President Carter[27]

But you are a shield around me, O Lord.
—Psalm 3:3a

As told by Igor

AFTER FOUR YEARS of study, I graduated from the technical college, and then I could put it off no longer—I had to fulfill my mandatory military service. Because of my aviation studies, the army assigned me to a helicopter unit as a mechanic and gunner.

At that time, the Soviet Union was embroiled in what our leaders called the Patriotic Afghan War. Many people privately called it "our Vietnam." For all young Soviet men serving in the military, Afghanistan was the scariest place on earth. Everyone had heard the stories. Our soldiers on patrol often stumbled on the bodies of our comrades who had been captured by the enemy, our comrades who clearly were tortured before they died, their bodies found without noses, ears, or skin. We all knew that our soldiers were prepared to kill themselves rather than be captured. I made every effort to escape being sent to Afghanistan. After all, there were so many other places I was needed: East Germany, Georgia, the Far East; capitalist enemies surrounded us on all sides.

Despite my arguments, pleas that I suffered from vertigo, and intercession from family connections, the army officers answered me sternly. "Young man, the Soviet Union is helping the people of Afghanistan in their struggle against the capitalist exploiters. If the Afghan people's movement fails, then America will move in, right into an area that will threaten the heart of the Motherland. We need young men like you in this struggle against the encroachment of the capitalists! This is a mountain war we are fighting, and we need every trained helicopter man we can find." With those words, I knew that there was no way out — I was headed for combat.

Fearing more for my parents than myself, knowing they would live in torment the entire time I was gone, I told them that I had been sent to Georgia. The entire two years I served I wrote letters as if I was near the Black Sea, and sent all my mail through the base there. My parents always wondered why I never answered the questions they asked in their letters, but I just couldn't tell them the truth. My mother had high blood pressure and a weak heart, and I wanted to protect her as much as I could.

Once in Afghanistan, it was clear that my fears were justified. The endless Afghan War was filled with searing heat, blinding dust, relentless mosquitoes, exhaustion, suffering, and death. Our crew of four flew every day anywhere the action was flaring up, often in the air from four in the morning to eleven at night. While we were in the air we shot at everything—bushes, trees, hills—because the enemy guerilla fighters could be hiding anywhere with surface-to-air missiles ready to fire. Many times we couldn't see the ground because of the dust, but those on the ground could hear us and had an idea of where to shoot. We suffered heavy losses of machinery and equipment; more troubling were the deaths of scores of my friends. As horrible as the helicopter service was, it was still better than being a foot soldier, an exhausted robot, mindlessly slogging over the mountains, numb with weariness. Every day I travelled between life and death, wondering if I would survive the next battle.

By the time I arrived in Afghanistan, I knew that God existed and is the Supreme Being in the universe. Now more urgent questions posed themselves: Does He care about me? Can there be a personal relationship between me and God? It wasn't enough for me just to believe in a Creator; I wanted more. What did God think about me? And what would happen to me if I died? I began talking to God, asking Him for help, unaware that this was what people called prayer. All I knew was that I needed help to get through this agony. "Lord, if you are there, just help me. Just protect my life in this difficult situation." This was my constant plea. At one point I made a promise to God that I would serve Him if He saved me during this war.

Mission after mission, even when our helicopter was full of bullet holes, I never had so much as a scratch on my body. Could it be true, I wondered, that God really cares about me? Is God answering my prayers?

Sometimes I talked with other soldiers about my questions about God. In any other place in the Soviet Union, such discussions were impossible; people asking such questions were mocked and shamed. But the soldiers facing death listened somberly, with a touch of fear, wondering what lay beyond. Have our leaders told us the truth, that this life is all there is? After watching the atheistic propaganda films, films shown to distract us from the war, we returned to the barracks, debating well into the night questions of truth and the existence of God.

The last few weeks of my tour of duty were quiet ones — we had not seen much action on our patrols. On the afternoon of my final day, consumed by an anxious sense of wanting to get out of there the minute we had permission to go, relieved that we were still alive, we started disarming our helicopter, preparing it for the flight home. We knew we weren't supposed to do this until just before leaving, but wanted nothing to delay our departure.

That evening, a helicopter full of gaping holes from enemy fire flew into camp, barely avoiding a crash landing. This helicopter had been ferrying a company of foot soldiers to a battle site. Instead of the expected safe landing, they were met by Afghan ground-to-air rockets fired from bunkers dug into the steep canyon walls. One helicopter was shot down, the other crippled so that it barely made it back to base. Now our soldiers were trapped on the canyon floor, surrounded by Afghan rockets and anti-aircraft and machine guns. Our orders: working with another helicopter, we needed to rescue the trapped soldiers.

The problem: the other helicopter crew was also finishing their last day. They had completely disarmed their helicopter. We had been a little slower in the disarming process and had two bombs left on board. There was no time to rearm—all the officers were screaming at us to get airborne. To confess that we had disarmed our helicopter early was unthinkable—we would surely be shot for dereliction of duty. It was our own fault we had no weapons. We all knew we were heading into certain death. Flying targets, that's all we were. I took comfort in the small machine gun I held. It would be useless in the battle we were heading toward, but sufficient to commit suicide with if I didn't get blown up first. In desperation I began to pray for protection.

From above, the green Afghan terrain with its yellow spots looked like rumpled camouflage, deeper red lines marking the canyons. As we made our approach, we knew enemy fire would greet us from every side; we saw no way we could avoid being shot down just as the troop helicopters had been. When we flew between the canyon's sheer cliffs jutting into the sky we saw caves dotting the rock walls; the gauntlet of gun emplacements at the entrance of the canyon were harder to locate. Just then, a stiff headwind sprung up that enabled our navigator to descend into the canyon without being heard. He dropped some flares, and we were able to spot the main bunker. The Afghans built these bunkers with only a small window and gun aperture, which limited their range of vision. Losing his nerve and shouting "Guys, we are all dead!" our panicked bombardier released one of our two bombs.

Miraculously, the bomb that measured about a foot and a half in diameter flew directly into the bunker's two-foot square window, wiping out that gun emplacement and a full crew. Seeing this, the gunners in the other Afghan bunkers held their fire so as to hide their locations. The next thing we knew, they were all fleeing for their lives. All we could figure out was that because our bomb hit the gun emplacement so accurately, the Afghans must have assumed we were equipped with guided missiles. Dumb bombs dropped from moving helicopters normally fell at an angle and could not be aimed with any precision. There was no way a dumb bomb could fly into targets the way ours did.

In any case, the area was now clear for us to land and complete the rescue mission, flying out about twenty soldiers that night. God had protected us from certain death; it was only much later that I learned what He had saved me for.

Alexei and Valentina's wedding, 1958

Valentina playing guitar while Alexei and Yakov listen

Alexei baptizing Yakov, 1978

Back Row: Yakov (20), Viktor (17), Lena (14)
Front row: Valentina, Alexei, Veniamin (11), 1980

Igor in Red Army uniform, 1980

Lena and Igor on their wedding day in
front of the Zaparozhye Oak, 1984

Orthodox priest congratulates Alexei on public
baptism held during the 1000 years of Christianity
in the Soviet Union, 1988

Alexei and Valentina, 2004

Alexei at work, 2006

Lena, Igor, Vika, 2007

CHAPTER 28

HOW GOD USED THE ATHEISTS TO HELP ME FIND HIM

Christianity, like all other religions, became a method of deadening the consciousness of the oppressed masses.
—Leon Trotsky[28]

For the grace of God that brings salvation has appeared to all men.
—Titus 2:11

As told by Igor

TAKING A BREAK from combat duties, my fellow soldiers and I had discussed what our lives would be like once we returned home, and we were all agreed on one thing: life would be different for us; it could never be the same after the horrors we had lived through. I knew that what I wanted was some quiet time with my family, some peace.

But it was not to be. Returning home from the foreign war, I found a domestic one brewing in our tiny flat. My mother had become a Christian, had been baptized, and was now attending Sunday services regularly. My father was bitterly angry. He felt they no longer shared a life; my mother had deserted him for Christ and split our family in two. She had different interests, different friends, and had become an entirely different person.

Even worse, my father believed that Mama had brought shame on the entire family by joining what everyone knew was a barbaric and ignorant cult called "Baptist." Everyone knew that Baptists held orgies at night behind drawn curtains, that they sacrificed babies during their worship services, and sometimes even ate them. The teachers in school told us these things, so there was no need to doubt these tales. Some of the smaller kids were so scared of the Baptists that they would run, not walk, past the churches, just in case they were looking for their next sacrificial victim. Baptists were also well known to be arsonists and vandals, seeking to destroy the Communist state.

I sided with my father in this dispute, keeping my own research into Christianity a secret, reasoning that belief in God is a private matter. I told my mother, "Believe what you want, just keep it inside your own head. It's nobody's business!" I pushed my promise to God to the back of my mind, saying I was too busy with my job at the factory; I didn't want to think about it.

That August, having no other plans, one of my friends and I decided to take the entrance exams for the university, just to see how well we could do. We hadn't studied at all. Both of us passed those intensely competitive exams and were accepted into the university.

By October, I began to feel guilty over my broken promise to God. I told everyone, my fellow university students, the people I worked with at the factory, that I was a Christian. Then I waited for the persecution. It never came. Many didn't seem to take me very seriously, some were interested in the Bible, and some were afraid to show any interest, but that was all.

Then I began to avidly research religion. One day I went to the university's library and asked to borrow a Bible. "We don't have such a book here, young man," the librarian told me.

"What? In such a big library there is no Bible?"

"During the Great Patriotic War we had a few. But they were burned up in a fire that destroyed many of our books."

I didn't believe that story. Either it was forbidden to give a Bible to someone, or the KGB had taken them all away. So I began to read atheistic books, the ones officially sanctioned by the state, hoping to find scientific arguments supporting atheism.

I never found any. Instead, I found absurdities, such as:

Instructions for Atheists, Questions and Answers:
Q: Is it a good idea to read the Bible?
A: No. It is best to avoid this entirely.

Some authors made clearly ridiculous claims that the Bible gave recipes for eating cockroaches. Others quoted a verse from the Psalms, saying, "See, even the Bible says there is no God." But in another book I found that entire verse quoted and read the whole sentence "The fool says in his heart, 'There is no God.'" Not at all the same as denying God's existence! Other authors quoted verses like "you must hate your father," without the surrounding context. Every argument put forth by those atheistic authors that quoted the Bible ignored the context. Instead of presenting concrete proof against God, all they wrote were sarcastic, unfounded accusations. For example: "What does it mean to turn the other cheek? Only weak losers would do that! And if someone asks you for your tunic, you should give your cloak as well. Fine. Does that mean if someone asks you for your shirt you should give your underwear? The Bible is teaching that you should run around naked! And Noah got drunk, but his son was cursed. God isn't fair! And where is the example of a happy marriage in the Bible? Anyone who is a believer is not happy." Or they pointed out the sins of the people in the Bible—Abraham's lies to Pharaoh, Judah visiting a prostitute, David, raping and murdering, Solomon's polygamy—and concluded "See, this is how the Bible teaches you to live. All Christians are immoral like these people." It obviously never occurred to these writers that the examples of people in the Bible were examples of how not to live, and why we need God's help. Most people, not having Bibles, wouldn't be able to check to see if these writers were correctly quoting the Bible. And none of their arguments directly addressed the question: does God exist?

In the end those writers did me a favor. By quoting so much of the Bible in their works, they gave me large portions of the Bible to read, to compare with the arguments of the atheists. Checking the accuracy of their quotations, reading the quoted versed in context, I realized the Bible proved the atheists' argument to be wrong. I began to wonder. If God is just a fairy tale, why is every Soviet university student required to take a course on atheism, and why is there a government Department of Atheism just to convince people that God does not exist? Why don't we have classes about why Grandfather Frost is just a fable? It seemed to me if it was true that God doesn't exist, there shouldn't have to be all these activities to persuade everyone.

The more I read of the Bible, the more it impressed me with its beauty and power, as opposed to the weak arguments of its critics. Through my reading, I gained some knowledge of Jesus Christ and Christian doctrine, that I was a sinner and needed to repent. Over and over, in science, in logic, in philosophy, in Afghanistan, and now in the pages of the Bible, I met God. My research gave me theoretical knowledge of God, my experience in Afghanistan gave me practical knowledge of God, and my Bible reading taught me the truth that God cared about me personally and that Jesus is His Son. I had found the right conclusion just like I knew when I solved a mathematics problem correctly—there can only be one true answer. I no longer had any doubts; it was time to act.

I knelt and confessed my sins, asking God for forgiveness and for help in starting a new life. A veil lifted from my eyes, I could see everything more clearly and felt God working in my life. My loyalties, values, and character began to change. Past interests no longer had any appeal.

I gradually became aware of my need to worship publicly among other Christians. Somehow I had to find a church. It was time to make that leap of faith and publicly expose myself as a Christian, a move that was almost as scary as a nighttime parachute drop into enemy territory. I had never imagined that I would do such a thing, and it was hard to conceive what my life was going to be like, just as a man born blind cannot imagine color.

The problem was that many of the churches were secret places and I had no idea where to find one. The only Christian I knew was my mother. Desiring to keep my religious beliefs a secret, especially from my father, one Sunday morning I covertly trailed my mother, keeping well behind her. Occasionally I hid behind a tree like a detective shadowing a suspect. At last I saw her go into the building that was used by the church.

I staked out the church, watching to see what kind of people went there. Suspicious of Christians in general, I carefully observed all of those going in and out. My expectation was that all of the church members would be old ladies or obvious social misfits who couldn't find a place in society.

But the people appeared normal enough, even smiling. None of them had blood on their clothing, so it didn't seem like they were conducting any sacrifices. I struck up a conversation with one young man as he came out of the building, and was surprised at how pleasant a person he was. Finally I got up the courage to attend a service.

Taking advantage of my mother's illness the next Sunday morning, I went to services alone. Well, not quite alone. Hidden deep in my pocket, I carried a nail. Unsure if the stories about human sacrifice during services were only lies, knowing it was illegal to carry a knife, I hid in my pocket the best weapon I could find—a large nail. Just in case I would need to defend myself.

When I arrived at the church, the believers greeted me warmly and invited me to sit in the front. *Right. That way I will the first to be sacrificed.* Instead, I sat in the last row, next to the door, fingers gripping the nail. Just in case.

The beauty of the service and the joyfulness of the people were the last proof I needed that all I had been told throughout my life were lies. With that, I plunged fully into the life of the church.

That very day I went on a charity mission with the church youth group. We traveled to a distant village to help a destitute old lady by digging her garden. This adventure moved me deeply. It was the first time I had seen what happens when Christian ideals are translated into action.

Later, I confessed my faith to my mother.

She listened to me in silence. "I don't believe you, Igor," she said.

"But, Mama, I thought you'd be happy…"

"You have never shown any interest in the church before, and even said your father was right to be angry with me for joining the church."

"That was earlier, before I understood."

"Or was that before you became a spy sent by the KGB to destroy the church?"

It was only after many months my mother decided I wasn't a spy after all. Instead of arguing with her, I was respectful. Instead of disobeying her rules, I submitted patiently. These changes convinced her more than any words of mine.

Through all this time, we hid my faith from my father. As we left the apartment together, I asked her questions like, "What time does the bookstore open?" questions designed to make my father think I was just going out for a little shopping. It was only after a full year, after I had been baptized, that we let him in on our secret.

Maybe the way I told him wasn't too wise. I left my baptismal card on the kitchen table and went out, knowing my father would soon find it. When I returned home, his reaction of rage and grief was just as I expected; in his anger he just about flew up to the ceiling. "You are throwing away your future, your education, your career, your whole life!"

"But, Papa, I have found the truth!"

"That doesn't matter. Don't you realize there is nothing but persecution waiting for you?"

There was a long silence as we looked at each other. Fury and disappointment distorted my father's face. "All my life I have worked for you, so you would have opportunities I never had, so you could have a better life. And now you throw it all away. For what? A fairy tale?"

He turned his back on me and his shoulders sagged. "I have been on my own since I was fourteen. I survived by finding any jobs I could—carpentry, building, even cooking! And now you are joining a cult, like those hypocritical Pentecostals from my village. Is that the life you want? You could not have disappointed me more."

While he never discussed the issue again, his anger didn't cool for years.

My father was partially right; I did experience some mild persecution at school and at work. But I would have to call it moral pressure, pressure to drink or smoke, or jokes that I wasn't fun anymore. While I wasn't in danger of losing my job, I could forget about promotions or better positions. These didn't matter to me. What was important was that I had found the truth that God exists, and that God loved me enough to die for me and my sin. Losing out on a promotion seemed to be only a slight inconvenience compared to the vast privilege and joy of my deepening relationship with God. I knew that my life was in God's hands; and that no matter what my circumstances, I would be His for eternity. Little did I know then the trials—and the blessings—God had planned for me.

PART III
BITING MY ELBOWS

Lena takes up the story, telling of her own struggles to remain true to her faith, though tempted with marriage to a non-believer. She and Igor take turns telling of their unusual courtship and their life in America.

CHAPTER 29

A SCANDALOUS ROMANCE

*It is much harder to supply the needs of the many
than to supply luxuries to the few.*
—Leon Trotsky[29]

*He upholds the cause of the oppressed and gives
food to the hungry.*
—Psalm 146:7

As told by Lena

THE SUMMER BREEZE blew through the windows of the church in irregular puffs, fluttering the pages of the songbook in my hands. "My house and I want to serve you, Jesus, you alone. Give me the strength to be your obedient servant." That morning we were singing one of my father's favorite hymns. *But how does He want me to serve Him? What is His will for me? What does He want me to do?* I wondered.

A few weeks earlier I completed the eighth grade. Some of my friends had already decided to find jobs and not finish high school; others had enrolled in vocational school. Another possibility would be to find a part-time job and finish high school in the night program, attending classes from six to nine in the evening. Other than deciding to repent and join the church, this was the first big decision I had to make in my life.

But how to know God's will? My brother, Yakov, always knew he wanted to go to the university, so he stayed in regular high school. Viktor didn't have ambitions for higher education and was content to follow our father and go into metalworking. It seemed so simple for them; they were both so sure that they knew God's will. I didn't have any idea what I wanted to do, and wasn't good at anything. Thinking it would be fun, I enrolled in the *uchilishe* to study baking. Before the first semester was over, I decided I had made a big mistake because all the bakers were so fat. That's not how I wanted to end up.

Now I needed to choose something else. How did people make such a decision, I wondered? I didn't want to commit myself to the wrong profession and be stuck in a job I hated. Then an idea struck me. From the time I was fourteen, using just two fingers and our illegal typewriter, I had been typing prohibited copies of Christian books and literature for my father. I knew that I could learn to type faster if I worked at the telegraph station. Then I could produce more copies of the literature in much less time. So that's what I did. Six hours a day I spent sending telegrams, and after work attended ninth grade in the evening.

That summer, a group of us from the telegraph station were sent to work on the collective farm. Since agriculture in the Soviet Union was so poorly managed, the government had to force people to work on the farms just so there would be a harvest. Usually one or two weeks' service was mandatory. Everyone had to do their part: teachers, factory workers, engineers, doctors. Everyone but the party bosses.

On the farm, the routine was up for breakfast at six, off to the fields by seven. At noon we would break for lunch and a nap, then return to work, tilling, weeding, and watering, mostly with hand tools.

But not only work was going on. All of the temporary workers were living in a kindergarten, men and women alike. With nothing else to do, drinking became a popular form of entertainment. And many people were sleeping together: some voluntarily, some not. The man in charge, fearing that someone would rape me, fearing the scandal that would result because I was underage, the scandal he would be blamed for, hid me in a wardrobe at night; a wardrobe meant to save me but felt like a prison. I was terrified that someone would find me, so afraid it felt as though frost was creeping over my skin. All through the dark nights I prayed, pleading with God to keep me safe. During the day when everyone else was in the fields, the boss let me sleep. At the first chance he sent me home.

Back in Zaporozhe, my boss at the telegraph station, not wanting to fire me, kindly gave me a choice: put in my two weeks on the collective farm or quit.

So now I was back where I started, with no idea what to do with my life. At sixteen, I was so shy the thought of trying to find another job scared me almost more than the idea of going back to the collective farm. Finally, my mother took me to the director of the second largest medical clinic in Zaporozhe, thinking somewhere they would find a job I could do, such as cleaning or answering the telephone.

In the Soviet system of universal health care, there were no private doctors' offices. People saw the doctor in a clinic and were treated by whoever was working that day. Some of the clinics were neighborhood clinics, for people who lived in that region. Others were attached to large hospitals, sometimes owned by factories instead of the city or *oblast*.

Mama took me to the clinic attached to one of the city hospitals. When the director of the clinic finally let us into her office, Mama explained why we were there. I was too afraid to say anything.

"What can you do?" the director asked me.

"I can type," I meekly answered.

"Go into my secretary's office and show me how you can type."

After I typed a few lines, she agreed to try me for a month, saying, "My current secretary can only type with two fingers. Maybe you'll do better."

On my first day of work, as I was leaving the house, I asked Papa if I should tell people I was a Christian.

"No, Lena," he said. "Don't say anything unless someone asks you. Just make sure you show them how much God loves them by how you treat people."

So I resolved to love everyone, showing kindness and concern to all, and stood out from the other workers by being courteous and respectful to everyone. Observing my polite and cheerful manner, the director of the hospital tried to convince my boss, Yulia Silvestrovna, to let me work for him. This man was Yulia Silvestrovna's boss, but somehow she managed to keep me.

Watching Yulia Silvestrovna handle difficult situations was an education in itself, and I learned many things from her, such as how to be direct with people courteously. Over time, we became very close, sharing our lunches nearly every day. Understanding that my family was poor, she brought meat for lunch, while I contributed potatoes, the potatoes Mama made in a way that Yulia Silvestrovna liked. Closing her office door, we ate and talked, mostly about personal things.

As time went on, she loved me like the daughter she never had. For the first time in my life, I felt as though someone outside of my family really needed me. Often when her husband was out of town, I spent the night at her flat. When she was getting ready for guests, I helped her clean and prepare the food. As a boss, she had the right to shop at special stores reserved only for the Communist Party elite. No one outside the upper ranks was allowed to even look into these stores, but we all knew that they sold things unavailable anywhere else. Yulia Silvestrovna often sent me to do her shopping in these stores, or took me shopping and picked out clothes for me. She even got me a *Komsomol* membership card without me signing any papers or going to any meetings. Sometimes I called her on the weekends just because I missed her.

As our relationship developed, so did her trust in me. I attended Health Department meetings and made tea for the Health Department inspectors when they came to our clinic. Many of the Communist officials called her for their prescriptions, and I delivered them. I knew a lot about the personal health of the officials, problems within the system, and the inner political intrigues of the powerful.

For the two years I worked for Yulia Silvestrovna, I never had any disagreements or problems with anyone. I kept wondering why I was not being persecuted. After a fire in the basement of the clinic, Yulia Silvestrovna said that it must have been Baptists who started the fire, since Baptists were trying to destroy the Communist state. In this way I learned of her feelings toward Baptists, since in all the time we had spent together the subject of faith never came up.

One day an acquaintance of Yulia Silvestrovna's came to the clinic, a government official in his late thirties who had broken his arm playing volleyball. My boss asked me to escort him to the doctor and to wait while the cast was put on. She often asked me to do this for important people so they wouldn't have to stand in line like everyone else. Whenever the doctors saw me escorting someone, they knew to take care of that person first. This man, who was named Dmitri, behaved so properly toward me, no hint of flirting, that I felt at ease around him. For my part, I was as respectful and compassionate to him as I was with everyone else. Each week when he came to get his cast checked I stopped by to see how his arm was healing. These visits were prolonged when the doctors realized the arm had healed improperly and they had to re-break it and start over. Dmitri and I became good friends during this time.

Soon after this, he was admitted to the hospital for two weeks, and I visited him in the ward every day. Then we started to go out for coffee. Dmitri never pressured me to date him or to even let him kiss me. Somehow he knew he'd lose me if he tried anything like that. He was old-fashioned at heart, and I was so different from all the other girls who were trying to attract him. We started to meet more and more frequently.

Then he invited me to celebrate the New Year with him. I knew my parents expected me to be at the New Year's service, but I went to the party anyway. Held at the flat of a factory director, attended by wealthy guests, the party, with all its caviar, assorted cheese, kolbasa, salads, and piles of fresh fruit out of season, more rich food than I'd ever seen in my life, fed my sense of guilt. Dmitri told all the people there that he didn't allow me to smoke or drink, protecting me from having to resist their attempts to get me to join in.

After midnight, I asked Dmitri to take me home, and then ran to the church so it would look like I'd been there the whole time. My parents weren't fooled. I knew they were praying that God would send a Christian boy my way to rescue me from what they thought was a dangerous situation.

Later Papa talked with me earnestly. "Lena," he said, "I am grieved to say this to you, but I might have to excommunicate you from the church."

"Papa! You wouldn't do that to me! I am your own daughter!"

"I have a responsibility to protect the congregation."

"But I haven't done anything."

"You are spending a lot of time with an unbelieving man. Am I right? And you know that marrying an unbeliever would be a very grave sin."

"That would be a sin. But I haven't married anyone. And I haven't decided to marry anyone. I'm not getting married for a long time, not for years and years."

"Lena, it seems to me you are walking down a path that will lead to marrying this man. You repented and were baptized. You chose to join the church, to be an obedient servant of Christ. If you marry this man, you will have chosen to disobey God's word. What choice will I have then? And what kind of example would that be for all of the others in the church? Maybe if you understand how serious this is now, you will repent of your actions before it is too late. You have to choose, Lena. Right now you are neither meat nor fish. Either be a believer or a non-believer, but make up your mind."

This might seem overly harsh, but I was not surprised. When I was in school, knitted tams were very fashionable. While my cousin Zoya wore hers the stylish way, tipped over to one side, I had to wear mine straight on my head. If I ever used hair spray, that was cause for a major scandal. We were not to take on the customs of the world, and certainly not involve ourselves closely with non-believers. Doing so could be taken as a sign that we really hadn't repented and given our lives to God. As a result, our church membership could be taken away.

In the turmoil that raged within me caused by the battle between my own emotions and my desire to please God and my parents, I knew I loved Dmitri, even though he was an atheist. On my eighteenth birthday, the seventh of January, he sent me eighteen red roses. Rejoicing in the first flowers a man ever sent me, I thought that I would probably marry him someday. He wasn't my ideal, since he was a widower and I wasn't his first love, and it bothered me that God wouldn't approve if I married an unbeliever. But I was only eighteen, and didn't think I needed to worry about getting married for several years. Neither of my older brothers had gotten married, so why should I be thinking about it? In the meantime, I was enjoying the relationship with someone who treated me so respectfully and was such a gentleman. He had never even tried to kiss me, knowing that I would consider that improper since we weren't married or even engaged. He loved my soul, not just my body, I was sure of it. I spent the next two months enjoying his attentions and not thinking about the future. It would be a long time, maybe a few years, I thought, before I had to seriously think about our relationship and its consequences.

The eighth of March was one of the biggest holidays in the Soviet Union, International Women's Day. All day, long lines of men waited outside the flower shops, because a gift of flowers was the minimum most women expected, and for most, about all they would get all year by way of appreciation from their husbands or sons. Dmitri went a step further and took me to a restaurant. This showed everyone how serious the relationship was. Yulia Silvestrovna encouraged me to marry him, thinking a life with Dmitri would be a life of material comfort and acceptance into influential circles.

Less than two weeks later, Igor came into my life.

CHAPTER 30

INSTEAD OF A CAMEL, I RODE THE BUS

Walk firmly in the path of life indicated by the great Lenin.
—From "Name-giving ceremony" certificate,
communist ritual created to replace baptism[30]

Your word is a lamp to my feet and a light for my path.
—Psalm 119:105

As told by Igor

AFTER MY CONVERSION, I immersed myself in the life of the church. Although my life was happy, I felt that at twenty-three it was time for me to find a wife and think about having a family. I was also profoundly aware of how unworthy I was to make the choice myself. Previously I fell deeply in love with a girl, and thoughts of her filled my mind day and night. I had certain knowledge that I absolutely could not go through my life without her by my side. Circumstances took us in different directions, and we were tragically separated. When we met again a few years later, I could not imagine what I had found so wonderful in her. Instead of mourning her loss, I was delighted and relieved we had parted.

• 197 •

Understanding that my emotions were as changeable as the weather, I resolved not to trust them. If I developed an attachment to the wrong person, my brain could invent any kind of story in order to justify my feelings, proving my mind was unreliable as well.

I was more than afraid to make a mistake—I was petrified. Marriage can turn your life into a mini-heaven, or an enormous hell. The best way to avoid making the wrong choice, I realized, was not to make a choice at all.

As I was searching my Bible for answers, the story in Genesis chapter 24 caught my attention like a searchlight in the night sky. Abraham wanted to find a wife for his son, Isaac, among his own people, not the Canaanite women of the area they were living. So Abraham sent a servant off to his relatives, riding a camel and bearing costly gifts. The servant prayed for guidance, and God led him to Rebekah, the granddaughter of Abraham's brother. She agreed to marry Isaac without ever having seen him, although it meant journeying far away from her family, believing it to be the will of God. When they returned to Canaan, Isaac married Rebekah, and for the rest of his life, loved the woman God chose for him.

What a perfect way to get married! Isaac had no chance of making a mistake because God chose for him. Just what I wanted for myself. Fascinated with the story, I read it several times, noticing that chapter 24 is the longest chapter in Genesis. In chapter 1, God is able to create the universe and every living creature in just thirty-one verses, but it takes sixty-seven verses to bring Isaac and Rebekah together. This story must be important to God, I thought, and I decided to use it to guide me in my quest for a wife. Maybe it was an unusual way to find a wife, but it was God's way, not man's. I got on my knees to ask Him to make the choice for me.

I was a new Christian filled with faith and trust, and fire for God burned within me. I gave myself to Him one hundred percent, and I said, "Lord, help me. I cannot handle this problem of finding a wife. I cannot make a choice. Because I know myself from the past, I know that if I choose, I will make a mistake, definitely. You need to do this. Show me the woman who will be the best mate for me."

I prayed about this for six months.

One Sunday, I visited a church that was about an hour away from the one I usually attended. After the service, I caught sight of a young woman in the crowd, and I felt something happen inside me. I did not know what this was—a sudden disturbance inside that I had not experienced before. It wasn't just because the girl looked pretty; there were many other attractive girls around. This was different.

I turned to my friend, Vladimir, who was acquainted with many church members in this part of town. "Do you know that girl over there?" I asked.

He answered that he did.

Emotions surged inside me, but still I wasn't sure if this came from God, or if it was just a momentary sensation. Mistrusting my judgment, I decided to do nothing about this girl, and dropped the subject.

What I did do was change my prayer. I asked God that if the feeling inside me really did come from Him, then please keep it going. But if not, then stop it. Take these feelings away from me, and rid my mind of all images of this girl.

Time went by.

God didn't remove my feelings for this girl. Her image flickered in and out of my mind like a reflection in a mirror. I continued to pray. "Lord, if this is from You, then please help me use the example of Isaac's story in my own life. Please take away all of the obstacles and stumbling blocks from my path. If this is not from You, then build these obstacles into a great force that will stop me."

I prayed this way for another six months, and nothing changed. So I decided I must act.

The problem was I had no idea who this girl was or where she lived or anything about her. I had seen the girl only once—at church six months earlier. She had never seen me at all. The girl looked about twenty-two, but that was only a guess. What sort of job did she have? Did she have brothers or sisters? Naturally, I was curious about those things, and I was tempted to ask my friend, Vladimir, but if I followed the Bible story exactly, I should not do this. Isaac and Rebekah knew nothing of one another.

There were a few basic principles that I drew from the story, and one of the most important was that the servant had to find the girl from within Abraham's people. Under no circumstances was he to bring Isaac a Canaanite wife. I took this to mean that I was to find my own wife from within the Church—she was to come from Christ's family and nowhere else.

Also, following the example of Abraham's servant, I must go first to see this girl's father and speak with him about my intentions before approaching the girl directly.

I reminded my friend, Vladimir, of the church we had visited six months earlier. "Do you remember the girl I asked you about?"

Vladimir thought for a second, and nodded. "Yes, I remember."

"Could you tell me who her father is?"

"Oh, certainly," he replied. "Her father is the presbyter of that church."

"Good! Then it will be easy to find him."

I asked no further questions about the girl, not even her name. After all, I reminded myself, Isaac and Rebekah had known nothing about each other. Also, it seemed unfair to me to have knowledge about her before she knew me at all. I wanted to do everything exactly as in Genesis 24.

Unlike Abraham, I had no servant to send on this errand—I must go myself in person. Nor did I have expensive gifts to bring, only the faith and abilities God had given me. And as I owned no camels, I did the next best thing and boarded the trolleybus one Sunday morning and rode to the small church where the girl's father served as presbyter.

I wish I could remember something about the service that day—what topics were addressed in the preaching or which hymns were sung. My whole being was overcome with fear over what I was about to do. I sat toward the back, conscious of nothing but shivering, shrinking dread.

When the service concluded, I stayed in my seat. The presbyter stood in the front, surrounded by members of the congregation, chatting and asking questions about the sermon. An older lady approached me with a smile and started to make conversation with me. I was nervous about getting trapped with her, that the presbyter would leave while I was stuck talking to this nosy lady who was asking me all kinds of questions. Hoping she would leave me alone, I told her I was waiting for someone.

"Who are you waiting for?" she asked.

"The presbyter."

"Oh?" Her smile broadened. "I am the presbyter's wife. I'll tell him you are waiting."

My intended mother-in-law! I smiled back at her. Now she seemed like a pleasant and helpful person, motherly, short and plump, her weight probably bearing tribute to her cooking skills. "He'll be free in just a few minutes," she added.

When the presbyter was free, I went up to him and introduced myself. Because I was a preacher in one church and he the presbyter of another, we were familiar with each other's work, although we had never met. His name was Brynza—Alexei Gavrilovich.

"There is something important I must discuss with you," I said.

"Fine," he answered. "Let's talk."

I glanced around at all the people milling here and there and decided it would be better for us to talk in private. "I think this is not such a good place to discuss what is on my mind," I said.

"All right." He looked a bit tired, with deep furrows in his forehead. "The walk from here to my home is about twenty minutes. If that's enough time for you, let's walk and talk together."

The church was located in a suburban part of the city, far from the downtown area where the large apartment buildings stand. It was quiet here, and we strolled along a one lane street lined with tiny wooden houses and their small, fenced yards. The March afternoon air breathed a promise of spring, as did the hint of green buds on the apricot trees. With a sense that once I started talking, the situation would be beyond my control, I launched my conversation with Alexei Gavrilovich.

I am twenty-three years old, I told him, and I am not married. Recently I have decided that it is not good for a man of my age to be alone in life.

"Amen to that," he said, nodding his head approvingly.

Then I told him that I thought I should use the Bible as my guide for finding a wife. What did he think of that idea?

"Of course, young man, you can never go wrong if you follow what the Bible says," he replied.

I explained that the first time I read the Bible, I was fascinated to discover how Isaac and Rebekah came to be married, and I vowed to use this story as an example for my own life. I wanted God to make the choice for me about who I should marry. Then I asked him, "What do you think of this idea?"

Alexei Gavrilovich looked thoughtfully into the distance. "Well," he said after a moment, "it's a bit unusual, but I see nothing wrong with it. This is in the Bible after all, so if that is what you want, I think you should go ahead with such a plan."

I thanked him, and said I was glad that he approved. Then I explained that I had seen the girl God had chosen for me. "Do you know who is this girl?" I asked.

"How can I know?" he answered. "You didn't tell me."

I took a deep breath of the spring air, and stood in silence for a few seconds. I felt nervous, but also jubilant. This was the last moment of one part of my life, and the first moment of the next, and I wanted to remember it always. Surely, the long winter of being single was passing, and God was bringing a new season to my life.

"This is your daughter I'm speaking about."

Poor man! His face turned red, almost purple, and he began sweating a great deal and gasping for breath. I feared for him that something might happen—a stroke or heart attack. I remained silent, and waited with him until he recovered. After a few minutes his breathing became a bit more normal, and I felt I could speak to him again.

"You know the story of Isaac and Rebekah better than I do," I said. "First I must ask permission from the father—from you. So what do you think about this? Will you permit me to marry your daughter?"

When we first met, he confidently looked straight at me. Now he did not know where to put his eyes. He kept shaking his head from side to side, as if to say, no, not my daughter. As I would learn later, Alexei Gavrilovich had three sons and only one daughter. Two of the sons were older than she, and neither had married yet. The girl's age surprised me—she had just turned eighteen and was still in high school. And although Alexei Gavrilovich watched over all of his children carefully, he was especially protective of his daughter. She wasn't even allowed to wear hair spray or makeup, let alone marry a complete stranger who appears out of the blue sky.

We walked along without speaking. His face was still crimson, and it was clear that he had no idea how to answer me. But he was a wise man. He said, "I have to talk with my wife about this."

We stopped walking when we arrived at his house. I glanced at the neat white brick home approvingly. It had a large garden and a green picket fence that had been carefully mended several times.

"Could you please come back in a week?" he asked. "I would like to see you…Monday. One week from tomorrow. We must have some time to pray about this."

I agreed, and we set a time for me to visit.

He was about to enter his house when I called out, "Oh, Alexei Gavrilovich?"

He turned. "Yes?"

"What is your daughter's name?" I asked.

Alexei Gavrilovich turned back toward his door, and I thought for a moment he wouldn't answer. He stood there another second not facing me, and finally said, "Lena. Her name is Lena." Then he disappeared into his house.

CHAPTER 31

ALL GOOD WIVES CAN MAKE BORSCHT

Man can do everything that he expects from God.
—Soviet Antireligious Newspaper[31]

I can do all things through Christ who strengthens me.
—Philippians 4:13 (NKJV)

As told by Lena

I WASN'T REALLY paying attention that Sunday when a young man I had never seen before walked home with Papa after church. There were so many people who wanted to talk with Papa that they stood in line to wait for a few minutes of his time like they would queue up for bread. Mama and I walked ahead and were busy making dinner when Papa finally came in the house. I could tell something was going on, because his face was as red as a beet. He was unsettled, like the chickens when they sensed a fox nearby. And while I couldn't be sure, I thought I saw tears in his eyes.

My suspicions were confirmed when he immediately said to Mama, "I must talk to you about something," and led her right into their bedroom. They were in there for a long time with the door closed, Papa speaking in a low voice to Mama. When they came out, Mama was the one who was crying.

Papa saw that I was distressed by this, so he came to me and hugged me.

"Papa, what's wrong? What has happened?"

"Nothing. Don't worry." He patted my shoulder. "Nothing has happened."

Over the next few days it became clear to me that whatever was going on, it had something to do with me. Mama would suddenly hug me for no reason and say things like, "You know, Lena, you should learn how to make borscht," or "it's time you started thinking about what it takes to be a good wife."

"Mama! I'm still in high school," I protested. I still had two more months before I graduated from the evening high school program.

"I know, but you are eighteen already. Some girls marry later than this—but some are grown up enough to marry earlier." Then she added, "You are grown up enough that you are already working in a professional job."

This was making me nervous.

On Friday, Papa met me at the door when I came home from school.

"Let's go into my room, Lena," he said. "We must talk."

My mood quickly became solemn to match his unsmiling countenance. We knelt on the floor by his desk and bowed our heads. Papa asked God to be with us during this time, to bless our discussion, to give us guidance. Then he opened his Bible and read aloud all of Genesis chapter 24—the marriage of Isaac and Rebekah.

"Papa, why are you reading this to me? Is this your favorite story, or what?"

"I want to ask you a question. Are you ready to use this story in your life?"

"What?" I could not have been more bewildered if he had asked me to use sand to make ropes. "What do you mean?"

"If someone came to me, and asked that you be allowed to marry him, and you don't know this person, would you say yes?"

"Of course not!" I looked at my father in disbelief. "I would like at least to know what he looks like."

He pursed his lips thoughtfully. "And if this man was blind?"

"No!" I wailed. "I'm not going to marry any blind man!"

"Lena," he said in gentle rebuke. "That is not what should matter to you the most."

"Papa! If I were a different sort of person, like an older woman, then maybe I would feel differently. But right now I'm not thinking this way."

"Well, it is clear to me. You are not yet ready to be married."

"Why do you say that?"

"Because your answer should be, 'Does this man have the fear of the Lord?' That is the most important thing. And then you should say, 'If this is God's will, then yes.' It makes no difference what he looks like, Lena, or whether he is blind or not. If he has the fear of the Lord, and it is God's will, then you should say, 'I am ready. I will go.'"

Seeing I felt his rebuke, he smiled gently. "Lena, this man is not blind. But even if he were, it should make no difference."

I could only regard my father in silence. All my life I had known the story of Rebekah at the well. Only I had not understood that it was really about knowing God's will and obeying it.

The next day Papa and I prayed again, asking God to reveal His will in this matter. Then Papa called the whole family together, except Yakov, who was in Moscow. For the first time Viktor and Veniamin heard about Igor and that he wanted to marry me. What they didn't know at the time were the details of Igor's strange way of finding a wife.

The next day Papa, Mama, Viktor, and I fasted and prayed. It was almost surreal to hear them praying that God would give them knowledge of this man who was interested in marrying their Lena—me! I think they were as stunned as I was. No one had been thinking that anyone would want to marry baby Lena for many years. We all beseeched God to tell us His will, whether I should marry Igor or not.

Papa told me to skip school the next day, and to come home straight from work. I was acutely aware that when I did return home, the man who wanted to marry me would be waiting for me.

Out of the house that morning, away from my family, I began to feel the dread that had been closing in on me recede. Some of the distress ebbed away, and I felt a little calmer.

Why all this anxiety? I asked myself. I had no reason to feel threatened by this man. I would meet him, we would talk, spend time together, get to know each other. Eventually I would make up my mind. My family would never pressure me into doing something I did not want; I was sure of that. I would have plenty of time.

It was not as though I had to grab at the first offer of marriage that came along. Hardly. I was comfortable and satisfied with my life. I had many friends at work, at school, and at church, and was involved in church activities, popular with not only the boys, but their mothers as well. And there was Dmitri, who made no secret of his feelings about wanting to be married. I just wished everyone would remember that I was only eighteen, and be a little more patient. There was no reason to take all this talk of marriage seriously, at least not yet.

All day my thoughts kept returning to this man who would be waiting for me at home. My father hadn't given me the slightest clue what he would look like. I found it hard to keep from wondering, imagining what color his eyes were, how tall he was.

Such an original idea of his, I thought, *to use the Rebekah story this way. Not so strange, really, once you thought about it, but ... interesting.*

Kind of romantic, in a way. Rather clever of him, I decided, *to use the story to meet me, instead of approaching me directly like anyone else.*

Should I be afraid? I didn't think so. No one would possibly expect me to make up my mind tonight. I had plenty of time.

All the same, I could feel my heart pounding when I walked up to my house, opened the front door, and walked into the living room. There he was, gazing at me. I didn't even have the chance to glance at his face before he spoke his first words to me: "My name is Igor and I am here because I want to marry you."

Shocked so that I could not speak, I couldn't grasp what was happening to me. The room was spinning, a mist was forming before my eyes, and I felt my strength leaving me like water running down a drain. One more minute and I will faint, I thought.

CHAPTER 32

I PROPOSE MARRIAGE

[T]he truth no longer need be sought...it is the Marxist-Leninst-Stalinist view of history and concept of the world...Whoever still seeks the truth is a heretic and damages communism.
—Yrjo Sirola,
trainer of Communist Party functionaries[32]

But seek first the kingdom of God and His righteousness, and all these things shall be added to you.
—Matthew 6:33 (NKJV)

As told by Igor

WHEN I ARRIVED at Lena's house that Monday, her father met me at the door. "Well," Alexei Gavrilovich said.

"Well," I replied, pleased that my voice came out sounding strong and sure. "You asked me to come back after one week, and here I am. Do you have an answer for me?"

"Come in and talk with my wife," he replied. We went into the kitchen where Lena's mother was waiting, seated at the kitchen table. After greeting her, I repeated my request.

At this moment, I am prepared for any answer. I have been praying that if this girl comes to me from God, all problems and obstacles will be removed from my path. But if not, then let her parents tell me, "No." I will assume their answer comes from Him, and I will say thank you. Then I will turn away, knowing this marriage is not God's will.

Alexei Gavrilovich took a deep breath. His face was set, stern and resolute, and I could feel the strength within him that sustained him through many trials. "Well, we have prayed about this for a whole week, and we do not have any reason to say no. But we also cannot say yes. Lena must speak for herself in this matter, and we will abide with whatever she decides."

"Wonderful!" I said feeling a big grin spread across my face because this is exactly the way it happened in the Bible. The uncle and brother ask Rebekah, "Will you go with this man," and they agree to honor her answer.

"Go sit in the living room," Valentina Grigorievna told me. "Lena will come home in a few hours, and then you can talk with her."

It seemed like such a long time, but also just a few seconds, before Lena came home and I asked her to marry me. I had expected that many things might happen the first time I met my future wife, but having her turn completely white in the face was not one of them. I took her in, trying not to stare. She had an ordinary pretty face, except for her lips, which were large and beautifully curved. Her thick brown hair was pulled back from her pale face, and her green eyes were large and frightened. I realized immediately that I was going too fast.

"Please sit down," I said to her. "Do you think it is going to rain tomorrow?"

We talked of the weather, my job, her job, about high school and how she was almost finished. After a while, her mother called us to join the family for supper. Lena's parents were silent, her brothers, Viktor and Veniamin, were somewhat suspicious of me.

I learned later that all they could think was, "Who is this stranger who wants to marry our baby, our Lena?"

After we finished eating, Lena and I separated from the others and sat together in the living room. We talked for a few hours, and as I got to know her a little realized this was an extraordinary girl. Generosity of spirit shone from her eyes and resonated in her voice in the most refreshing way. When she smiled, I felt as if she had given a wonderful, private gift to me and me alone. I had seen movie stars whose smile made you feel that private bond, but I had never met anyone in life with that ability. My wife-to-be was an incredible girl. I was so happy God had selected her for me.

Knowing the hour was late and I had to go home, I didn't want to leave before having a concrete agreement with Lena. I am a man who likes to settle matters quickly and then move forward with a plan, and something as important as this shouldn't wait. "Do you remember why I came?" I asked her.

Lena nodded.

"Your father said that the decision to marry me was up to you," I told her.

Lena nodded again.

"How long will you need to think about it?"

Instead of answering, she made a sound like when you are drinking milk and it goes the wrong way up your nose. I waited for a few seconds, but she still didn't give me a specific answer, so I decided to let the topic drop for now. Her reluctance to tell me when she would have an answer probably had something to do with her being a woman. I had noticed they were less direct.

Not wanting to leave on a tentative note, I suggested that we pray together before I went home. We knelt, and I closed my eyes so that her small, pale hands folded on the couch in front of us wouldn't distract me. Lena had bitten her nails down to the quick; even the skin on her fingers around the nail looked chewed. I found this endearing for some reason.

I thanked God for His blessings, for the hospitality and fellowship of this warm family, and asked Him to protect us all, to guide my relationship with Lena.

Her prayer was as traditional as mine, but at the very end, she suddenly said, "…and God bless our life."

Our life! How simple and beautiful this girl was! A wonderful electric current passed through my whole body, because I understood that this was how she had chosen to give me her answer. Our life! I had to struggle not to laugh out loud in exultation. She had said yes to my marriage proposal, yes to our future together.

I turned to Lena with a big smile, but she wasn't smiling back. She put her finger up to her mouth and began to bite on the nail, then quickly stopped herself, clasping her arms together tightly against her body as if they were trying to fly away. *Better to wait,* I thought. She has just said yes to a marriage proposal. This must be a big moment for her, a moment of joy but also some anxiety might be mixed in as well. This was normal for a young girl. I could wait patiently now, since I had received her answer.

I happily told my mother the next morning that I was soon to be married to a Christian girl. As expected, my mother was delighted, and was especially joyful that Lena was a presbyter's daughter. Then I had to find a good time to tell my father. "Papa, I have news for you," I told him one evening. "I have finally found someone, a Christian girl I want to marry."

"Great idea. I am glad for you. When I was your age I had a lot of girls, some to drink with, some to sleep with."

A few days later he was not so enthusiastic. Once he remembered the part about Lena being a Christian, his mood deteriorated. Not only was he a strong atheist, he had come to hate everything about Christianity. It was his perception that the religion had taken his wife and split his family. My father's big hope was that I would pass through this "phase" and come to my senses. He understood that marrying a Christian girl made this impossible. Moreover, living permanently as a Christian meant saying good-bye to all chances of a good career and decent place in society. And now I was marrying "the pope's daughter" as he called her. My father was not an easygoing man, and the more he talked about how marrying Lena would ruin my life, the angrier he became.

"Papa," I said. "If I could bring God right into this room, and show you exactly what He wanted you to do, would you do it?"

"God isn't real." Papa smacked the table hard enough to shake the glasses on it.

"I know you think that." I struggled to keep my own voice calm, since allowing oneself to become emotional in an argument never accomplishes anything. "But let's just say for a moment that He is real, and I had the power to actually bring Him to you. If you saw God here, would you do what He told you?"

My father drew deeply on his cigarette. "Well, yes," he answered hesitantly.

I ran into my bedroom, and came back a moment later with my Bible. "God is in this book," I told him. "This is His Testament. The word "testament" means to witness, or to make a will. The Bible is an actual written record of His will, and if you read this book you'll see that worrying about a good job or a place in society is silliness."

"Don't tell me about this!" His face framed with white hair seemed so old and defeated. "I don't want to hear another word." He ground the cigarette he had been smoking into the ashtray as if to destroy it. We stared at each other for a moment, and I saw terrible fury in his light blue eyes. And just before my father turned away, I saw something else there as well. I saw fear.

When I told my best friend, Vladimir, that I was going to get married, he was happy for me, asking questions about Lena, her family, and what had happened between us. After I told him about the way I had proposed, and how she had said "yes" in her prayer, his attitude changed.

"All she said was 'God bless our life?'" he asked, staring at me skeptically. "And you think you are now engaged?"

"Well, what else is needed?" This was distressing. I had been visiting Lena every day believing that the question had already been settled. Could there be something about marriage proposals that I didn't know—some sort of code or sign? No, that was impossible. I was a grown man, and an intelligent one at that, and would have found out such a thing by now.

Vladimir's expression changed to one of sympathy, which made me feel even worse. "I think you should check with her again," he said. "Definitely. Check again."

I said okay, I would do it. But I had no idea how to arrange to ask her such an awkward question.

As told by Lena

When I thought back over my first meeting with Igor, I realized I only had the haziest notion of what he looked like. My mind was curiously blank. Tense throughout our entire encounter, I had never settled my gaze on him or even allowed our eyes to meet; I did not have the nerve to look directly at him.

At dinner I had been careful to notice everything he did, watching out of the corner of my eye to see exactly how he was eating, if he chewed nosily or talked with bread in his mouth.

Later, when we were alone, talking about whatever nonsense came to mind, I felt a bit better, more like we were just friends. I still couldn't look at him. Then Igor brought up the question of marriage. Was I ready to give him an answer, he wanted to know.

I could only wonder at this guy. We had spent four hours together and I was supposed to tell him that I would join him for the rest of my life?

I really doubted it. Why would I want to? How could I know?

We prayed together, and as I prayed I said something about God blessing our lives, thinking in my mind that our lives would most likely be separate. Afterward, Igor suddenly seemed to be in a wonderful mood. I agreed to meet with him regularly, and he promised to return the next night after ten o'clock. He left smiling, mysteriously elated. He was definitely not an ordinary sort of man. I had never met anyone like him before, that much I knew for sure.

The next evening he came back, and the evening after that, and after that; he never missed. Always he came with flowers and his Bible. He read to me from places in the Bible where it speaks about marriage, like Ephesians and Corinthians, and the way he believed most deeply our marriage ought to be, and would be.

"What do you think the apostle Paul means by this, Lena?" he would ask me. "Do you agree with this, that you are to be a submissive wife?"

At eighteen, submission wasn't exactly what I was thinking about. "It's in the Bible, and I agree with the Bible," was all the answer I would give him. *This shows he has the fear of the Lord,* I thought. *But why does he keep coming back?*

I could feel the pressure mounting every time he came to see me. Before this week I had not given serious thought to marrying anyone; only now did I appreciate how carefree those days had been. Igor allowed me to think of nothing but marriage, marriage, marriage, and the strain was getting to me. He ignored any of my hints about how young I was or how I wanted to take some time to let our feelings for each other develop naturally. He knew what he wanted, was sure it was God's will, and I just needed to realize it. I went to my parents to plead for help.

"I don't know what to say to him, Papa. Mama, tell me what I should do!"

"We cannot." Resigned, my father shook his head. "If we say to you, 'Go ahead and marry him,' and it turns out badly, you will blame us for it. Or suppose we say, 'Send him away.' If that turns out to be the wrong choice, and you are lonely and miserable all your life, it will be hard for you to forgive us. So we cannot tell you how to decide."

"I'm so afraid I will do the wrong thing."

"You must discover God's will," Papa answered. "If Igor is from God, you must marry him, and there will be no mistake. Pray and work earnestly to discover God's will."

Many years later I found out that by this time Papa and Mama were already well on their way to believing that Igor was the answer to their prayers that God would keep me from Dmitri. As bizarre as the situation was, they didn't want to interfere with God's plan or their own hopes for me.

There was only one hope, and I seized it. *God will give me wisdom if only I ask for it*, I thought. I began to pray. Papa and I prayed together every night before Igor came to visit, and my parents prayed with us before Igor went home, asking God for insight and guidance.

I also launched my own investigation, seeking information about Igor. Because of my father's position as senior presbyter, my family had contacts and friends in all the churches in the *oblast*. I spoke to some of the deacons in the church where Igor preached, to my aunt and cousin, Pasha, who attended this church, and to everyone else I could find who knew Igor. All they could say was "He is a good preacher." No one could tell me anything more. He had come to faith only two or three years earlier, and none of the people in his church had known him long. There were times I feared he was a KGB spy.

At first, I didn't breathe a word about Igor to anyone outside of my immediate family. When my father invited Igor to preach in our church the Sunday following our first meeting, I asked Igor to go to the church without me to be certain that no one saw us together.

All this intrigue may have made Igor nervous during his sermon that day. Something did, anyway. He seemed unable to look people in the eye. Instead, he preached to the rafters in the ceiling, up over their heads.

He acted almost as nervous a week or two later, one night when he had come as usual. Oddly, it seemed as though something was threatening his confidence. I'd noticed this on and off the last two weeks, but hadn't thought much of it. We decided to take advantage of the warm April evening to take a walk through the neighborhood.

"You know..." Igor began, then stopped, then tried again. "You know, not long ago I was talking with my mother. I said to her....I have asked you to marry me. And I said you told me yes. Am I right about that?"

I was still agonizing over this question. Several times a day I asked God if He had sent Igor to me. Was it His will that we be married? God hadn't answered me yet, and I was not at all certain what His answer would be.

If I told Igor the truth, that I had not agreed to marry him, then he would immediately ask me again. I wasn't ready to answer this question! But if I said I didn't want to marry him, then he would go away. Forever. Putting an end to the pressure. Putting an end to all his attention to me. Putting an end to these confused feelings I had for him, and the fun we had together. And I'd never have the chance to get to know this man, whom I respected for his wholehearted zeal to do God's will and who had so freely opened his soul to me.

So I said in a tiny voice, "Yes."

"Wonderful." I could hear the relief and pleasure in his voice. He seemed to expand, growing visibly larger as he walked beside me.

Well, all right, I thought. *It's only as binding as words written on water with a pitchfork. I could withdraw at any time if marrying Igor turned out to be outside of God's will.* I had told Igor yes, and meant it sincerely enough, but that did not necessarily make it the final answer. Only God knew what that would be.

Now that we had this clear understanding, the proper thing was to announce in church that we intended to marry. In the Baptist churches of Ukraine, it is customary that before young couples begin courting and are seen keeping company together, their intentions are made known to the whole congregation. The presbyter makes an announcement, giving official status to the young couple's relationship. Everyone who sees the couple together then knows they are not just "having fun" with no strings attached. Rather, it is understood they are seriously working toward marriage. Once the announcement has been made in the church service, a couple is more or less engaged.

We looked forward to the end of the secrecy, which was becoming a burden. It would be fabulous to go about together without fear of discovery, and to talk and laugh openly as a couple, in the company of friends. Coming as a total surprise to everyone, the announcement of our engagement would cause a stir in the Baptist community, which could be fun.

Before the announcement was made, however, there was someone else I had to tell. My suitor, Dmitri, who had treated me so tenderly, so respectfully, deserved to know that I had agreed to marry someone else. While I could see the pain in his eyes, he was not surprised. He knew I'd been seeing another man. "If you change your mind, Lena, please tell me," he said. As the months went on, his hope dwindled, and his melancholy deepened. Being the man of dignity that he was, he did not pressure me or cause me any pain. He discreetly stepped into the background. I also struggled, mourning his loss, wondering if I had said goodbye to a man who loved me unselfishly in exchange for one I hardly knew.

Meanwhile, Igor arranged with the senior presbyter at his church to announce our engagement at a Saturday evening service. I'd known this presbyter since my childhood, and he was amazed at our news. We could tell he was looking forward to amazing his congregation, too.

I was present for that service, as I had been for the past three weeks. Being careful to preserve our secret, I arrived alone and sat far away from Igor. No one had any idea that we were together.

At the end of the service, the presbyter said, "Brothers and sisters, I have one more announcement to make. Our youth leader and preacher, Igor, is planning to be married. Igor, will you please stand?"

Igor stood there alone, smiling. Where was his fiancée? All the people looked at each other, murmuring, glancing around the room. A young woman sitting next to me leaned toward me. "Who is the bride? Do you know her?"

I wanted to grin, but held myself back. I smiled vaguely at her and shrugged my shoulders.

The presbyter beamed at the congregation. "Can you guess who is his bride? No?" He paused, toying with his audience, and said, "Well, it is Lena. Would you stand please?"

They all looked at the Lena they knew, a young woman who regularly attended this church. But she didn't move; she just sat, looking confused.

So I stood up and smiled, and they greeted me with a gasp of surprise. For many I was a total stranger. I knew what they were thinking. How could Igor marry a girl from some other church, and not from within their own congregation? After all, believers had to be constantly on guard about KGB spies or people who were spreading false doctrine. It was important to know people, for them to become part of the church community, to demonstrate how solid their commitment was. Marrying someone from another church that no one else knew could be very risky.

I wasn't too worried about Igor's church. Sooner or later, they'd find out who my father was, and I would become more acceptable in their eyes. It was thinking about the reaction from my own church that made me nervous.

Unfortunately for Igor, many in the congregation of my church thought of me as their princess. Part of this was because I was the presbyter's only daughter, but I never did fully understand the rest. I certainly didn't think of myself as beautiful. And why I had so many friends was a mystery to me. After all, I was very shy. People told me I had inherited my father's kindness and sensitivity to others, and my mother's warm, hospitable personality. Maybe they were right. All I was sure about was that for whatever the reason, people in the church were not going to be happy with me marrying an outsider.

Another problem for Igor stemmed from the fact that he hardly thought at all about how he looked or dressed. I spent an entire week searching for something to wear the day our engagement was announced, choosing a dark blue dress, the first new dress I'd had in a very long time, and it cost half my father's salary. Igor arrived at my church that morning wearing an old zippered jacket that was a relic of the Afghan War, and it looked the part. Clothes and appearance were always important to me, and my embarrassment over what Igor was wearing didn't calm my nerves any.

When one of my father's deacons made the announcement that I was engaged and asked me to stand, there was a pleased murmur among the congregation. And what lucky guy was going to marry their Lena, daughter of the presbyter they loved so much? They all looked around in pleased anticipation.

When Igor stood up, the murmurs abruptly ceased, leaving only a shocked silence. Not only was he a stranger, he obviously came from some uncouth and shabby world. He made them uneasy. Not one of them believed that this young man could be a fit match for me.

Thus began the time of our betrothal.

CHAPTER 33

BITING MY ELBOWS

*Naturally, the class enemy attempts
by all means to sneak in to our ranks...*
—Georgi Dimitrov[33]

But love your enemies, do good to them.
—Luke 6:35

As told by Lena

THE MUTED, if not patently insincere congratulations coming from members of my church were no surprise to me. How could I blame them? They barely knew Igor, and he came to church that day wearing unkempt clothes fit only for hard labor. For him to show up in front of Papa's whole congregation dressed that way on that day of all days! No wonder people were taking him as a personal insult.

It was a shock when my uncle and aunt, the aunt who attended Igor's church and had told me he is a good preacher, spoke against Igor.

"You know, Lena, you are making a big mistake," she said.

"Why do you say that?" I asked her.

"Did you know he was in the war? In Afghanistan?" She gave me a dark, ominous look.

"I didn't know about this," I replied. Igor rarely spoke about himself, and had told me nothing about being in the war.

"Your aunt and I have discussed this matter," my uncle said. "We believe he is probably disturbed. Mentally ill from so long in combat."

"Thousands of these boys are coming home with mental problems," my aunt added. "Why do you want to marry one of them? There are so many other boys around, friends from your childhood, who you have known a long time. Why turn your back on them?"

How I wished I had an answer for this question, not just for my aunt and uncle, but for everyone else who came to me demanding answers. I had no idea that so many people would be disappointed in me. Women came to me, one after another, as if they had formed a queue outside my door. "Why are you doing this to us? How could you?"

The women who questioned me were mostly the mothers of the boys I had grown up with in the church, boys I'd played with, sat next to in children's Bible study. While I knew that people nearly always married within their church, I had never thought seriously about the fact that I was supposed to marry one of those boys. Their mothers would draw me aside after church services, at church suppers, or prayer meetings, or even when they happened to see me on the street.

"Lena, I must talk with you…" They made appointments to come and see me on weekends or when I came home from school.

"Lena, you are making such a mistake!" they said. "You don't know this young man at all."

"You could do so much better, Lena! The way he looked in church, like he had just walked in off some battlefield!"

"No one understands you at all, Lena. You chose this person none of us know. He could be anybody. And you are so young! You have no reason to make this decision so soon in your life."

"I think there is something not right about this boy, Lena. Is it true he was in Afghanistan a long time? He is possibly a little bit crazy."

"Such a shame to disappoint your father and mother in this way."

"Lena, you could choose from anyone at all to marry, anyone! Some well-established person in our church, for example, from a family you know well. You would be so much happier, and much more secure."

"This cannot be God's will, Lena. God would never wish on you such a risk. Don't marry him!"

"Who can know where he might lead you? He may be really dangerous, this young man."

Through all this turmoil, I could always escape to my job. No one harassed me about Igor, and I could rest in the love and support of my boss. But one Monday morning I went in to work and Yulia Silvestrovna would not talk to me or eat lunch with me. For two days she was an iceberg to me, as if I were someone she had never met or didn't want to know. How could I have offended her?

On Wednesday morning she yelled at me to come into her office and to lock the door behind me. After I sat down, she started to shriek at me, so angry she was throwing thunder and lightning. "Why didn't you tell me who you are? I knew you were different, but why didn't you tell me you are a Baptist?" Then she put her head down on the desk and sobbed.

Through my own tears I said, "You never asked me."

"I almost lost my job, and my husband might lose his. What about Dmitri? Does he know?"

When I told her I wasn't seeing him anymore, she got even more irate and snarled, "I don't know if I ever loved you."

After she calmed down a little, she told me what had happened. Many times in the course of my work in the clinic, we received telegrams from the Communist Party. Usually these were just informational notices, letting us know such news as the weather service had forecast a big storm, and that we should close all the windows. I was often the person who answered the telephone when the telegram station called and had to give my last name so they would have a record of the person who took the call. Because of my father, the name Brynza was well known. And because of these telegrams, there was plenty of evidence about the importance of my job and how long I had worked there.

One of the Communist Party bosses who had met me in one of his visits to the clinic was a womanizer and wanted to have some fun with me. Several times he pulled me into an office and locked the door, telling me no one would know what we did. I always told him that I would know. After he found out my identity, he was so embarrassed that descended on Yulia Silvestrovna, making angry threats to expose her and the scandal she had created by hiring me. A Baptist girl, a member of the sect that was working against the building of Communism, had learned many things that most people didn't know. Not only did I know a lot about the bosses' medical conditions, I had seen their flats and what was sold in the special stores, and observed the favored treatment they received in hospitals, like never having to wait in line. I could expose the lies they told about the classless society that supposedly existed in the Soviet Union. And to make matters worse, they found out from a member of the church that I was in fact the daughter of the senior presbyter of the *oblast*. That was enough to convince them that the Baptists were actively seeking information to bring down the Communist government.

"He and the others interrogating me threatened me and my husband with all kinds of horrible things," Yulia Silvestrovna said. "I can't believe they ended up not doing anything. They must have believed me that I really didn't know who you are."

Soon after, the director of the hospital found me another job as a typist for the Director of Gastroenterology, which was a less visible position. I think Yulia Silvestrovna forgave me because we still ate lunch together every day. But those cozy chats weren't comfortable for me; Yulia used every opportunity to tell me I had chosen the wrong man.

Now I had nowhere to turn. My friends at church, my boss and colleagues at work, anyone I might rely on for support only had negative advice for me. My parents refused to tell me what to do. I felt as isolated as a stranger in a noisy crowd.

I told Igor nothing about the mud people were throwing at him with their insinuations. Why disturb him with gossip? I did care for him, and felt encouraged that he loved the Lord. I concealed from Igor how the negative opinions were planting doubts in my heart and shaking what small confidence in our relationship that I had. There were many things about him that did seem odd. Not that I believed he was crazy; I felt certain he was not. But I found him stranger than anyone I had known. *Different.* I almost felt afraid of him, though this fear was less than my fear of disobeying God's will. I couldn't send him away until I knew that was what God wanted me to do.

Toiling to find God's will, I spent hours praying and reading the Bible. I thought about the people in my family and in the church, who seemed to know just how God wanted to be served. My grandfather, who went to the firing squad because he was convinced God didn't want him to risk fighting in the war and killing someone. The many people who suffered in prison and labor camps for their faith. Sometimes God's will wasn't pleasant, sometimes God saved people at the last minute. How was I to know what to do? I had become engaged to Igor, gotten myself into this predicament, now I was biting my elbows, frustrated with myself for committing myself without thinking.

After we became engaged, I expected more affection from Igor. It seemed to me that in the normal scheme of things, a girl would welcome some show of fondness from her fiancé. When he came in the evenings, for example, I thought he might say, "I love you" once in awhile. But he didn't say this at all. Sometimes it seemed as if he had no idea what I was feeling, or that it even mattered to him. Instead, he continued teaching me from the Bible about the life he wanted us to have together.

At the same time, everything about the way Igor acted when he was near me sent the message that he loved me. Just the look in his eyes when I met him at the door, taking the flowers he brought me, seeing his eyes overflowing with love for me made me think that he was up to his ears in love with me.

Still, every evening he spent most of our time together explaining his new, deep thoughts about our future. More than a month passed in this way before he finally spoke to my need for reassurance.

"I want you to know," he said at last, "that it isn't because I don't love you—I do. You just don't know how much I love you. I love you with all of my heart and with all of my being. But I'm not going to kiss you; I'm not going to hug you until we are married. I want us to be doing everything together for the first time after we are married."

Hearing these words relieved me of some of my worries. Rather than forcing our relationship ahead of God's blessing, Igor was waiting with me, choosing to spend his time sharing with me his dreams for our life together, opening his soul to me. It felt wonderful to listen to him express his feelings, almost as if he knew the precise words I needed to hear. This was love, surely; wasn't it?

While that weight was lifted, others remained. I knew so very little about him, and he was rarely serious when I tried to find out about his childhood or life experiences.

"Well," he said one evening, "there was a period in my life when I was really interested in eastern religions, especially Hinduism."

I looked at him wide-eyed. "Hinduism?"

He smiled. "And yoga. I probed deeply into yoga. It is a very exacting discipline."

That frightened me. Everyone knew that doing yoga is inviting the snake demon into your body. "Yoga!" At that I stood up. "Excuse me a minute. I'll be right back."

I ran into Papa's room, where he was working at his desk, and shut the door behind me.

"Papa! Igor was into yoga!"

"So?"

"Yoga!" I repeated. "With all those bad spirits! How can I marry such a man?"

"Well, he's not into yoga now, is he?"

"No."

"Now he is in Christ, yes?"

I nodded.

"So I wouldn't worry about it."

"But couldn't there be lasting effects from the yoga? Some bad things may show up later in his life."

"Lena," he said, "Igor has the Lord to help him. I believe together they can handle this."

Another time, I pressed Igor to tell me some war stories, even though I knew he preferred to avoid this subject. His wit helped him distract me from my questions.

"Lena, you are so bold. Can you really trust me so easily? A stranger you never knew? Actually," he said, "it was the KGB that sent me here to Zaporozhe."

"No. I don't believe you."

He shrugged. "It's true. The KGB wants information about the church. They sent me here as a spy, to learn about your family."

"About Papa?"

He nodded. "The truth is that I have a wife already. She lives in a city some distance from here. I can't tell you exactly where."

I rose to my feet. "Excuse me just a second, Igor."

I rushed to find my father. "Papa! He says he's from the KGB! He's a spy!"

Papa looked at me and smiled. "I don't think so."

"He has a wife in some other city. He told me that."

"And do you really believe him?"

I looked at my father and was silent.

"Lena, he's teasing you," Papa said.

"At a time like this, he teases me?" I pressed my lips together fiercely. I was really angry with Igor this time.

CHAPTER 34

TESTING GOD

In increasing its battle power, the Soviet Army is ... protecting the security of all mankind and serving as a strong barrier in the battle of peoples against imperialist export of counter-revolution.[34]

*Unless the L*ORD *watches over the city,*
the watchmen stand guard in vain.
—Psalm 127:1b

As told by Lena

I FOUND MYSELF living with so much stress that often I lost track of what I was really feeling. The unfavorable opinions about Igor others constantly drummed into my head caused my own doubts to grow and magnify. A thousand questions filled my mind, and not one answer came to me. In desperation, I began testing God. I knew it was wrong to do this, but I saw no other choice; I simply did not know what else to do. I had no doubt that God's love for me was sure and that whatever His will was for me, it was the best for me. If God intended for me to marry Igor, then I could be certain that God would bless our lives together. The difficulty I was having was that I couldn't figure out what His will was. Testing God seemed to be my only hope.

That spring the weather was fitful and often rainy, as unsettled as my own moods. One night, a truly savage storm moved in. The wind howled and great shards of lightning split the darkness; rolling crashes of thunder shook the house and an unending deluge of rain soaked the yard and garden. It would be unreasonable, it seemed to me, to expect anyone to venture outdoors on such a night. The trolleybuses, if they hadn't been stopped by downed power lines, would be empty for sure. Even though Igor had not missed coming to see me once since our relationship started, I was convinced this storm was enough to stop him.

I closed my eyes and prayed: "God, please help me. Show me Your will. If Igor does not come tonight, it means I must tell him, 'No, we cannot be married.' I pray for Your wisdom and Your guidance. Amen."

At that precise moment the door flew open.

"Hi, sweet girl!" A drenched Igor stepped into the room, wiping soaked hair from his eyes. Water sluiced off his raincoat as from a duck's back and formed puddles on the floor.

I could only stare at him, powerless to speak.

Another evening I was studying, waiting for Igor. I sat on my bed and opened one of my books, but couldn't focus on what I was reading. Instead, I decided to ask God again for guidance. Taking a blank sheet of paper from my notebook, I cut it into forty or fifty pieces. With a pencil I wrote "yes" on one of the pieces. The others I left blank. I spread these bits of paper face down on the bed and mixed them around and around for a long time while I spoke intensely to God.

"Help me please, Lord. Let me know Your will because I do not know what I should do. I feel I am being torn this way and that way by Igor and the others, and I am so confused. Tell me if it is not Your will that I marry this man. Give me a clear answer, Lord, if I should not marry him…"

The public announcements we'd made in church hardly mattered to me; I was prepared to cancel our engagement in a minute. All that I cared about was that I not commit the error of my life, which in my heart I feared might very well be marrying Igor. I made a definite commitment in my mind: if I drew a blank piece of paper, I would take it as God's message regarding Igor, and be able to say to him, "I'm sorry, Igor, but I will not be able to marry you. It is not God's will."

I turned my eyes up to the ceiling so I could not see my hands as they mixed the scraps of paper thoroughly one more time. Holding my breath, I picked up one of the pieces of paper and looked at it. It read "yes."

Igor's shift at the aircraft factory broke for lunch each day at noon. He was in the habit of telephoning me in my office at this time, just to hear my voice and talk with me for a few minutes. One night as he was leaving to go home, he told me he would be unable to phone the next day.

"We'll be working out in the countryside," he said, "at least an hour from the city. There aren't any phones out there in the wilderness."

His entire shift was scheduled for a nuclear training drill, a precaution against the imminent nuclear bomb attack our leaders assured us the Americans were planning. All factory workers received this training. These drills were normally conducted in open wilderness areas, well away from population centers.

"I'm sorry I won't be able to call," he said. "I'll miss talking with you."

"I understand," I told him. "No problem."

In the back of my mind I wondered: could this possibly be something that God had arranged?

It seemed to me that all control of my life had been taken away from me. I felt cornered, trapped by circumstances and my own confusion about what to do. I knew I couldn't move without God's help, and I prayed for it earnestly.

"Please send me the sign I need, Lord. Help me! If he will not call today at noon, then it means I must tell him no, that it is not Your will that we get married."

I was convinced this time the Lord would answer me with a clear sign and tell me that Igor was not meant for me. Then I would be free.

CHAPTER 35

A SMOOTH COURTSHIP?

In the event of the unleashing of a nuclear missile by the imperialists, [the] task is to destroy the aggressor's nuclear weapons, large concentrations of troops.[35]

Some trust in chariots and some in horses, but we trust in the name of the LORD our God.
—Psalm 20:7

As told by Igor

HAVING MET THE girl God had chosen for me, I made sure I visited her every day so we could get to know each other better. These were full days for me, working full time at the factory and preaching in the church, devoting spare minutes to sermon preparation. In addition, I attended the university in the evenings and Saturdays, studying aircraft engineering.

After classes finished at 9:00 PM, I rode the trolleybus for about an hour to get out to Lena's place in Upper Khortitsa. Once there, I chatted with her for an hour, or sometimes two, and then returned home. Often, I didn't get to bed until two in the morning, and I had to get up at 5:30 to go to work. I was exhausted, but it was worth it. What a wonderful girl! True, Lena often seemed nervous and distracted, but who wouldn't be, knowing their marriage was coming soon, and all of the changes that would bring.

There was only one thing that mystified me about Lena—her lack of punctuality. We liked to meet downtown on the weekend and walk around looking at stores or sit in the park. Often she was an hour late, leaving me standing on the sidewalk waiting for her. I never let this bother me too much, since in all other ways she was so wonderful, but it seemed strange to me. Why say you will be somewhere and then come an hour late? Not wanting to make problems with Lena about this, I took to teasing her instead. She would finally be coming up the sidewalk, and I would hide the bunch of flowers I bought behind my back. "You are so late," I'd say, smiling. "You don't deserve this." Then I gave her the bouquet and I could see she was happy.

"Oh, thank you," she would say, and smile shyly.

One Saturday morning she met me at the university after my classes were finished for the day. Having some extra time, we walked back to her house, Lena wanting to go by foot so we could talk privately, away from her family. The distance to her house was more than fifteen miles, and we walked for nearly six hours, walking at first past tall apartment buildings with shops on the first floor, all government owned shops named after what they sold. No brand names in the Soviet Union: the store named "Bread" sold bread, the store "Books," books. Inside, clerks totaled sales on a wooden abacus. There was not much traffic, as most people rode the bus or trolleybus, or occasionally took a taxi; only the elite or those persistent enough to wait in line for ten years drove cars. We left the city behind, crossing the bridge over the wide Dniepr River, to Upper Khortitsa where most people lived in small houses on narrow roads. Lena was wearing a pair of new shoes that day with a bit of a heel. She did not complain, even when I noticed she was limping and asked if she wanted to stop.

When we got back to her house, Lena took off the shoes and I saw the insides of them were covered with blood. Her feet were bloody as well—both heels, and most of the toes. I wanted so much to take those swollen little feet in my hands and wash off the blood, but this would not be proper. Her mother filled a small tub with warm water and made Lena sit at the kitchen table. She cast a reproachful glare at me as she eased Lena's feet into the warm water, a glare Lena must have seen because she said, "Oh, Mama, don't blame him. It was my choice to keep walking."

I looked down at her feet in the washtub. The water had turned a faint pink, and seeing it made me think of things that were soft and pale and perfect. This girl was crazy with love for me.

The next week, I told Lena we could not have our usual lunchtime phone call on Monday. This was an important chat for both of us since we had so little time together. I explained to her that the factory where I worked was participating in some civil defense drills on a deserted stretch of land outside the city, competing with groups from other factories to prepare for a surprise attack by the Americans.

The next day, I stepped out of the bus onto dry, sandy soil and gazed around at nothing but rocks and a few scattered weeds stretching clear to the horizon in all directions. We learned how to put on gas masks and ran through a tent filled with foul-smelling gas. Anyone who smelled the gas hadn't put on the mask properly. We were instructed on how to quickly don suits for protection against radiation. We put them on, ran for several kilometers through the fields, then went through simulated decontamination procedures.

Around mid-day, a contingent of army troops suddenly arrived in this same area, probably to conduct military training exercises.

I watched them set up a temporary field headquarters not far from where I was standing.

Soldiers quickly brought out a table and chair for the high-ranking officer to use as his command post. This captain sat there watching imperially while foot soldiers unspooled yards of electric cable that ran from a mobile truck generator parked nearby. He was a red-faced man, and I noticed with some amusement that he looked sweatier than the soldiers around him who were actually working. *Perhaps being an important official makes one very warm,* I thought. As I watched, the soldiers connected their cable to a large field telephone, which they placed on the table in front of the officer.

Without really considering it, I walked over to him. "Captain," I said. "May I use your telephone for a moment?"

The officer looked at me as if I had lost my mind. "No, you cannot," he said and gave a sweaty little sneer. "This phone is for military purposes only."

"Of course," I answered. "I understand. Sorry to have bothered you."

The officer nodded, and I turned to walk away. But before I could go two steps, the man halted me with what sounded like a sharp military command. "Make your call. Do it quickly."

We looked at each other for a moment. "Thank you," I said. He didn't answer. There was nothing on this man's face that implied sympathy, camaraderie, or even interest, and I had absolutely no theory about what could have made him change his mind.

I picked up the phone and dialed Lena's number.

"Hello?"

"Hi, sweet girl," I said. "How are you doing today?"

"Igor!" Her voice sounded a little squeaky. "Where are you calling from? You told me you would be out in the field today!"

"Here I am," I told her, "calling you from the middle of the wilderness. This is something, eh?"

There was complete silence on the other end of the phone. I waited for a few seconds, and when she still hadn't spoken, I asked, "Is everything all right?"

Instead of answering Lena began to laugh. "Yes," she said, and then laughed some more.

"Well, what's so funny?"

Lena just kept giggling, and after a moment I started to laugh as well although I didn't know why.

Not long after this, one Saturday afternoon, sitting at Lena's kitchen table, we discussed the wedding date with Lena's mother. While the wedding had been set for July 21st, Lena's mother thought we should move it back to August or even September.

"We have seven hundred guests coming from all over the country," Valentina Grigorievna said. "It would be nice to give them more time to make their arrangements."

I replied, "If we must change the wedding date, then let us make it earlier, please, not further away."

Valentina Grigorievna stared at me austerely; her features set in a stern, almost military look that could have scared Stalin himself.

"How will we obtain all the different foods we need by July 21?" she asked. "Harvest time is still a long way off."

I did my best to remain strong. "Please," I said, thinking of Abraham's servant in Genesis 24. *Do not detain me now that the Lord has granted success to my journey.*

Valentina Grigorievna wouldn't relent. "We have so many guests coming, Igor! We must put up a tent in the yard where we will have the reception. But now all our vegetables are growing there—tomatoes, cucumbers, carrots, beets, cabbage, and potatoes. Nothing will be ripe by July 21. Everything will have to be destroyed. How can we waste all this good food? That just isn't right at all! Now, if we wait just one month for the wedding, we can harvest our crops first. Yes?"

I looked at the worn rug on the floor that the family was too poor to replace. How had this happened? Now, all of a sudden, the fact of my getting married when I wanted to meant the wasteful destruction of a huge amount of food. I wished Lena was there to somehow smooth this over, but she was out on an errand with one of her brothers. For months, I had been living on less than four hours of sleep a night. All aspects of my life—work, school, the church, and Lena were suffering. I couldn't focus, was losing weight, and last week on the trolleybus I had seen the famous astronaut, Yuri Gagarin, playing a piano, rather badly I thought. It had taken me a few minutes to realize I was hallucinating. I didn't think I could go on much longer. Yet, they had worked hard to plant and care for that garden. I bent my head, and asked God for guidance.

The following Saturday afternoon, I borrowed a sickle and went out into the Brynzas' yard. We had agreed that if the vegetables were to be sacrificed, I was going to have to do the job. It took longer than I thought, although once I found the right motion the work was not so hard. Inside the house, Lena's brothers watched me silently. I mowed down every plant in that yard until nothing was left but moist, springtime soil.

CHAPTER 36

"WE CAN TELL IGOR TO GO AWAY"

Superstition, which lies at the root of [church] ritual, must, of course, be opposed by rationalistic criticism, by an atheistic, realistic attitude to Nature and her forces.
—Leon Trotsky[36]

He ransoms me unharmed from the battle waged against me, even though many oppose me.
—Psalm 55:18

As told by Lena

IN UKRAINE, PRESBYTERS like my father do not have the authority to perform legal weddings. Usually the couple, dressed formally as bride and groom, goes to the ZAGS (City Agency for Government Services) office for the civil marriage ceremony. Along with two friends acting as witnesses, they sign various documents. The couple's internal passports are stamped and sealed with the information that they are now husband and wife. For most people, there is no more to it than that: they are married.

For Christians, the civil ceremony is the prelude to the real wedding, merely a legal necessity. Only in the church will God put His blessing on a union and seal it officially for a lifetime.

On the day of our civil ceremony, two days before our church ceremony, heavy rain drenched the streets of Zaporozhe. "If it rains on the wedding, the marriage will be happy," Mama repeated the old saying to me as I walked out the door.

Crossing the street as we approached ZAGS, I was preoccupied, barely noticing where I was walking, my wedding gown trailing through a wet patch of mud.

"Igor, what is your last name?"

He looked at me oddly. "What?"

"I don't know your last name."

"Yaremchuk. Igor Yaremchuk."

"Oh, good." I smiled radiantly at him, pleased. I never liked my own last name, Brynza, as it happened to be the name of a salty variety of a popular whitish cheese. One advantage of marrying Igor meant I would be freed from that name.

I remember little else about the civil ceremony, which held no great importance for me. I was not accepting it as necessarily final. A new prayer formed in my mind.

"Lord, help me, I pray this one last time. If this is after all Your will, then I am ready to marry Igor. But if it is not, then please change his mind. When the pastor asks him in the church, 'Do you love this woman?' let him answer 'No, I do not.' Then I will know for certain that we should not be married, and everything will be cancelled."

For the next two days, this prayer repeated itself in my mind, over and over again. There was still hope, there was still time. Years later I listened, horrified, as Igor pointed out to me that backing out after the civil ceremony would have meant we would have needed to obtain a legal divorce. At the time, this thought never entered my mind. All I was focused on was that God would keep me from making a mistake, and that He could stop the wedding if it was His will.

Yakov Kuzmich Dukhonchenko was having difficulty grasping what I was telling him. He had journeyed 500 kilometers from Kiev to perform my wedding ceremony. My parents were two of his oldest and dearest friends, and he'd known me since I was a baby.

Before joining a couple in matrimony he usually talked with the bride and groom separately, first one and then the other. He used these confidential chats to determine their state of readiness for marriage. Have they deeply and prayerfully considered their decision? How certain are they of their love for one another? Are they truly prepared to spend the remainder of their lives together?

He had interviewed Igor the day before, who had been clear and certain on all counts. "No problem!" he said happily.

I was different. Yakov Kuzmich could not imagine how he would have handled things had my parents not made an effort to prepare him beforehand. Even then he found his brief interview with me unsettling.

"Tell me, Lena, do you truly love him?"

"Well, I don't know."

"You don't know? How can that be?"

"I still have time," I said.

"But the wedding is tomorrow!"

"There is still time..."

The presbyter hesitated, frowning a little. "Try to explain to me, please, what do you mean?"

I finally made him understand that I was half expecting Igor to deny me in the middle of the ceremony. I was prepared for Igor to tell me no, he did not love me, in front of the 700 guests who had traveled from all parts of Ukraine and Russia, some of them taking several days to arrive, and who were now looking forward to the day-long celebration and six course wedding feast under the tent that occupied our yard. And Igor was to say, "Why, no, I don't love this woman."

In other circumstances, Yakov Kuzmich might reasonably have postponed the wedding until the bride was a little more certain of her feelings. But in this situation, how could he? As a houseguest and lifelong friend of my father, he had no choice but to await the next day's ceremony in a state of unprecedented suspense.

The day before, after the civil ceremony, Igor's parents hosted a small reception for their non-believing friends and relatives, and told me that Igor was going to stay home the next day. They insisted on it. He should not set eyes on his future wife again until the ceremony in church, his mother said. Anyway, Igor was too tired, so exhausted he had no legs left, they said. He must rest up for the wedding festivities, otherwise, he would surely become ill with fatigue. They would put him to bed immediately, and allow him to sleep as long as he wanted for a change.

One look at Igor and I had to agree; he appeared to be sleep-walking. But the thought *what about me?* crept through my mind. I felt at least as worn out as he did. Between misery and fear, I was feeling far beyond tired.

I smiled and said good night to the man I had promised to marry. The next time I would see him would be just hours before our wedding ceremony.

During those last few days before my wedding day, old family friends and well-wishers from Zaporozhe and from towns and cities hundreds of miles away had arrived at our house. They paraded in and out the front door, crowding into our small house. They gathered under the tent in the yard, calling greetings to one another, hugging, trading news, examining each others' faces to see what the years had done. What a great and glad occasion for all of them.

Except for the bride.

I was now surrounded by the same mothers and fathers I had offended by my "thoughtless" action of forsaking their sons to marry that strange Igor. I had wounded them, insulted them with my disloyalty. Sensitive as an exposed nerve, I perceived their disappointment in every glance they gave me, every small twitch of their lips as they tried to wish me well. Sensing the disapproval of people I loved so much gave me the feeling of sinking into a bottomless morass, which I struggled to hide by smiling constantly.

Hoping for a moment of peace, I escaped to the kitchen. Three relatives stood at the table across from the sink sorting through vegetables. People from churches all around the *oblast* had sent food: piles of tomatoes and cucumbers, pyramids of melons stacked on the floor, chickens heaped high on the table in two piles, some plucked, others awaiting a similar fate. Beets, cabbages, and loaves of bread. Several 50-kilogram sacks of potatoes stood by the door.

My brother, Viktor, poked his head through the door. Seeing me, he came into the kitchen.

"You're hiding," he said.

"I'm just so tired!"

"Have you seen Sasha?"

"Sasha Voslov? Is he here?"

"His whole family. You must talk with him, Lena. He's a desperate man."

I laughed, then wished I hadn't. My brother was giving me a hard look. Viktor and Sasha were the same age and had been close friends since the summer Sasha spent in our house a few years earlier. I had always thought of Sasha as another older brother.

"It's not funny, "Viktor said. "This is serious. I promised I'd find you. He's waiting in our room."

I bumped into Sasha's mother the moment I stepped out of the kitchen.

"Olga Alexandrovna! Hello!"

"Oh, Lena. None of us can understand why you are doing this. Poor Sasha is so upset. We all are!" She looked at me with pleading eyes. "Speak with him, Lena, won't you? Be kind."

Sasha was sitting hunched on the edge of my bed staring glumly at the door. He rose quickly to his feet when I stepped into the room and closed the door behind me. He put his hand on my shoulder and looked longingly into my face. His cheeks were red and mottled and I saw dark circles of fatigue under his eyes. I sat on the chair by my desk and tried to smile.

"Well, Sasha, it's been such a long time."

"I've been in Kiev, studying in the technical college. I only found out three days ago that you are getting married."

"Everything has happened so fast."

"I don't even know this guy. His name is Igor? I've been looking for him. Where is he?"

"Home asleep. He's exhausted."

"I'm surprised he isn't here. I want to speak with him."

"What would you say?"

"I would begin by threatening him. Maybe I could scare him away."

I smiled at the thought of scaring Igor. I could not imagine him frightened by anything. "He's really very good."

"You smile, but I am serious," Sasha said. "You know, I have always been expecting to marry you."

I looked at him in wonder. "How could I know this?"

"Because I told you! Plenty of times."

"You were teasing me," I countered.

"I pretended that, because you were so young. But I was serious, even when you were a little girl. Ask Viktor if you don't believe me."

"I thought of you more as my brother."

"I would be your brother! And your husband, and your father. I would be everything for you."

"Then why didn't you say so? You might have let me know. I haven't seen you for nearly a year."

He flashed me an angry look. "Who could imagine you getting engaged? It is like Veniamin telling me all of a sudden he has found himself a wife."

"Sasha, Venya is only fifteen."

"You are not so much older," he said. "I thought we had plenty of time. Oh, Lena!"

He dropped suddenly to his knees in front of the chair and took hold of my hands. "Please!" He turned his face upward, imploring me.

It startled me to see tears filling his eyes and running down the sides of his face. I wanted to run away from him, from everyone.

"Don't marry him, Lena. You don't even know this man. Who is this Igor, anyway? Break it off. Listen, marry me tomorrow, instead. We could do it, Lena. Really."

In a daze, I shook my head. "I think it is God's will that I marry Igor."

"How can it be God's will? Igor is not even here, at this time when you need him so much."

"Igor is very strong in his faith," I said. "God has given him many signs that we should marry."

"Then why is Igor not here? Lena, what do you expect your future life to be like? I have watched you in the other room, among all the people. You smile and pretend everything is wonderful, but I know you too well. I can see you are not happy. You are suffering! Isn't that true? I dare you to deny it!"

"Sasha," I said softly, "it may be true. But God's will is all that matters." I looked down at his face and longed to dry his tears, but stifled the impulse. I touched his hair with my fingers. "You know, it still could happen that God will act to change Igor's mind. I have thought about this, and I believe it might take place during the wedding ceremony."

"Tomorrow? In the church?"

"I believe it could happen."

"With all the people there? It would be terribly embarrassing, I think."

"Well, yes. But so what? If this is what God wishes, it will be the right thing to happen, and perfectly natural. It cannot be a mistake. What is it to be embarrassed, compared to doing God's will? It is nothing."

Sasha pulled himself to his feet. He took out a handkerchief and wiped his face. I saw a glint of hope in his eyes, which was a relief to me.

I rose and opened the door in such a way that I was able to edge Sasha out of the room. I smiled at him and said softly, "I'll see you in a little while," and closed the door.

Alone, I fell onto my bed and lay there in a crumpled heap. I felt like crying, but couldn't summon the energy. I also had too many details to think about.

I had promised my mother that I would see about the flower arrangements. Who could I ask to take them to the church and place them properly? If only Igor were here! He could at least entertain the guests while I tried to make the last-minute preparations. And what about my wedding dress? I had washed out the mud that got on it the day of our civil ceremony, but I hadn't ironed it. The photographer would be here at 8:30 in the morning. And where had I put my veil? It was tucked away somewhere, but where?

I was startled out of a sound sleep by a knock on the door. The room was growing dark, and I had no idea how long I'd been asleep. As I got up to turn on the light, my brothers, Yakov and Viktor, came in, filling the room with their presence. From the way they were looking at me, I knew this conversation would be as enjoyable as a KGB interrogation. "We have a suggestion," Yakov said.

"We've been talking with Sasha," Viktor said. "He told us you are not happy."

I shrugged. "You know how it has been."

"You still have strong doubts, right? That's not how a bride should be feeling," Yakov said. "That's what Sasha believes, and we think so too."

"He's so in love with you, Lena," Viktor said. "Now he has this crazy hope that Igor will change his mind at the last minute. It's pathetic."

"It could happen," I said. "I've had feelings about this."

"Do you want it to happen?"

"If it happens, it will be because God wills it. So then of course I want it to happen."

Viktor scratched his head thoughtfully.

Yakov asked, "Have you told this to Igor, what you wish would happen?"

"No, of course not. I couldn't."

Yakov looked at me for a long moment. "And yet you have a terrible fear that you are making a mistake."

I nodded my head miserably and said nothing.

"Here is our suggestion," Yakov said. "We will go to Igor, Vitya and I. We will tell him ourselves, 'Lena feels she does not really love you. She cannot marry you, but has been unable to tell you this.' We will say it for you. We'll tell him everything, and the wedding will be canceled. No problem, yes?"

"No!" I cried, my eyes wide with alarm. "Please promise me you will say nothing, not a word to Igor. Promise me you'll be quiet as fish!"

"But why?"

Because God would be greatly displeased, I thought. "It would be terribly wrong," I said. "The worst thing you could do. So make me this promise: you'll keep your tongues behind your teeth, all right?"

Neither of them spoke. They just looked at me, reluctant to give up their plan.

"You must promise," I said to them evenly. "You will say nothing to Igor."

Finally they nodded and agreed to leave matters in my hands.

"I hope you know what you are doing," Viktor said as he followed Yakov from the room. They closed the door, leaving me alone with my confusion and doubts, and the feeling that even my brothers were disappointed in me.

CHAPTER 37

I STILL HAVE TIME

The thoughts of Lenin will live forever
—Soviet banner[37]

"For my thoughts are not your thoughts, neither are your ways my ways," declares the Lord. "As the heavens are higher than the earth, so are my ways higher than your ways and my thoughts than your thoughts."
—Isaiah 55:8-9

As told by Lena

IT WAS NEARLY midnight before all the visitors left. Papa had gone to bed an hour before, as had Yakov Kuzmich and his wife, who were staying at our house.

Having failed to convince myself that I could put off ironing my wedding dress until the morning, I changed into some old clothes and took the dress and veil into the kitchen, leaving our room free for my brothers to go to bed. I spread the dress out on the ironing board and nearly fell asleep waiting for the iron to heat up.

My mother and her sister, Aunt Fenya, were working like horses, surrounded by the mountains of food they had to prepare for the 700 guests. They calculated the number of hours they and their helpers would need to cut, slice, chop, cook, boil, and bake everything and prepare it for serving, garnished artistically with fresh parsley and dill. As it turned out, they figured they would have to start cooking at two in the morning. Going to bed hardly seemed worthwhile. They only had time for a nap.

Mama watched me iron my dress. "When you finish," she said, "you'd better try it on again."

"Oh, Mama, why? It fit fine two days ago."

"Just do it. And did you find your veil?"

"It's here. I was careful with it like you told me. I folded it, and put it on the back of the shelf to keep it safe."

After I finished ironing, I shook out my veil and in horror saw that it was torn. My brother, Viktor, had stepped on it during the civil ceremony, but I hadn't noticed any damage then. In dismay I looked at the rip in the delicate white netting, which made a prominent hole just at chin-level. I could not possibly wear it like this, yet to be married in a torn veil was unthinkable, as bad as not having one at all.

Already alarmed, I put on my wedding dress and discovered another disaster. Even without a mirror I could see that the dress was drastically changed. The lower part of the skirt, where I had washed out the mud, had shrunk by several inches.

"Mama!" I spun around to show her my ruined dress. "Look at this! And this!"

"Oh, it's a pity. Let's see." Mama examined the damaged dress and veil carefully. I had hopes that her experience as a seamstress would end this nightmare. "Oh, Lena," she said. "You surely have sat in a puddle this time."

I watched her with anxious eyes. "Can you fix them?"

"I cannot," she said. "You need a new section of fabric here, for the skirt. And you need some filament thread to mend the veil. Very delicate white thread." She raised the veil to the light and looked unhappily at me. "See how fine the netting is? I don't have anything like it."

I could barely listen to her next words. "It's after midnight, and by the time the stores are open in the morning, it will be too late."

Mama and I looked at each other helplessly. We were silent for a long moment, until at last Mama spoke in a thoughtful voice. "I have an idea," she said. "What about Aunt Tanya?"

"My friend Olya's mother?"

"She's been invited to the wedding. It's not so bad that we ask a favor."

"What favor?"

"I'm sure she can help you."

"At this time of night?"

"You'll have to wake her up. And you've got some walking to do."

"They live way out in the country!"

"A little more than three kilometers."

"But Mama, it will be so dark!"

"Lena, there's nothing else to be done. You'll have to go now, and let me get back to cooking." Mama was so distracted by all she had to do that night she didn't consider what she was asking me to do.

It was dark! There were no streetlights, and the moon wasn't out, only starlight. The little points of light in the sky only deepened my sense of groping blindly through the night, like walking on the bottom of the sea. I couldn't even see my feet. For a time I was able to discern the general paleness of the dirt street where I was walking, but it changed into black pavement. Further out of town, the pavement ended. The earth became rough beneath my feet and I nearly stumbled. I moved forward uneasily on the dirt road, darkness pressing against my face like a blanket.

I would have liked someone to come with me, but Mama had all the wedding food to prepare. Papa's health was not too good, and neither of us thought for a second that he should be awakened. As scary as a walk alone at night was, it was less daunting than the thought of several hours alone with one of my brothers. I knew that Yakov or Viktor would spend the whole time trying to talk me out of getting married, which was worse than going alone. I was afraid if I tried to wake up Veniamin, one of the others would wake up and insist on going with me.

I carried my folded wedding dress in two hands waist-high like a serving tray so as not to crease or wrinkle it. The veil was folded flat inside the dress. It troubled me that both my hands were occupied. If a leafy branch brushed my cheek or a bat flew at my face, my hands would fly up in alarm to protect myself. The dress and veil would go sailing into the night and end up right in the mud.

I had always felt threatened by the dark. My earliest memory was lying in my crib wailing in terror, waiting for someone to turn on a light. Now I could wail all night and no one would hear.

This is all Igor's fault, I thought. *Thank you so much, Igor. I hope you are sleeping well.*

It seemed to me less and less likely that God wanted this marriage to take place. If God were behind it, then why was I plunged into such misery? Why did God, from the beginning, and especially right now, make it horribly difficult and uncomfortable for me? Was He telling me, "Don't do it, Lena!"

As I trudged through the darkness with my ruined wedding dress, Sasha's question flew into my mind, complete with its own answer: If Igor really loved me, wouldn't he be here right now to help me?

Of course he would. Was this so complicated to figure out? As I had long suspected, and what Yakov Dukhonchenko and all my family and friends must eventually understand, was that Igor did not love me.

Whatever he might have believed until now, Igor would discover the real truth in the morning. Standing in God's church before His people, Igor would be unable to announce, "Yes, I love this woman." He could not tell such a lie before God, I was certain.

Without noticing it, my eyes had grown accustomed to the dark; I was able to identify Aunt Tanya's cottage when I came to it. I knocked hard on the wooden door for nearly a minute before an outside light was switched on above my head. Squinting my eyes nearly shut from the sudden brightness, I saw Aunt Tanya pull aside a curtain and stare at me from a front window next to the door. I gave a brief smile and held up my wedding dress. Aunt Tanya moved cautiously to the door, opened it a crack and stood there waiting.

I spoke in a half whisper. "I have an emergency with my wedding dress. Mama thought you could help…"

Aunt Tanya did not react, just stood there in silence. Did she hear me, I thought, and raised my voice. "Mama thought you could help—"

"Sshh!" Aunt Tanya opened the door wide. "Why do you shout? Come in."

Aunt Tanya's long white hair hung down her back almost to her waist. She wore a pale cotton robe that made her look ghostlike until she turned on a lamp in her room. Then she spread out the wedding dress on her worktable under the light. She put on her glasses and bent closely over the table to examine the skirt.

"You washed it, didn't you," she laughed. "But this part is new cotton! Of course it would shrink."

I put on the dress and stood without moving while the seamstress knelt and took measurements front and back with a threadbare yellow tape measure. Together we chose a panel of cream-colored felt to be added to the lower part of the skirt. Aunt Tanya attached the new piece using her hand-powered sewing machine, quickly finishing the dress so that it looked perfect and new again.

"Now this veil…" She picked up the white netting and turned it this way and that under the lamplight, frowning.

I watched her anxiously. "Mama said it needed filament thread. Do you have that?"

"Eh, I don't," she said.

"Oh, no!" I groaned.

Aunt Tanya looked at me and smiled. "Don't worry; we have a few tricks left."

Reaching behind her shoulder, she pulled forward a strand of several long hairs and examined it under the light. Selecting a single hair of exceptional whiteness, she gave it a sharp yank, plucking it from her scalp. She threaded this hair into a fine small needle. Holding the white netting close to her face, she worked her needle back and forth through the mesh. At last she gave a sigh of satisfaction, tying a final knot. With a pair of tiny sewing scissors she cut off the white hair she'd been using as thread. Then she snipped off the broken bits of the original netting and displayed the mended veil for me to see.

It was amazing, a miracle. The veil looked perfectly whole from just inches away. I had to hold the netting almost on my nose before I could see where it had been mended.

"I can hardly believe this," I said. "Aunt Tanya, how can I ever thank you?"

"My wedding gift to you, dear. I hope it goes well for you tomorrow."

Walking home in the darkness, I started to regret my impulsive decision to come alone. Now that the crisis was over, I had more time to think about how scared I was to be out so late at night.

To distract myself, I thought about other weddings I'd seen. How I loved weddings: the church decorated with flowers, filled with loving friends and relatives and happiness. I had seen at least half a dozen of my brothers' friends married. Everyone would be dressed in their best, wearing their widest smiles and most buoyant moods. The plainest girls, when they became brides, all turned radiantly beautiful from the joy shining from within. All my life I had dreamed of the day when I would be a bride, and be so happy that everyone would think I was beautiful, for once. I wasn't expecting that to happen today.

How wonderful it was for those other brides, who were waited on and protected, their future husbands hovering by their sides, doing their errands and little jobs, whatever needed to be done for the wedding, making sure the bride was not disturbed in any way, or under pressure, so she would be fresh and rested for the ceremony.

Tears welled up in my eyes and overflowed, flooding down my cheeks. I blinked them away, but made no effort to stop them as I continued walking through the night. It was probably after three in the morning, but I was beyond caring about the hour. I was also past caring how vulnerable I was, walking alone at this time of night. Thieves, hoodlums, and drunks sometimes attacked lone people on the streets at night. *Let them come,* I thought. "God, just take me home," I prayed. "I am so tired."

All the same, I was relieved when I saw the light streaming out of the windows of our kitchen. It was the only sign of life on the dark street. I felt as though I'd been away a long time, and my step quickened as I passed the last four or five houses. Pausing on the doorstep, I wiped my eyes and cheeks, adjusting my face into a smile as I opened the door.

Our kitchen was steamy and warm, with huge cauldrons simmering on the stove, stirred with clanking metal ladles.

"Well, see who's finally here!" someone called out when I appeared in the doorway. There was muted cheering.

Mama and her helpers, bustling back and forth between the long kitchen table and the stove, simmering soup, tossing chicken parts into various pots, cutting up beets and potatoes, slicing onions, were in a party mood, festive and convivial, already celebrating the wedding.

"Just look at all this work you are making for us," Aunt Fenya said. "I hope you are pleased with yourself."

They all laughed.

"Are you sure you want to do this, Lena?" Mama looked at me, pretending great seriousness. "Why don't you just change your mind so we can all go back to bed!"

Gales of laughter.

"I myself have been wondering," Aunt Luba said, "because you are so young. Why would you want to get married so early in your life?"

Their laughter rose to even higher levels.

I could think of nothing to say that had enough bile to express my mood. Anyway, they were laughing too loudly to hear me. I retreated from the kitchen without speaking.

Scheduled to appear at my house at eight that morning, Igor had not appeared when the photographer came at 8:30. He took some pictures of me and my family, and the tent with places prepared for 700 guests.

I wandered through the house and yard in my wedding dress, smiling. I picked up my bridal bouquet, then set it down, picked it up, set it down. The moment I sat in a chair, I felt like standing, then wanted right away to sit down again. Where was Igor?

I knew I wasn't sleeping, but I wasn't quite awake either. I was not entirely certain that I was still alive. It was as if I were absent, just watching someone else get ready to be married.

One hour late, Igor finally showed up.

"But how am I late?" he asked. He turned to my father. "You said ten o'clock, right?"

Papa smiled at him. "Well, ten is when we all go to the church. No matter, we are all here now."

For a brief moment before we left for the church, I found myself alone with Igor. He smiled at me warmly.

"You look so beautiful, Lenichka. How are you feeling?"

"Fine," I told him. "And you? Did you have a good rest?"

"Wonderful! I am fresh as a cucumber. And so happy we are getting married finally!"

It was then that I began to feel the heavy thudding of my heart inside my chest. I could hear it too, the heartbeat thumping relentlessly in my ears, marking off the rapidly vanishing minutes before the wedding. I didn't have much time left.

I had prayed almost continuously for many days, and now prayed with intensity and desperation that if this wedding was not His will, God would change Igor's mind. He would just cause Igor to answer, "No, I do not love her" when that particular moment came in the ceremony, so that I would know for certain that we should not be married, and all this would be past and forever done with, and I could have my life again.

Just before the ceremony began, Yakov Kuzmich came to me for a final hurried consultation. We were in the anteroom at the back of the church, where the presbyter and preachers usually met before the service to pray together, out of sight of the wedding guests who were now filing into the sanctuary and taking their seats. Idly I thought that the church wouldn't hold 700 people, and that those who came later would be standing in the lobby or out in the yard, unable to see, unless they were able to catch a glimpse of the proceedings through the open windows. Of course, not all those invited would attend the ceremony. Most of the non-believers we had invited would come to the reception later.

Yakov Kuzmich leaned close to me and spoke in a whisper no one could overhear: "Tell me, Lena. Do you love him or not?"

"I don't know yet," I said. "I still have time." I smiled vaguely and went on praying, my heartbeat thudding louder in my ears. As I floated down the aisle on Igor's arm I could hear the woosh-woosh of the blood pumping through my veins.

Then I was standing at the front of the church next to Igor, with Olya as my witness and Vladimir as Igor's. Yakov Kuzmich did not follow the normal order of a wedding. Instead, he started with a question. He looked directly into Igor's eyes and asked him, "Do you love this woman?"

"Yes, of course," Igor replied. I could tell from his tone he was surprised, thinking, "Why else would I be here?"

And in that instant, everything in my world changed. I felt a wall inside me collapse, and my confusion was gone. All my doubts vanished as if they'd never existed. My heart ceased its hectic thumping and a feeling of serenity spread over me. I had been so blinded by my fear that Igor did not really love me, I couldn't see all the ways God was showing me that this was His will for me, including my own growing affection for Igor. Such a peace in knowing that this was God's will! And it was God's will for Igor. God Himself had chosen me to be Igor's wife. All my doubts had been foolish and wrong.

"And Lena, do you love this man?" Yakov Kuzmich was waiting for my answer, wondering just what I was going to say.

"Yes!" I said slowly, and nodded at him, to reassure him. For the first time in many weeks I knew that my smile was truly radiant.

While that trial ended in joy, I had no idea what trials lay ahead.

CHAPTER 38

A PREMONITION OF DEATH

And what about equipment? We don't have any...all we get is syringes—we don't even have scales for the pregnant women.
—Soviet hospital manager[38]

*My comfort in my suffering is this:
Your promise preserves my life.*
—Psalm 119:50

As told by Lena

FOLLOWING OUR WEDDING, Igor and I settled down to live in my parents' summer kitchen, all fifteen square meters of it. Originally, the summer kitchen was one room of a small building that included a tool shed and chicken coop. Having moved the chickens and tools to other places in our yard, Papa renovated the vacated space into a bedroom, kitchen, and sitting room. We were delighted that we had our own place, surrounded by the vegetable garden and sheltered by cherry trees, three tiny rooms that were our little island. The last four months had been constant storms for me; now I was basking in sunny days. That first year of marriage was so idyllic, I felt as though I were already in heaven.

How could I have been reluctant to marry Igor? Overwhelmed with happiness, I was drowning in love for Igor, and my life revolved around him. Nothing was as important to me as Igor.

During our honeymoon, I shocked him profoundly when I told him of my doubts and fears before our wedding. "I cannot believe you never told me," he said. "I had no idea you were under such stress."

Four months after our wedding, I realized that I was pregnant. Seeping under my happiness, filling me with a profound peace, was the knowledge that soon I would be living with God, fed by a premonition that I would die in childbirth.

I tried to convince my mother that I was going to die. "Mama, will you promise me something?"

"Anything, my daughter. What do you need?"

"Will you take care of my baby after it is born?"

"Of course, Lena, I'll help you. You know that."

"No, Mama, you don't understand. Will you take care of my baby?"

"Oh, you mean once you've gone back to school. I'm so glad you've decided to study to be a nurse. That will come in handy when your own children are sick."

"No, Mama, you aren't listening to me. I know that I'm going to die in childbirth, so I won't be here. Igor won't be able to do everything himself. Please, Mama, promise me."

Deciding that that I was scared of the delivery, Mama humored me. "Lena, it's normal to be a little nervous. But no one dies when they have a baby. Of course I'll do whatever needs to be done. You can count on me." Mama had no idea just what she was going to be called on to do just a few months later.

As the months passed, my happiness with Igor increased, as did my sense that my life would end once I gave birth. While my feeling of deep peace never wavered, I grieved at the thought of leaving Igor and my unborn child. When I told him that I was sure to die in childbirth, Igor took me seriously, and for the first time, I saw him cry.

Maybe Igor believed me more than Mama did because he saw how ill I was throughout the pregnancy, suffering from morning sickness nearly the entire time. At three months the doctor told me the baby had died. After a few days of mourning, I felt movement. The baby would live, I was sure. I was the one who would die.

Over the next few months I collected things for my baby, green and white swaddling clothes, green baby carriage and blankets, thinking green and white were good colors for either a boy or a girl. My due date came and went as I continued my preparations, making sure everything in our little house was clean and welcoming for my new baby. To leave it all dirty was unthinkable.

On the first Sunday in July, nearly a year after our wedding, Igor paused on his way out the door, asking me how I felt. I told him to go; I felt fine and didn't want him to miss the baptism that was to be held early that morning. He came back a few hours later to check on me, but nothing was happening, so I sent him to the church for the regular service. While he was there, my labor started. I used the time waiting for him to return home to write him a letter, expressing my gratitude that I got to know him, thanking him for the year of happiness he had given me, telling him how much I looked forward to seeing him in heaven, closing with "please take care of the baby."

When I finished the letter, I walked across the yard to find Mama, who had stayed home from church in case I needed something. She called for the ambulance to come, which was normal procedure in Ukraine. Many of the neighbors came over to say good-by to me, some of them in tears. While they thought they were just seeing me off for a few weeks, I believed they all knew I was going to die and were paying their final respects to me.

Seeing my face, Mama said, "Lena, I wish I could take your place. Never did I have such fear as you have now." Once the ambulance came, Mama gave Venya a note to take to Igor at the church, letting him know that I had been taken to the birth house. Receiving the note, Igor quickly wrote out a request for the church to pray for my safe delivery and then rushed over to the birth house.

In the Soviet Union, women gave birth in special hospitals called birth houses, which for many were places of secret dread. No visitors were allowed, especially not husbands. I lay in a room with several other laboring women. Having received no medicine for pain, some of the women in the room with me were pulling their hair out, others were banging their beds. Through my sobs I heard my name being called.

It was Igor, standing in the street. For all husbands and relatives, the only means of finding someone in the birth house or even any news of her was to walk around the building calling her name. Igor despaired when I didn't answer him, and stood there in the street, publicly praying with his hands clasped tightly together, not caring if anyone saw him or reported him.

On the way to the delivery room about six hours later, I told my doctor, Natalya Ivanovna, that I knew I was going to die. She told me the same thing my mother had said, that people don't die from having babies. When Natalya Ivanovna delivered the baby's head she said, "It's so big, it must be a boy."

I immediately said, "Name him Vitaly." A few minutes later, the baby was born, and she told me that I had a girl. The feeling of having given birth was such a relief.

The doctor started to deliver the afterbirth, and suddenly she was covered in blood. Feeling weak, craving sleep, I felt a warm flow going out from me. I could hear my daughter crying and asked God to save my life. Faintly, as if they were far away, I heard the doctors and nurses shouting at me to stay awake. Someone hit me in the face with a folded newspaper and screamed, "Stay awake! You cannot sleep!" They were all yelling at each other as they moved me to surgery, where they did some kind of operation without giving me any anesthesia.

While they worked, I felt that I was in a tunnel, watching my life go by like a living photo album. The further I went into the tunnel, the faster I traveled and the brighter the light became. Then at the end of the tunnel I saw my funeral and Igor holding the baby, crying. I was so glad to approach the end. Jesus would be waiting for me there.

Meanwhile, Igor was waiting, pacing around the lobby of the birth house, where he was allowed to wait once I'd gone to the delivery room. The doctor told him that a daughter had been born and that his wife was in bad condition. As he waited, he noticed all kinds of activity. First an ambulance sped up, and a nurse jumped out, carrying some tubes of blood. Then another drove up, and a doctor leaped out and rushed inside. What Igor didn't know was that all of this was for me. Five hours later, two doctors came out of the delivery room with sad faces and hanging heads. The chief doctor approached Igor and asked him how old he was.

"Twenty-four," he replied.

"You are so young," she said. "I am so sorry, we did everything we could. But her heart stopped. Your wife has died."

Igor watched numbly as the nurse wrote out a death certificate. He walked home alone, feeling a knife in his heart. None of this made sense to him. He kept asking God why He would choose this wife for him, and then take her away after only one year. As he walked, he prayed out loud. "God, hear my voice. Hear my prayer. I just don't understand. Please give Lena's life back to her, and give her back to me."

It was late when he got home, and the first my family knew that he had returned was when they saw the light on in our window. Then they saw Igor, pacing back and forth. They could even hear a few words. He was praying, beseeching God for someone, that

God would spare someone's life. At first they didn't realize that he was praying for me. Only after over an hour of agonized prayer could Igor bear to face my family and to tell them that I had died. Viktor told me later he had never seen a man cry so much as when Igor told them of my death.

Early the next morning I woke up alone in a dreary room, with no feeling in my legs or arms. The only sensation I had was my head on the pillow. I could hear the director of the department shouting at someone over the phone saying, "She's alive, but she's going to die because she lost so much blood. We couldn't get to her in time, and she's only nineteen."

I looked at the doctor and asked her why they had cut my legs off. Until they lifted the sheet from my legs and showed them to me, I didn't believe them when they said they had done no such thing.

I found out later that the EKG had gone flat during surgery, causing them to conclude that I had died. Soon afterward, a nurse happened to come into the room and noticed that the EKG had started again. All of the staff were astonished and did everything they could to revive me. After bringing me to consciousness, they put me on a ventilator, but didn't believe that I would survive.

Later that morning, Igor and my parents returned to take my body away to be prepared for my funeral. The nurse told them that I was still alive, and that Igor could see me for one last time. They weren't supposed to let in visitors, but they made an exception for him, probably because they were feeling guilty for the mistake they had made that was costing me my life. Igor came in the room and laid down on top of me and cried so much they made him leave and wouldn't let him back in. I asked to see my baby, but they refused.

For an entire month I lay in the birth house, healing from the large incision they had made when they opened me up for a partial hysterectomy that was necessary after the doctor had perforated my uterus accidentally. They had inserted so many IVs and I had developed some kind of hives from all of the drugs they were giving;

any touch was painful. I dreaded the daily pain when the nurse tore off the old bandages from my various wounds and applied new ones of fresh cheesecloth, but was glad for it, because it assured me that I was still alive.

When I regained consciousness the day after my daughter's birth and heard the doctors and nurses saying I was going to die, I began to fight for my life. Praying fervently, I asked God why all this had happened to me. He answered with a gentle rebuke. Since my marriage, I had made Igor my idol and worshipped him in place of God. My deepest devotion belonged to God, not to any man, no matter how much I loved him. I promised God that if He gave me my life back, I would never stand in Igor's way if he entered full time ministry. No matter what he felt God calling him to do, I would put up no obstacles or objections. I knew from my mother's life just what kind of sacrifices this might require me to make, but I was willing to submit. I only wanted to live.

The day I left the birth house, the chief doctor called me into her office. Looking sadly into my face, she said, "I know you are only nineteen, but I have to tell you this. Do not tell your husband or even your mother what kind of surgery you had. If your husband knew, he would divorce you tomorrow. He's a young man, and it is natural for him to want more children. I know it will be hard for you, but don't tell him anything."

Hearing those words, I lost all desire to go home. Would Igor really cast me off if he knew the truth? Shuffling slowly, hunched over because of the pain from my incision, I walked out of the birth house right up to Igor before he recognized me. He had been looking for a tall girl, not someone bent nearly double, and I had lost about one third of my weight, dropping from about 165 pounds to 99. I was also covered with bruises from having fainted and fallen so many times in the birth house while walking to the room where they fed us or to get some treatment. In the Soviet Union, patients were expected to take care of themselves, and to walk on their own to the toilets, washrooms, and procedure rooms. Those who were too weak depended on the other patients to help. Mama and Igor's mother were also there waiting for me, and they didn't recognize me at first, either.

As she had promised, Mama took care of my baby, Victoria, or Vika, for short. Igor had his hands full with me. He had to do all the work around the house, to help me dress, and even to bathe me. I simply didn't have the strength.

While I was still in the hospital, Yakov married my best friend Olya, who had been a witness at my wedding. In September, Viktor married Luba, and by then I was strong enough to attend. To cover the wounds on my legs left over from my stay in the hospital, Yakov and Olya brought socks from Moscow for me, socks for women that were not available anywhere else.

That fall, I started attending medical college in the evenings to study nursing. My maternity leave exempted me from any work requirements during the first year, so all I had to do was attend classes, which was about all I had strength for. The second year I worked as a nurse's assistant. And the last two years I worked full time as a nurse while studying at night. We would work for twenty-four hours, then have two days off. I loved the work, helping people. Most of the other nurses slept when they were not caring for one of their sixty patients, but I used my extra time to chat with them.

One way I endeared myself to my patients was the technique of giving shots that I perfected. In the Soviet system, most medications or vitamins were given by injection. As a result, many patients had to get as many as four shots at a time, several times a day. I placed four syringes between the fingers of one hand, slapped that hand against the patient's rear end, depressing the syringes one by one, surprising the patients that I was finished so quickly. "But, Yelena Alexeiyevna, I only felt one." was the typical response.

Two years after I started in the medical college, I fainted at work, numbness spreading over half my body, my vision deteriorating. After they ran test after test, the doctors diagnosed me with multiple sclerosis. Not willing to accept this, Igor took me to a hospital in Kiev where they performed all kinds of tests, only to come up with the same diagnosis. In all, I had been in the hospital for five months.

The doctors said there was nothing they could do for me and sent me home. Two-year-old Vika didn't know me. In her mind, Igor was Papa, and my mother was Mama, so many months my mother had cared for her. Even though the doctors gave me official invalid status, which meant I didn't have to work and could collect a small pension, I went back to work anyway, working only the day shift, one day a week. Over time and with much prayer, I got better and the symptoms went away.

The next few years passed quietly. Gorbachev was in power and life was a little easier for believers. Once during an exam on Atheistic Philosophy, one of my professors tried to harass me. "What is your last name?" he asked me.

I knew he recognized me, but didn't let on. "Yaremchuk," I replied.

"That's not your name. What is your name?"

"Yaremchuk. Why do you ask?"

He said to me, "I know who you are, and just because you got married it doesn't change anything. I am going to give you a three for this exam."

Some of the other students, and even some teachers, came to my defense, and convinced this man to give me the five I deserved. Five years earlier, very few people would stick up for believers in public. Conditions in the Soviet Union were definitely changing.

CHAPTER 39

IF YOU FLY, YOU DIE

To obtain a…visa, the average Soviet citizen needed to fill out numerous questionnaires…be totally loyal, have no unauthorized contacts with people in other countries, leave close relatives at home as hostages.
—Yuri Tarnopolsky[39]

You are no longer foreigners and aliens, but fellow citizens with God's people and members of God's household.
—Ephesians 2:19

As told by Lena

ONE OF THE positive changes during this time in the Soviet Union came in the form of government permission granted to the Baptist Union to start a seminary in Moscow. The Union leaders quickly invited pastors and leaders to attend. They wanted only pastors with at least five years' experience and a university degree. Igor was one of the few men in Ukraine who fit these requirements, so he was one of ten from our republic who were chosen to attend the new seminary. All of them were told to quit their jobs before traveling to Moscow.

Igor decided not to give up his job. "I want to see if this is a serious seminary or if it is just for show. Maybe the government is only letting them do certain things, which wouldn't really be of much use," he explained to me.

"That's true, Igor," I agreed. "Then you'll have a job to come back to if it doesn't work out."

Neither of us had to say out loud our other reason. Due to the chronic lack of housing in the Soviet Union, we were still living in the summer kitchen four years after getting married. Most people had to work for one organization for ten or twenty years to get their own apartment. As a war veteran, Igor only had to wait five years, and the five years were nearly completed. We were not about to risk losing our place in line for an apartment.

When Igor arrived in Moscow, he discovered there was no seminary other than on paper. The Baptist Union had all the government documents stating they were operating a seminary and had a building, but that was about all. It turned out that once the government gave the Union permission for the seminary, the leaders decided it was best to start quickly and publicly, so that it would be harder for the government to close the seminary if they ever changed their minds.

They didn't mean to deceive anyone, but the result was that students came and there was no curriculum, no books, and no place for students who had traveled from all parts of the Soviet Union to sleep other than in the faculty members' offices.

Many of the students were the sons of senior presbyters of *oblasts*, like my father. These students complained to their fathers, who complained to the leadership. Hearing of this predicament, the Slavic Gospel Association offered to provide for five of the thirty students to study at Moody Bible Institute in Chicago. Three criteria were set: the candidate must have a university degree, five years' experience in ministry, and a small family.

Again, Igor was one of the few who met all the criteria. At that time, it was unusual for a Christian to have attended, much less graduated from a university, but Igor had been a non-believer when he began studying. Most Baptists had large families; we only had the one daughter, and there was no chance for any more.

We had never dreamed that such an opportunity would be possible; we were stunned at the choice ahead of us. Was this God's will? After we prayed, we decided that if Igor got a visa to go to America, then we would know that it was God's plan.

Receiving the American entry visa was fairly simple, but obtaining the Soviet exit visa took nearly a year. Our government investigated to find out if we were working for the CIA or if Igor would be trained as a spy. Finally, I was summoned to the Department for the Affairs of Religious Cults. The official informed me that Igor could have his visa as long as I signed documents saying I would not attempt to leave the country to join him for four years. They were afraid that if we all left, we would never return.

Four years! Such a long time. But Igor was only supposed to be gone for two. *They needn't worry,* I thought. *I have no desire to live in America.* Realizing immediately what I had to do, I signed the papers, remembering that I had promised God that if He gave me my life back after Vika's birth, I would never stand in Igor's way for anything related to ministry. I knew I had to let him go.

"Lena, I really don't want to leave you. You are still not well."

"Igor, you need to go," I told him. I explained the deal I made with God, and told him that if he stayed, then God would probably take me to heaven. Looking back, I wonder: would God really have taken me? We never do find out what would happen if we had made a different choice in life. All I know is that I had made a promise to God, and needed to keep it.

So in May, Igor quit his job, giving up his place in line for an apartment, and traveled to America. After only one week, he realized that he would not be able to endure life in that alien culture.

He just couldn't understand Americans and the questions they asked. Do you have grass and trees in Ukraine?" one would ask. *How can they not know that Ukraine is the breadbasket of the Soviet Union? How could we not have grass and trees?* Igor thought.

Or, "In Ukraine, are there stars in the sky?" He didn't know what to think of people who would ask such questions.

Not only was everything strange, but he didn't know any English. Like anyone trying to learn a new language, he made embarrassing mistakes. One of his new friends introduced Igor to his thirteen-year-old daughter, Emily. Igor called her "Enema" for three weeks until someone corrected him and informed Igor what he had been saying. Another time he was offered a hot dog. "No," he answered. "And I don't eat cold dogs, either." Although most people's laughter at such mistakes was good-natured and sympathetic, Igor felt humiliated. Racked with guilt over having left a wife in poor health alone with a small child, filled with doubts over having left Ukraine just when there was freedom to preach openly, he wondered why he was stuck in America trying to learn English. My husband realized he would not be able to survive alone, deprived of the support of his family. He decided that Vika and I must come to America.

Igor prayed, asking God for mercy, that He would send Vika and me to him. He asked some of his new American friends to pray with him. They all told him it was impossible, that the Soviet government would never allow me to leave the country. Igor felt that God was telling him that we would see each other by the end of the year, so he asked me to apply for an exit visa. Several times over the next six months I applied for that vital piece of paper, which would let me leave the country, and each time I was denied.

Every time they brought up the documents I had signed, saying I had promised not to leave, and shouldn't even try.

In the meantime, I was in an uncomfortable half-way position in that I was married, but had no husband, and felt almost like a widow. Some of the women in the church, whom I had considered friends, with whom I'd laughed and cried with, and stood with through adversity, were not kind at all. Walking home from church, leading Victoria by the hand, I overheard their comments. "I'd rather have an uneducated husband at home than an educated one far away." It took a few years before I could truly forgive them, realizing that they spoke more out of jealousy than out of truth.

Igor, when he wasn't calling me to ask about my visa, was studying and working hard. News of more religious freedom and the spiritual hunger in the Soviet Union caused Igor to yearn to participate, to help others come to faith. God answered that prayer when Slavic Gospel invited him to preach Sunday sermons in Russian for broadcast to the Soviet Union. The tapes of his sermons were sent to Saipan, Monte Carlo, and Quito, Ecuador, and were broadcast by Trans World Radio and JCJB Radio, covering all eleven time zones of the Soviet Union. It is no surprise that I listened to every one. Igor's father, while hating the message, listened avidly as well, just to hear the sound of his son's voice.

In mid-December, Igor grew more insistent that I "do something" to get my exit visa. I applied again, and was rejected almost immediately. I was pained to have to tell him the bad news; I could tell he was so disappointed.

"Maybe God meant we would see each other by the end of next year," I suggested.

"No, Lena, I felt the Holy Spirit so clearly. By the end of this year. I know."

I submitted yet another request for an exit visa. Without warning, around the 28th of December, I received a phone call. My exit visa had been approved. Vika and I left the next day for Moscow, where we spent the day getting our foreign passport and exit visa. Once we had these documents, we went to the American Embassy for our entry visa, which was also granted. We arrived in Chicago on December 31, true to what God had told Igor.

In his joy, Igor wasn't expecting a sick child and a wife in near hysterics. Travelling to America, I had to face one of my deepest fears. "I had never been on a plane before, Igor," I told him. "You know the saying "if you fly, you die. Now I know it's true!"

"Lena, you know that's not true…"

"Oh, so you think that? We get on the plane, and Vika has the whooping cough. I thought she was too sick for the flight, but I knew that if we waited until she was better, our exit visas would have expired. There was no telling when we'd ever get new ones."

"No, you were right to come anyway."

"Then she threw up on the plane. None of the stewardesses spoke Russian, and I had a hard time getting any help to clean up Vika."

"It must have been horrible."

"A nightmare. And then it got worse. I met a Russian lady on the plane, an older woman. She was also going to Chicago, and she helped me to find our plane in Frankfurt."

"So that was good, so nice of that lady."

"You don't know the whole story. At first I was relieved that I found someone to help me. Then on the plane she said she didn't feel well. Her color wasn't too good. Neither of us knew any English, so we couldn't tell anyone. She said she thought she'd just go to sleep and maybe she'd feel better."

"So?"

"Igor, when I went to check on her a few hours later, she was dead. She died of a heart attack right there on the plane. So you see, you fly, you die."

"Lena…"

I cut him off. "I'm leaving to go home as soon as I can. And I'm not going to fly."

"But how will you get across the ocean?"

"I have it all figured out. I'll take a train to Alaska. There I'll find a dogsled to take me to the sea…"

It took some time for Igor to calm me down and convince me to give America a try.

I soon understood why Igor was so adamant that we join him. The effort of learning English was so tiring that it was a relief to be able to speak in Russian, without having to labor over every word. And Americans had such strange ways. "How are you?" they always asked me. *How kind of them to care about me,* I'd think, and then I would try to answer their question. It didn't take me long to realize that the only answer most people were willing to listen to was, "I'm fine, thanks."

Most surprising of all was how Christian and non-Christian culture was blended in America. We thought of America as a Christian country, because nearly all the Christian books and Bibles we read in Ukraine were from America. The first time I heard someone ask for prayer for an unsaved family member I was shocked. How can there be unbelievers in this Christian country? More puzzling was that American Christians didn't seem to live much differently than their unbelieving neighbors. In Christian circles in Ukraine, divorce was almost unthinkable. Not so in America. How could people with such freedom to serve God not take seriously their responsibilities to live as holy people? We were so confused and many of our illusions were shattered by the reality of life in America.

Even with my support, Igor's struggles continued. Required courses included Greek and Hebrew so the students could read the Bible in its original languages. Not only was Igor trying to learn these languages, but the classes were taught in a language he didn't know. He studied English by comparing Bible verses between the Russian and English. Every night he listed to the lectures he had taped, and would look up every unfamiliar word in a dictionary. After he wrote his papers and went to bed, I would sit up late typing them.

In the end, Igor managed to complete his studies and graduate. Expecting him to follow in a few weeks, Vika and I went back to Ukraine. I told Igor that if someone were to pay my way to return to America, I wouldn't go back there. Just before he was to leave for Ukraine, he called me.

"Lena, you are not going to believe this. I received a phone call from Dallas Theological Seminary. They invited me to enroll in their International Leadership Program and offered me a scholarship that includes full tuition and living costs."

"Igor, why you?"

"I think my grades from Moody were a big factor. And that our family is so small. They know they will only have to support three of us, not like the others with four or more kids."

"Are you going to accept?"

"I am so confused by this offer. I was set to go back to Ukraine, to start ministry again. We need to pray about this."

Soon Igor felt God leading him to accept. Recalling my promise to God, I knew I could not stand in Igor's way, so Vika and I joined him in Dallas.

Living in Texas was like living in a new country, and it almost seemed like we had to learn a new language. Somehow we had an easier time than in Chicago. Despite all the hard work, we were grateful for the blessing of Igor's education. Contacts he made in America led to ministry opportunities after we returned to Ukraine, such as the time he went on a mission trip to Africa, where he nearly lost his life.

CHAPTER 40

IGOR MEETS A WITCHDOCTOR

The struggle will end only when Marxism-Leninism triumphs everywhere...Both history and the future are on the side of the proletariat's ultimate victory.
—Nikita Khrushchev[40]

Why do the nations conspire and the peoples plot in vain?...The One enthroned in heaven laughs; the Lord scoffs at them.
—Psalm 2:1,4

As told by Igor

OF COURSE I would go to Cameroon. The invitation came from a group of men from a church in Dallas going to preach for two weeks in rural areas of the country. They knew about my burning desire to share with people the love that God has for them, and to tell them of the miracles that God has done in my life. They knew that I would be very willing to travel with them for such a purpose. So of course I would travel from Ukraine to Cameroon.

They didn't know about my secret hope to see a witchdoctor. The existence of powerful witchdoctors was the only thing I knew about Cameroon. Such was the education I received in the Soviet Union—a lot about Marx and the glories of socialist achievements, not much about other countries that refused to join in the fraternal struggle to build world communism.

Maybe, I thought, *I'll even get to take a picture of a witchdoctor.* No one I had ever known had been to Cameroon. A photograph of a witchdoctor would be such an interesting souvenir to share with all of my Ukrainian family and friends. I could imagine how amazed my mother would be, how all my friends would gather around to study the picture and ask me so many questions, thirsty to know about life in other lands. My students in the seminary where I was teaching would then see that witchdoctors still wielded power in some parts of the world.

In Cameroon, our group of fifteen preached about the love and power of Jesus. After a few days, I learned more about witchdoctors and how they must be respected. The witchdoctors could punish, curse, or kill people, and no one would do anything about it. Taking pictures of witchdoctors was not considered to be respectful.

Most of our time was spent in a small town in the north of Cameroon called Kumbo. We walked along the dirt roads of the village, past the huts of clay bricks and straw roofs. This was a poor area; there were no animals in the village. All of them had been eaten for food. As we finished our preaching in the market on our last day, while we were packing up the vans in preparation for leaving, we saw the funeral procession of a witch doctor approaching. Six witch doctors were walking slowly through the village. They wore their traditional regalia—scary masks painted in bright colors decorated with feathers, black robes with strips of cloth hanging from the chest—and were carrying long spears. Many of the villagers had gathered to watch. While most of my friends were climbing into one of our two rented vans, I hid behind a car with one of my friends. The biggest and fiercest-looking witch doctor was standing to the side, as if he were supervising. I had a good angle to take a picture of him, and was hoping no one would notice me. As I was taking the picture, I could see through the camera that he saw me. He raised his spear in anger and started to run toward us. When I lowered the camera, I realized he was a lot closer than I thought, and approaching rapidly.

My friend and I had only a few seconds to decide what to do. We knew the witchdoctor could put a curse on us, but we weren't afraid of that. The spear was a different story. If we ran away, that would destroy two weeks of preaching that Jesus is more powerful than witchdoctors. But an angry man waving a nine-foot-long spear was running at us. All we could think of was to shout, "Jesus is Lord" and wait to see what would happen. Maybe he would kill us, but we couldn't run away.

"Jesus is Lord!" we yelled. The witchdoctor kept running. "Jesus is Lord!" The witchdoctor ran even faster, shaking his spear at us. Now he was almost on top of us. "Jesus is Lord!" The witchdoctor fell to the ground and started twitching.

We decided this was a good opportunity to casually stroll to the van and get in. The other witchdoctors gathered around the one on the ground. They tried to get him to stand up by sprinkling water on him. When that didn't work, they poked him with their spears. As we drove away, we could see him slowly stagger to his feet. The people who had witnessed this scene began to run behind the van shouting, "Jesus is Lord!"

I don't know if the people really believed, or if they just didn't want to be lying on the ground twitching, and thought shouting, "Jesus is Lord" was a good way to prevent that. But maybe many did believe, after seeing God's power to save us from the witchdoctor.

Confronting the witchdoctor taught me that the miracles God did for others in the past, for the people in the Bible and Lena's relatives, were not gifts for another generation, but that God's power flows through the life of any obedient believer. This power sometimes shows itself through an amazing rescue, sometimes it reveals itself through changed hearts and lives, and sometimes in the rise and fall of governments. When we returned to Zaporozhe after I earned my master's degree in theology in 1995, our passports still said *Union of Soviet Socialist Republics* but that country had ceased to exist four years before. Freedom we had only dreamed about was granted to believers, and the churches were adapting to the new openness.

Lena and I had changed as well, in ways we had not expected. I still joke that I want the shy girl I married. Where did this confident, outgoing leader of a woman come from? "This is what America did to you," I tease Lena, knowing that it was God who changed her.

She was not the only one who had changed.

PART IV
COMING HOME

Veniamin, the youngest Brynza, narrates his journey from incorrigible schoolboy, to member of the criminal underworld, the Red Army, and marriage to an unbeliever, sharing his thirst for acceptance in a culture that categorically rejected all believers. His wife adds her testimony to the story of their journey.

CHAPTER 41

THE TERRIBLE RABBIT

Remember, the Church is separated from the state—and the schools are in the hands of the state.
—Comrade Mironov, Communist Party Official[41]

Assemble the people before me to hear my words so that they may learn to revere me as long as they live in the land and may teach them to their children.
—Deuteronomy 4:10

As told by Veniamin

ONCE THERE WAS a group of little animals who lived in a forest near a mountain. The squirrels, hedgehogs, rabbits, and birds all played happily together except when they heard the howls of a wild monster, stalking the mountainside. Then they huddled together, one trembling mass of shaking fur and feathers. When one of the little animals went close to the mountain by mistake, the others yelled to him, "Run away! The monster is going to eat you up!" They didn't know that the monster was really a little rabbit dressed up in the skins of savage animals, roaring ferociously. The rabbit disguised himself so he would feel big and powerful instead small and vulnerable.

I read the story "The Terrible Rabbit" when I was about twelve. By that time, I was the rabbit: angry and rebellious on the outside, scared and craving acceptance on the inside.

From my early childhood, the taunts of non-Christian neighbors and classmates embarrassed me more than my older brothers and sister. I never understood how they could hear the sneers of the other kids and not be wounded to the core. Sometimes Yakov, Viktor, or Lena would come home, angry or in tears. A few minutes of conversation and prayer with our parents were enough to give them strength to go on. I was determined that when I started school, everyone would like me and never tease me. During my first three years at school, I studied hard and earned high grades. If anyone teased me, Lena or Viktor were usually around to defend me. Then I started fourth grade with a different teacher.

On the first day of school Mama laid out my school clothes: dark pants, white shirt. The first day was festive like a holiday, and all the children dressed up for it, the girls with large white bows in their hair. Just before leaving to walk to school with Lena and my mother, I carefully picked an apple from a tree in our yard for my new teacher. I so much wanted her to like me!

We walked to Elementary School Number 81, enjoying the warmth of the sun. As we entered the red brick building, Mama greeted many of the other parents and children gathered for the first day. I couldn't help but notice that they didn't all seem friendly or respectful to Mama, not the way the people at church were. When we arrived at my classroom, my new teacher, Olga Borisovna, turned to us with a smile. She was in her late forties with brown curly hair and a pleasant face.

"And who is this?" she asked.

Mama answered, "Veniamin Brynza." I watched in confusion as the friendly smile on the teacher's face froze into place and the warmth in her eyes turned cold as if September had turned into December. "I am Valentina Grigorievna, and my husband is Alexei Gavrilovich," Mama continued.

"I know of your family," the teacher said. "Baptists." She looked at me for a moment and said, "Veniamin, sit over there. I don't want any trouble from you."

Mama kissed my forehead and said she'd see me at home after school. I sat at the wooden desk the teacher had pointed out to me, wondering what I had done to displease her. *It's all right*, I thought. *I'll make her like me.*

By the middle of the day, my hopes for approval had shriveled like old potatoes. "Give the paper to Veniamin," the teacher told one of my classmates.

"Which Veniamin?"

"Baptist."

On the playground, the teasing continued. "You're a Baptist and Baptists can't play ball," the kids yelled at me. "You wear poor-people clothes."

My soul was so sensitive it bruised as easily as an overripe pear. I was powerless to defend myself. Lena was in class somewhere; Viktor had graduated and no longer attended the same school. I slunk away from the other kids, my head hanging, my mind churning to come up with a way to earn respect and acceptance.

I tried to study hard, to earn high grades, and became a leader in the games of the class. But the teachers would never let the class forget that Veniamin the Baptist was among them. Shame turned into anger and I decided to find another way to get my classmates to stop teasing me. I would make it so they not only respected me, but were even afraid to risk offending me.

And what was my solution? I beat up the kids who made fun of me. If someone laughed at me, I'd make him feel my inner pain, only his would be physical pain. If the teachers were going to reprimand me, it would be for something I had done, not the label they gave me because of my family. So I started skipping classes, gradually daring more, pushing back at the teachers who mocked me. Sometimes I'd talk so much during class that the teachers couldn't teach.

Within a few years, I began taking risks outside of school, reveling in the thrill like a hungry man salivates for his soup. When I was eleven, I would volunteer to watch the cars of church members during my father's service. When everyone was inside, I would take one of the little Zaporozhets cars for a drive around the city, sitting on a pan to make me appear taller. Somehow, I was never caught. The excitement of getting away with delinquent behavior made up for the constant dread of being teased or laughed at and took some of the sting out of the taunt "Baptist." One of the few times I actually attended church services that year, I prayed, repenting of my sins. But as I grew older, the less I wanted to be around believers, to be tainted by association with them. By the time I was in the sixth grade, I completely stopped going to church.

Releasing my shame-fueled fury like an erupting volcano, I fought more and more, sometimes to punish someone who teased me, sometimes as the aggressor. I always said the other kid started it to avoid getting in even more trouble, and several times was rewarded with a trip to the juvenile department at the police station. Papa and Mama felt helpless. Reining me in was like trying to harness a tornado. The methods that had worked with my brothers and sisters—talking, praying, reading from the Bible, corporal punishment—were useless with me.

Then I noticed that the teachers were suddenly asking me all kinds of questions. Who had I talked with? What about? This made no sense to me. What business of theirs was it? And why did they care? Were they that interested in what I was doing? Or were they that stupid that they thought I would tell them who I was planning to fight with next? My grades, which had been poor for some time, became much lower than I actually deserved. Papa saw me crying about my grades a few times, but he could not help me. Neither of us knew the plans the teachers were preparing for me.

CHAPTER 42

SAVED BY A COMMUNIST

We cannot remain indifferent to the fate of children whom fanatical religious parents are virtually raping spiritually. We cannot permit blind and ignorant parents to raise children like themselves and thus transform them.
—Leonid Ilichev[42]

Do not conform any longer to the pattern of this present world, but be transformed by the renewing of your min. Then you will be able to test and approve what God's will is—his good, pleasing and perfect will.
—Romans 12:2

As told by Veniamin

RIGHT AROUND THAT time, Papa's mother died. Papa held her funeral in our yard, complete with the church orchestra, hundreds of mourners, and preaching, and got in all kinds of trouble with the authorities for breaking the laws regarding public worship and proselytizing. One night they took him away in a police car. The rest of us huddled together until morning, crying and praying that God would return him to us. When Papa came home the next day, shaken but unharmed, I assumed everything was fine and went back to my life, which was more important to me. Wrapped up in my own internal struggle, I had no idea that I was the authorities' next target.

One evening when I was doing math homework, Papa came to me and said, "*Sinok*, you will go to a different school tomorrow."

"Papa, what do you mean? What are you talking about?" I answered.

"There have been too many problems at your old school."

"So?"

"My son, there have been too many warnings, too many reprimands. They are forming a committee to take you away from us if you can't behave better."

"They can't do that!" As ashamed as I was of being a Baptist, to be torn from my family was a frightening prospect. "If they take me away, where will I live? In a government orphanage?"

"Venya, they can. They have the right. If they take you away, you will have to live in an orphanage."

"Papa, you have to fix it. I don't want to go live there."

"The only thing we can do is send you to a new school. Now you must decide how you will choose to live your life with this clean slate you have been given, not only as a believer, but simply as a person."

I didn't know what to think about that. The thought of living in an orphanage was terrifying. The stories we heard about those places were horrible: never enough food, workers cruel to the children, older kids ruling tyrannically over the younger. Attending a new school would be a small price to pay for being able to live at home.

They never did take me away. The authorities had made the decision, the parents' committee had made the recommendation, but they couldn't get the evidence they needed. At that time, the Soviets told the world that our country had religious freedom and they were afraid of any publicity that might prove they were lying. Taking a child away from his family without any proof of wrongdoing was too risky. It was only many years later that I learned what Papa went through for me, how he had suffered, and the anxiety I had caused my whole family. At the time I felt only my own pain. I agreed to change schools but wasn't planning on changing my life.

In the new school, I continued to pick fights and break as many rules as I could. Even my fear that the director, Nina Afanasievna, an ardent Communist, would find out did not restrain me. What I didn't know was that she took pride in turning around problem kids. Trust was one of her weapons.

One day she called me to her office after lunchtime. Nina was a heavy woman with short blond hair and an aura of authority an army general would envy.

"Venya, I've just gone out and bought some milk. Here are the keys to my flat. Will you take the milk home for me and put it in the refrigerator?"

Silently I took the keys and listened as she explained how to get to her flat. In a daze I walked along the street. How could she trust me? No one liked me, the other kids feared me, the teachers said I was no good, my family thought of me as a disappointment. But this woman gave me her keys!

Nina's flat was cozy, with real wallpaper instead of whitewash, tiles on her kitchen walls and all her possessions obediently in their places. Exactly as she had asked, I put the glass bottle of milk in her refrigerator. As I turned to go, I started thinking. Maybe I should look around a little, see if she has anything interesting I might want. Or maybe mess up her beds or throw her pots and pans on the floor. Somehow none of those pranks appealed to me. I locked the door carefully behind me on the way out. Returning to school, I found Nina Afanasievna and returned her keys. She thanked me politely, as if she were not at all surprised that I had done as she asked, confident that I had not let her down. Countless times during the next two years Nina Afanasievna entrusted me with similar errands or to take her dog for a walk. I could have done anything I wanted in her flat, but never abused her trust.

I finished the eighth grade with dreadful marks. A student with all 5's (the highest) was labeled an *otlichnik*. I was labeled *zhakhlivo*, or terrible. Because I liked mechanics, especially anything to do with transport, cars, trucks, or trains, I planned to study in the same *technikum* that my father had attended. My parents didn't try to influence me, and I didn't ask anyone's advice. *It's not their business,* I thought. Although I was often punished with the belt, I wasn't afraid of my parents. I considered them to be silly, weak people who were afraid to acknowledge their part in any success, saying instead, "that was pleasing to God." What did they mean by "it was all for God's glory?" Didn't they deserve some recognition for anything they had done? Also, if something turned out badly, they considered it a punishment because of a flaw they had in God's eyes. In reality, no one in the family thought this way, but this was how I convinced myself that rejecting their faith was a sensible decision.

Papa went with me when I asked Nina Afanasievna to write the reference I needed to submit with my application to the *technikum*. She smiled at me and said, "Yes, it was bad, but it wasn't all bad. There are some good characteristics." She sat at her black manual typewriter and typed a reference for me. "Wherever you go, always remember me, Venya," she told me as she handed me the document. Consistently kind to me despite my aggressive rebelliousness, she looked deeper than others and could believe in something good even in the midst of terrible circumstances; she looked into my soul and saw a reason to hope that no else could see.

CHAPTER 43

CARDS, CRIME, AND THE ARMY

*Stealing obviously offers a better livelihood than honest labor.
Only in that way can we explain the outcome of this great
[Communist] experiment.*
—Soviet Official[43]

*Ill-gotten treasures are of no value,
but righteousness delivers from death.*
—Proverbs 10:2

As told by Veniamin

ON THE 1ST of September, I was walking to the *teknikum* to start classes when I saw some guys I'd gone to school with. "Where are you going?" they asked.

"To the *teknikum*."

"Why are you going there? You'll have to do all kinds of work. At the *uchilishe* you don't have to do anything, and you still get the same diploma." I went straight to the *teknikum*, took back my documents, and enrolled in the *uchilishe*. I never bothered to tell my parents and still don't know when they found out. It didn't do me much good, studying in the *uchilishe*. I worked on electrical machines, but to this day don't know how to turn on a lamp properly.

That winter I worked nights for a small grocery store, unloading bread trucks, trucks labeled in stark, military letters "Bread." My friends, some of whom were older than me by ten years or more, came by late at night, and we would drink till early in the morning. The place was weakly lit and smelled of old cheese and fish, but we didn't mind.

Then a man appeared among us, an artist named Grigorii. He had a friend living alone in a flat, which was very unusual in the Soviet Union. My buddies and I started to hang out in this flat and drink beer. We didn't have to worry about food because we could persuade girls from the *uchilishe* to come and cook for us. Instead of going home after classes, I would sit in the flat for hours, feeling like a grown man.

One evening Grigorii suggested that we play cards. Having grown up in a family that never touched cards, I considered this to be really wicked. Nervously, I listened as Grigorii taught me the rules. At first we played for matches, but then the stakes got higher, all the way up to ten kopecks. For me, these were new thrills, all the more enticing because I knew it was all so sinful.

Several months later, Grigorii invited me to a restaurant, saying he would introduce me to some new friends. At that time, just about the only people who ate in restaurants were powerful in either the communist party or the mafia. The place my friend took me to wasn't even in a public location. It was more like a small private house.

We walked into the dimly-lit room filled with small tables and the pulsing beat of western rock music. The people wore tailored western clothing, the women had bright red lips and twinkled with expensive jewelry. My new friends at the restaurant said, "Today you play cards and risk a few kopecks. Maybe it's time for a bigger risk?" These people who played cards all day were not communist party officials. I may have been innocent in many ways, but even I knew that. As the game progressed, I realized that many of them were helping me to win, even my opponents. They all flattered me, commenting how wonderfully talented I was. "*Ukh ti*! He has shaken even me," said one man when I won a hand. The excitement of gambling and my conscience battled within me, the pleasure obscuring guilt as makeup hides a blemish.

Over time, I made more friends among these people, and always they were so agreeable and courteous. When Grigorii and I went to a restaurant together, entire tables bowed to us. As constant as the flow of a river, people approached our table.

"May I join you, Veniamin Alexeievich?"

"Let me buy you a drink, Veniamin Alexeievich."

"Veniamin Alexeievich, I need your advice."

Finally people recognized how important I was, how clever. At last I had found something to take away the shame that had dominated much of my life. No longer would I lie awake, writhing at the memories of being teased, humiliated by the sarcasm of the teacher, or cringing as the word "Baptist" was thrown at me as the worst insult my tormentors could muster. No longer would I try to think of ways to get people to like me. I was respected, admired, and even feared.

My parents suspected I was involved with unsavory people. Over and over we had the same conversation. "Venya," Papa said, "I don't understand something. How is it that you can spend all this time in restaurants and take taxis home late at night? Where is the money coming from?"

"Don't worry about it, Papa. My friends are happy to help me out."

"But who are these people? I don't think they are a good influence on you."

In exasperation I lash out. "Why are you talking to me like I am a small child? I know life. I am popular. You just can't imagine. You have no idea of the power and influence I have. More than you."

Mama didn't try to reason with me. Instead, she cried and prayed. Years later, Lena told me that when I was sleeping, Mama came into our bedroom, got on her knees by my bed, and knelt there for hours, crying and praying silently. Sometimes Papa came in and told her to stop. She always answered, "How can I stop praying, when my son is not walking with the Lord?"

One day, there was a big high-stakes poker game. The room was noisy with people and music. I remember singing along with Abba, laughing with my friends. Right in the middle of the fun, the police came to arrest everyone. The guy who was running the game slid the tray holding the salt and pepper shakers aside, revealing a hole in the table, shoved all the rubles through the hole into a sack, and passed the sack to me under the table. I hid the sack under my coat.

The police checked everyone's internal passports, the standard form of identification in the Soviet Union. When they got to me, they were surprised at how young I was. I told them that my father was the senior presbyter of the *oblast,* which surprised them even more. "How is it you are in a café gambling with criminals?" one of them asked.

"Look, I just came in to buy some mineral water," I said, staring at the buttons on his uniform. "I don't even know these guys."

The police told me to go, and I obeyed, still holding all the money. On the way home it suddenly dawned on me why my "friends" had been so obliging the whole time. I was the perfect accomplice to their crimes. I was from a Christian family and had never been called in front of a judge. Those criminals knew of my parents, and chose me especially because of them. Whenever the police came I could tell some story of how I ended up there: I was walking past and wanted something to drink. The money would always be safe with me. While they may have actually liked me as a person, their biggest reason to have me around was that I served as a useful tool.

Soon after, I finished my three years in the *uchilishe* and confronted a dilemma. I was due to fulfill my mandatory military service. In the army I could test myself, feel confidence in myself. At home my father was always ready to help me; in the army, I would stand alone. Holding me back was the thought that if I joined the army, I would lose any chance of rising in the criminal world. To serve on the side of the USSR was a betrayal of the criminal's code, an immoral act. My need to prove myself won out and I signed up. I knew my parents were praying that army discipline would help me make changes in my life, and I shared their hopes. We all thought I'd be sent to the Siberian tundra, the Kazakhstan desert, or some other awful place, but to everyone's relief I ended up in Moscow.

Once in Moscow, I was sent to the Main Training Center to learn a trade. Other soldiers told me stories of how horribly strict the Training Center was, and how the older students persecuted the newer ones. "The sergeant is a *khokhol* like you," they said. "He is harsh and respects no one." *Khokhol* was the name of the Cossacks' long pony tail, and is also derogatory slang for "Ukrainian."

Soon I met the sergeant. "Where are you from?" he asked.

"Zaporozhe," I replied.

"So am I," the sergeant said in surprise. "This is the first time in my two years of service that someone else has come from there." We talked about all the people we both knew. By the end of the conversation, I was calling him by the familiar form of his name, Lyosha, and he offered me cigarettes and wine. I was amazed. Everyone else was terrified of him. For me, Lyosha was like a long-lost friend. He even appointed me commander of my group.

So I began to think that life in the army wouldn't be too bad. If anyone gave me any trouble, I handled them the way I always had, with a fight. Sometimes I just picked a fight for the fun of it. There were a lot of guys from Central Asia in our group, and they could barely speak Russian. I offered to teach them Ukrainian, telling them it would help them with their Russian. In reality, I couldn't speak Ukrainian myself. Whenever they mispronounced a word, I hit them. One night when I was drunk I hit one so often he ended up in the hospital. For that, the army put me in the punishment block at a nearby base.

After five days, I was released from the brig. The guard told me I had a visitor. *Who could possibly come to see me? No one knows that I am here,* I thought. When I found out it was Papa, shame ate at my soul as acid corrodes stone. Adding to my embarrassment, he'd waited for two days to see me, as I couldn't have visitors until my release. Papa had sent me to the army, hoping that my life would change. Now he was visiting me at the army jail, proof that I had not changed.

The feeling of shame didn't last long. All during my army service, I picked one fight or another, beating people up just because I enjoyed the sense of power over others or because I didn't want to follow orders. My parents almost despaired that I would never repent of the life I had been living. When I returned from the army I attended church my first Sunday at home. Each week people wrote prayer requests or other notes and put them in the offering plate to be read aloud at the end of the service. Even I could see the tears in Papa's as he read the note I had written: "Dear church, I ask you to give thanks to God that for two years He protected me in the army and allowed me to successfully return home. Brynza Veniamin." With that one glimmer of hope to encourage them, my parents continued to hope and pray that their youngest child would find his way.

CHAPTER 44

THE END OF THE SOVIET UNION

Remember man's fortune is in joyful labor for the glory of one's people, the battlefield for the beautiful future of mankind—communism.
—From "Name-giving ceremony" certificate, communist ritual created to replace baptism[44]

For our light and momentary troubles are achieving for us an eternal glory that far outweighs them all.
—2 Corinthians 4:17

As told by Veniamin

IN THE YEAR 988, so the story goes, Vladimir, King of all the Rus, decided to abandon pagan worship and find a new faith. He sent envoys to learn about the religions of Moslems, Jews and Christians. One legend says that at first, Vladimir was intrigued by Islam, which allowed four wives, but he lost interest when he found he would have to give up vodka. Others say that the envoys witnessed an Orthodox ritual in Byzantium and were so taken with its beauty that they convinced Vladimir to adopt that faith.

However it happened, Vladimir converted and forced the entire city of Kiev to be baptized in the Dniepr River. Christianity had come to Russia and Ukraine.

One thousand years later, in 1988, the Soviet Union marked the anniversary of this event with a celebration. That the atheistic government would allow and even sanction anything related to religion showed just how much perestroika had changed the country.

In preparation for the 1000-year festivities, the believers in Zaporozhe prayed about holding a mass public baptism. After all the persecution that had gone on in the past, this was an astounding idea for them to consider.

On receiving approval from the authorities, my father found an appropriate spot on the shore of the Dniepr River and arranged for the baptism to be publicized on the radio and in the newspapers. More than three thousand people gathered on the shore of the river that day, the first to be baptized openly after decades of secrecy. The Orthodox priest of the *oblast*, sharing a rare moment of common victory with my father, came and congratulated him, expressing his joy for my father's success.

A year later, supported by Slavic Gospel Association, the presbyters in Ukraine decided to start a seminary near Kiev and asked my father to organize it and be the first rector. Papa, suffering from diabetes, didn't think his health would allow him to take on this new challenge. Mama opposed the idea, not wishing to move all the way to Kiev. Life had finally become good in Zaporozhe after all the years of struggle. There was freedom to preach and to worship, and my father felt that he was reaping the reward for the suffering that had gone on before. At the age of fifty-six, having spent his entire life in Zaporozhe, Papa didn't want to move either.

Disappointed, the brothers called him nearly every week for a year with pleas to reconsider. Then my father attended a meeting where a man from America told how he, his wife, and three children had moved twenty-five times, to Alaska, Africa, Indonesia, and many other places, to do the work of the Lord. Most people would be full of worry about such a life, but this man was never concerned because he trusted God.

Papa went home and said, "Valya, my dear, let's go to Kiev. God has convicted me. When I heard this brother I was ashamed, thinking how we are so upset about moving one time in our lives. It's wrong to be so worried about little things. God will accompany us."

In September of 1990 my parents moved to Kiev. The seminary, with the help of the Slavic Gospel Association, opened on February 15, 1991, with fifty-seven enthusiastic students.

Training new church leaders wasn't the only reason Papa and Mama decided to move to Kiev. Seeing me struggle after I returned from the army, my parents prayed that God would separate me from my unbelieving friends. They felt that maybe the Lord wanted them to take me to Kiev, since there were more believers there, and perhaps I would find some new friends among them. They didn't realize that I could easily find new friends just like the old ones, and that among them, I would find my wife.

CHAPTER 45

A CHILDHOOD DREAM

Lenin even now is more alive than all the living.
—Banner in Moscow school[45]

I am the resurrection and the life. He who believes in me will live, even though he dies; and whoever lives and believes in me will never die.
—John 11:25-26

As told by Ruslana

MANY PEOPLE LOOK back to their childhood as a joyful time, but in general I was unhappy, lonely, and living in fear of my alcoholic, abusive father. He was a communist and brought up his children as atheists. Years later, I tried to remember all the happy moments from my childhood, but they were very few. When I was small I read and re-read the book *The Little Princess*. The girl in the story lived a very hard life, surviving only because of her dreams of the loving father who would come and rescue her. I imagined myself to be that girl in the story who had a kind father whom she could trust and count on. She dreamed about having a different life than the one she was living, longing for a family filled with love and acceptance instead of fear and anger. How happy I would be if I could have even a part of this dream come true!

Sometimes I attended the Orthodox Church with my grandmother. I knew that God existed, but He had no relevance to my life. My grandmother also told me wonderful stories about Daniel being thrown in the den of lions, Moses parting the Red Sea, David slaying Goliath, and she told the stories so vividly that I thought these things had all happened no more than ten years earlier.

My dream was to be an actress, playing in the starring roles. I would be a princess and have a life most people could taste only in fantasy, and a man to love me and care for me, giving me a life of comfort and happiness. Instead, I went to study in the medical technical school because my father forced me to. He thought nursing would be the best career for me and was not interested in hearing any ideas I had for my own future.

After graduating I began working at the hospital, and met Venya's parents who came as patients. I learned that all their children were believers except the youngest son, that they had such good daughters-in-law, such a good son-in-law. I told them it was rare to find relatives like them. Usually people talk about the deficiencies in their children-in-law, and how wonderful their own children are. I had no idea that later I would become acquainted with their son. At the time I felt about believers the way most other people did; they were broken people. Orthodox was the true faith, if someone felt the need to be religious. Baptists were some kind of extreme sect or just a bunch of illiterate old women. I never imagined I would know any, and really didn't want to.

Once Venya and I started living together without being married, neither Venya nor I cared much about what his parents thought of our relationship. We knew they were not pleased; they didn't know this non-believer girl who was sure to lead their son further away from God. From all sides, with all their strength, they had tried to get him to like girls from the church, but Venya wanted the exact opposite.

Like others of our generation, we were living for ourselves. After the sadness of my childhood, I determined to make a better life for myself, convinced I knew exactly how to achieve it. I never thought about God and what He might think about what we were doing. In my own eyes I believed it right. Venya felt the same.

Talking with Venya, being silent with Venya, it all felt so easy; I realized I was in love with my best friend. Even though we hadn't gone through the legal formalities, we considered ourselves married, and lived as we pleased. Then I became pregnant. Our joy in each other was soured by confusion. Pieces of advice swirled around us like autumn leaves in the wind. Many of our friends assumed I'd get an abortion. I knew that Venya's parents, terrified that I would abort my child, still opposed our relationship. They begged Venya not to marry me many times, asking him, "Do you really want that kind of a girl to be part of our family?" During my pregnancy Venya went to America to visit Lena, who convinced him that if he did not want to give me up, it would be best if we got married.

On his return we registered our marriage in a civil ceremony. That evening we visited Venya's parents, our first meeting since the relationship began. I was as nervous as if I were going to court, to be tried for a horrible crime. What would Venya's parents say to me? What a disappointment I must have been to them. Instead of the bride they had dreamed about for their son, they ended up with me, and pregnant on top of that. My fear grew as we approached their house, certain I was in for an evening of loud shouting and angry accusations. How could I face that? Climbing out of the taxi, for one crazed moment I thought of turning and running down the street, and clung to Venya's hand as the only way to prevent my flight.

Greeting us at the door, Alexei Gavrilovich said, "Venya, now you are married. And your wife is Ruslana. For us, she will be your wife forever, your only wife. No matter if you live with her or not, we will always consider her your wife. And she is now a Brynza, one of our daughters. We will only receive you with her. If you argue with her and want to come home, we won't welcome you without her."

I was stunned, unable to think clearly or come up with anything to say. These people were welcoming me as if I were a valuable gift. Years later, they told me they had decided to receive me warmly so that there wouldn't be any bitterness. They didn't want to make the bad relationship they had with Venya worse.

That night, Venya's parents listened to me and encouraged me as they would a dearly loved daughter. They gave us a Bible and prayed with us. From that moment my perception of them began to change. I was amazed by the caring atmosphere of the family I had married into. Having seen the terrible quarrels of my parents, having endured beatings by my father, beatings given many times for no reason, I was mystified at how Venya's parents could live together without yelling at each other.

For the first time I heard people pray over a meal and express thankfulness for the smallest of things; for the first time I saw the presence of God in someone's life. For me, this was as exotic as if I had married into a family from Sri Lanka.

After that, Venya and I visited his parents at least once a week. The more I saw of Venya's family and their relationships, the better I understood what God could do in people's lives. Previously, I had thought my family was normal, that the Baptists were abnormal; now my thinking was turned upside down.

Slowly, my heart began to change. Unable to understand the adult version, I started reading a children's Bible. Then I got up the courage to ask Venya's mother all kinds of questions and we began to talk seriously about God.

On New Year's Eve, 1992, Venya and I decided to go to church. The service, with its beautiful choral singing and quiet prayers, was completely different from what I had expected, and gave me a sense of hope and peace. That night in church, I heard about the birth of Jesus Christ and why we celebrate it, and for the first time I understood the significance. This was the first New Year since I was a child that I didn't go out drinking with my friends. To my surprise, attending church fulfilled me more than all the nights of partying.

Throughout the winter, God continued to work in my heart. I began listening to Christian music and psalms on tape and found myself crying as I listened to the words. A feeling of shyness welled up within me, as if something deep inside me was being expressed. I didn't want even Venya to see the overflow of my emotion. I always waited for him to leave for work to listen to those tapes. Then I would sit and sob, praying to God for forgiveness.

That spring I gave birth to a healthy boy we named Yaroslav. In church, Yakov Dukhonchenko laid his hands on the baby and prayed over him. I prayed silently with him that my son might have a better childhood than I did, and that he would grow to love and respect the Lord.

Later I asked Venya's mama, "Why are there so few believers?"

"It's because people are proud and sure of themselves. They don't want to recognize the authority of God."

After a minute I quietly asked, "Am I like that, too?"

Mama replied, "Yes."

Another minute passed, and I said, "When I am in the church service, I watch how people kneel, and I sit in the seat like I'm nailed down, too proud to acknowledge God's greatness and glory."

From this Mama knew that the Holy Spirit was truly working in my heart.

Soon after, on June 30, I found myself weeping through the entire church service. I didn't know why I was crying or why everything within me was trembling from some internal earthquake. At the end of the service, my father-in-law, who was preaching, asked if anyone wanted to repent. Before I knew what had happened, I walked forward in response. Through my sobs I praised God for my husband's family and that through them I had come to know the Lord. Joy burst from me as a flooding river bursts a dam. God forgave my sins, and gave me peace and the loving family I always dreamed of. How Venya would react was in God's hands.

CHAPTER 46

GOD'S PLAN REVEALED

Who shall prevail?
—Lenin[46]

But thanks be to God! He gives us the victory through our Lord Jesus Christ.
—1 Corinthians 15:57

As told by Veniamin

I WASN'T AGAINST moving to Kiev. After I betrayed my old friends in the criminal world by joining the army, I knew they wouldn't accept me back. I had some drinking buddies, but nothing to tie me to Zaporozhe. Papa got me a job working as Yakov Dukhonchenko's driver, so there was no reason to not go with them. I knew Papa and Mama wanted me to go to Kiev with them to get me away from friends they saw as a bad influence. Instead, I continued on the same path, hanging out with others who also believed in living for themselves.

As often happened in the Soviet Union, it was hard to find gas for the car. Among Yakov Dukhonchenko's acquaintances was a chief doctor. Even though the man wasn't a believer, he superstitiously treated Christians for free because he thought God would reward him with protection. His status as an important physician meant he usually had fuel.

One day Yakov Dukhonchenko sent me to this man's office to ask for some gasoline. The sultry brunette receptionist told me the doctor wouldn't be back for thirty minutes. To pass the time, I started chatting with her. Before I left, I asked her out. We went to a café that night and saw each other the next day and the day after. It was the first time I had been around a woman I could really talk to and not just use.

Then Papa and Mama noticed that I had a girlfriend. This was disturbing for them, not only because as Baptists we didn't date like non-believers, but also because they wondered what kind of a girl I would find among my circle of friends. I came home very late or sometimes not at all. "How can I be rector of the seminary, an example to others, with a son who behaves like this?" my father asked. Determined to live my life as I saw fit, I felt no one had the right to tell me any differently.

Eventually, I was spending so much time with Ruslana that I decided to leave my parent's home and live at her place. Once I moved in with Ruslana, the rift between my parents and me deepened like a canyon. My parents told me not to come back until Ruslana and I were legally married. "We will recognize a wife, not some temporary girlfriend. So as things are now, Ruslana is not welcome in our home." Outwardly I made no response; inside I felt despised and rejected.

Ruslana and I lived happily together for four months. Then she gave me news that changed everything: she was pregnant. We didn't know what to do. Many of our friends thought she should just have an abortion, but even I knew that would be wrong. My parents called Lena in America to ask for her help. Years later, Lena told me they started the conversation by saying, "Venya has died!"

Lena immediately invited me to visit her in Chicago. It was amazing how three years into the Gorbachev years, exit visas were easy to get. I went there, knowing what Lena was thinking, that she had to protect her little brother, and that maybe I would forget about my girlfriend. I didn't want to discuss it with her.

One day after I'd been there a few weeks, we took a walk in the neighborhood. "What is going on in your life?" she asked me.

"Nothing."

"No, something is going on. You'd better tell me, Venya."

"I have a wonderful girlfriend, and I love her."

"Venya, I know she's pregnant. How do you know it's your baby?" Lena started crying as she said this, and I tried not to show how insulted I was that she would suggest the baby wasn't mine.

I turned to face her directly. "Lena, you know the family we grew up in. And you know that I would not lie. I would not tell you the child is mine when it isn't."

Lena knew that my mind was made up. I wasn't going to abandon Ruslana; she couldn't stop me any more than she could stop the wind from freeing her hair from its pins. "If you feel that way, Venya, then you need to marry her." By the time I left Chicago about two and a half months later, Lena had convinced me to marry Ruslana. I knew that years would pass before Lena stopping feeling that Ruslana had stolen her baby brother.

Legally marrying Ruslana meant that I could reconcile with my parents, and Ruslana and I began to spend more time with them. I knew that Ruslana was asking Mama all kinds of questions and was reading the Bible and praying. I never lost my faith completely, but I wasn't quite ready to change my life, to give up some of the things I loved, like drinking and expensive clothes. Too many people were pushing and pressuring me. Someday I would repent. Not now.

The night our child was born, I went out drinking with my friends, bragging all night about my new son. Inside, I knew my need for God. Arriving home, still drunk, I knelt on the tile floor of our bathroom, begging Him to protect Ruslana and little Yaroslav.

One Sunday late in June, Ruslana went to a church service while I stayed home with the baby. Papa came to me after the service was over and announced, "Today is a big holiday. Ruslana has been born again." In shock, I stumbled into the bathroom and collapsed on the floor, sobbing. Hot shame washed over me in waves. I was the one raised in a Christian home; my wife was raised as an atheist. I was one who knew about God; she had never had any interest in Him. Yet it was my wife who repented first, my wife who was able to make that public commitment to God, my wife who renounced our old life. Once she understood the truth that Jesus died for our sins, not just to save us from hell, but so the Holy Spirit could make us more like Christ, she acted on it; I had heard this countless times and put off my response, waiting for a more convenient time. Pride kept me from admitting my family had been right all along; humility admitted her into the family of God.

The shame of being taunted for being a Baptist was nothing to the shame engulfing me now. My defenses dissolved like smoke in the wind, my resistance melted like ice under boiling water. That night we all went back to the evening service where I publicly repented. No longer would I hide behind a façade of worldly toughness; Jesus had become my strength.

While my entire family rejoiced, my parents' joy surpassed them all. Despite the pressure of the government, the constant anti-religious propaganda, the taunts and teasing, all four of their children had come to faith. And after twenty-two years, Papa and Mama finally understood God's plan. For many years they questioned God. Why did they have such a son? Why did he behave so badly? Now they knew. They repented before the Lord that they had asked Him to save only me, when all along God had wanted Ruslana to be saved as well.

Ruslana and I were baptized together a year later, Papa preaching at the service. When Mama looks back, she remembers the joy she felt each time one of her children came to the Lord, but this feeling was especially strong with me. She says it's written in the Bible that God gathers up our tears in a vase. If the tears she shed during those twenty-two years before I repented could be collected, there would be enough for her to swim in.

EPILOGUE

*Since my youth, O God, you have taught me, and to this day
I declare your marvelous deeds. Even when I am old and
gray do not forsake me, O God, till I declare your
power to the next generation.*
—Psalm 71:17-18

As told by Igor

THE SEVEN-HUNDRED-YEAR-OLD OAK tree of Zaporozhe is dying. The tree lived through the Mongol invasion, the oppression of the tsars, and the enslavement of the communists. Ukrainians joke that having survived all that, it could not survive democracy.

My father-in-law, Alexei, told the joke a little differently. "The tree endured everything, but when Brynza left, it died."

Alexei himself died on October 3, 2008, after serving as rector of the Irpin Biblical Seminary for seventeen years. He lived his final years like a burning candle—steadily giving light, until he could burn no more. Before his last trip to the hospital, knowing he was failing, he prayed with all his children, telling us, "Be faithful to the Lord, and keep your eyes on Jesus."

Breaking with Ukrainian tradition, he requested that no one wear black at his funeral, because he knew where he was going and wanted people to rejoice. Instead of black scarves, all the women wore blue, to honor his wishes. Many of his colleagues spoke at his funeral, commenting that Alexei was one of the few people whose life was more beautiful than his words. The last speaker was Alexei himself, in a video he made a few months earlier in preparation for his funeral. He preached his final message, exhorting his listeners to not become materialistic but to keep their eyes on heavenly things.

When she got married, Valentina asked God for three years of life with her husband—she fully expected him to be imprisoned or killed. Instead, they had forty-seven years more than she had asked for. She lives in their house in Irpin, near the seminary, and is trying to encourage others to follow Christ, while mourning the loss of her husband.

Yakov resides in the family's old house in Zaporozhe with his wife, Olya. While he may have felt he lost something during the years of persecution, now he sees he's been given more than he lost. He works at a Christian radio station and is pastoring a church of about 180 people in downtown Zaporozhe. In the course of his work, he often deals with high officials in the city, many of whom were his father's enemies under the former government. Now they politely address Yakov as "Yakov Alexeievich" and offer help, because of the respect they have for Alexei and the way he lived with integrity and strength through all the persecution. Yakov and Olya's two sons have both pursued university educations.

Viktor lives nearby. He pastors a church in the suburbs and works for Hope International, a Christian organization that gives small loans to business startups. He and Luba have two married daughters.

Veniamin works as an administrator at the seminary and pastors a church in a small town near Irpin. He and Ruslana have a daughter, Diana, and a son, Yaroslav.

When we returned to Ukraine, Lena and I settled in Zaporozhe. After a few years, we moved to Kiev, and I began teaching in the seminary with my father-in-law. When he retired on May 31, 2008, I became the rector of the seminary, overseeing the education of our 300 enrolled students. Among our 1100 graduates is Lena. She teaches in the Christian Education department and is active in women's ministry in the church where I am pastor. Vika married June 14, 2009. Lena says it was easier to endure persecution than to see her daughter marry an American and move to California—so far away.

For all of us, the loss of Alexei was like the loss of the Zaporozhe oak—we lost someone strong, who could weather adversity. All of his children and grandchildren looked to him as a source of wisdom, like Daniel, and up to his death we sought his advice and prayers. Whenever any of us went to him, telling him our difficulties, saying it was too much and that we couldn't go on, he would tell us to use the persecution or trials as a tool. "What is God trying to teach you here?" he would ask.

We also thought of him like Job. Whenever the whole family got together for holidays, Alexei prayed for us all, just in case we had done something displeasing to God.

When asked what was the biggest challenge facing the Ukrainian church, Alexei answered that it is the question of what to do with our freedom. Earlier, any person who wanted to be baptized was thoroughly taught what they were getting into. Now it's much easier. Even with religious freedom, Alexei felt pastors should never aspire to baptize large numbers of people, but should make sure that those being baptized are serious about their faith. Repentance is much more than raising a hand and shedding a few tears.

We have seen many things come to us from the western churches, and not all of them are worthy of imitation. Many preachers came from America, trying to make things comfortable, so the people have no sense of conviction, no urge to repent. Alexei carefully studied the teaching of many Americans, and came to value the preaching of men like John MacArthur, because of their serious attitude toward the Word of God. If people have the right relationship with the Word of God, he knew, they will have the power of the Holy Spirit and can stand against the influences of the world or the flesh.

During the era of persecution, Alexei preached about the prophets who had suffered through trials, or the specific difficulties facing the congregation at the time. Once freedom came, he preached about submission to Jesus Christ. We are not saved just so we don't end up in hell, but so that the Holy Spirit could change us to be more like Christ. When the believer realizes he is saved to be transformed and sanctified, he begins to understand that all events, and the people in our lives, are God's instruments for our sanctification.

The Ukrainian church has had nearly twenty years of freedom, and we are grateful for the resources that have come to us from the west. But we do not want to lose our closeness with God, our adherence to His Word, and desire to be more like Christ. In my time in America I was amazed. In a country of religious freedom, why weren't more people flocking to the churches? And how could people be so careless with God's Word? In a land of material plenty, it seemed that the thirsty Americans were chasing after salt water, and missing the true, living water that was so abundantly available to all.

Now in Ukraine we have religious freedom—probably the most in the world right now. When I think of life during the time of persecution compared to life with freedom, I can say that freedom is good for the body but bad for the soul; persecution is bad for the body and good for the soul. During freedom, the church becomes big and fat, attracting many members. Persecution causes the church to exercise and burn off the fat, becoming healthy and strong. Freedom results in growth, persecution, purification. In speaking of the time of persecution, Alexei often pointed to the words of Paul: "I know what it is to be in need, and I know what it is to have plenty. I have learned the secret of being content in any and every situation, whether well fed or hungry, whether living in plenty or in want" (Philippians 4:12). Whatever our circumstances, Alexei would tell us, whether freedom or persecution, Jesus—and His promises—are still the same.

Above all, Alexei tried to be faithful to God and have a tender heart toward everyone, including those who would be his enemies. Throughout his life he gave thanks to God, utterly convinced that "the boundary lines have fallen for me in pleasant places; surely I have a delightful inheritance" (Psalm 16:6). At the last commencement of the Irpin Biblical Seminary that he attended, Alexei said in his address to the graduates, "I am begging you—acknowledge His presence every day of your life, and you will see how your life will be changed. The more you acknowledge His presence, the more you will learn of His promises." Alexei stands as an example of one who lived the way he taught, and looked beyond his trials to God, where he found victory and peace.

ENDNOTES

1. Shaw, George Bernard, *The Rationalization of Russia* (Bloomington, IN: Indiana University Press, 1964), p. 90.
2. Hochschild, Adam, *The Unquiet Ghost: Russians Remember Stalin* (New York: Viking [Penguin Group], 1994), p. 81.
3. Lenin, in March 19, 1922 letter to Molotov, www.loc.gov/exhibits/archives/ae2bkhun.html.
4. Kravchenko, Viktor, *I Chose Freedom* (Garden City, NY: Garden City Publishing, 1946), p. 162.
5. Gorbachev, Mikhail, Izbrannye rechi i stat'i, Moscow, 1985, p. 9, quoted in Volkogonov, Dmitri, *Lenin: A New Biography* (New York: The Free Press, a division of Simon and Schuster, 1994), p. 469.
6. V. I. Lenin, Collected Works, Vol. 14, p. 70, in Braun, Leopold L. S., AA, *In Lubianka's Shadow: The Memoirs of an American Priest in Stalin's Moscow 1934-1945* (Notre Dame: University of Notre Dame Press, 2006), p. 324.
7. The Hoover Institution Archives, Poster Collection, RU/SU 650, in Peris, Daniel, *Storming the Heavens: The Soviet League of the Militant Godless* (Ithaca: Cornell University Press, 1998), p. 80.

8. Leo Trotsky, quoted in Hochschild, p. 81.
9. The Hoover Institution Archives, Poster Collection, RU/SU 1916a, in Peris, p. 113.
10. Nikita Khrushchev, November 10, 1954, in Braun, p. 327.
11. Deyneka, Anita and Peter, Jr, *Christians in the Shadow of the Kremlin: The Truth About Life in the Spiritually Starved Soviet Union* (Elgin, IL: David C. Cook Publishing Company, 1974), p. 60.
12. "A Program for an Atheistic Society," *Nauka i religiia*, September 1961, translated in Joint Publications Research Service, 10, 899, No. 5 (11 Jan 1961), p. 6, in Constantin de Grunwald, *The Churches and the Soviet Union* (New York, 1962), pp. 61-64, in Donald A. Lowrie and William C. Fletcher "Khruschev's Religious Policy" in *Aspects of Religion in the Soviet Union 1917-1967*, Richard H. Marshall, Jr., ed. (Chicago: University of Chicago Press, 1971), p. 146.
13. Quoted in Weeks, Albert, in a review of Volkogonov, *Lenin* in the *Washington Inquirer*, August 26, 1994, cited in *The Rise and Fall of the Soviet Union*, Brian Cozier (Rocklin, CA: Forum, an imprint of Prima Publishing, 1999), p. 36-37.
14. Deyneka, *Christians in the Shadow of the Kremlin*, p. 60.
15. M. Sheinman, Nravstvennost' religioznaia i nravstvennost' proletarskaia, 2nd rev. ed, (Moscow/Leningrad: Gosizdat, 1930), p. 29, in Peris, p. 95.
16. *USSR—Questions and Answers*, trans. David Sinclair-Louti, (Moscow: Progress Publishers, 1975), p. 133.
17. Quoted in Brzezinski, Zbigniew, *The Grand Failure: The Birth and Death of Communism in the Twentieth Century* (New York: Charles Scribner's Sons, 1982), p. 82.
18. *Pravda*, October 18, 1962, in Lowrie and Fletcher, p. 134.
19. Agitprop, To: Stalin, "Proekt Ustava Kommunisticheskogo Universiteta," F. 17, Op. 84, Doc. 419, p. 72 in Brovkin, Vladimir, *Russia After Lenin: Politics, Culture and Society* (New York and London: Routledge, 1998), p. 89.

20. *USSR—Questions and Answers*, p. 133.
21. *USSR—Questions and Answers*, p. 94.
22. Antireligioznik, No. 2 (1926), p. 4, in Brovkin, p. 99.
23. Sign on factory in Vladimir, Russia, observed by author.
24. Quoted in Kravchenko, p. 425.
25. Mandelstan, Nadezhda, *Hope Against Hope*, trans. Max Hayward (New York: Atheneum, 1974), in Konchanlovsky, Andrei, and Lipkov, Alexander, editors, trans. by Jamey Gambrell, *The Inner Circle: An Inside View of Soviet Life under Stalin* (New York: Newmarket Press, 1991), p. 55.
26. Soviet newspaper *Bezhbozhknik u stanka* (Godless at the machine), 1923, no. 3, in Peris, p. 94.
27. Politburo minutes containing Brezhnev's reply to President Carter, December 29, 1979, Hoover Archives, No. P177/220, in Crozier, Brian, *The Rise and Fall of the Soviet Union* (Rocklin, CA: Forum, an imprint of Prima Publishing, 1999), p. 663.
28. Trotsky, Leon, "The Metaphysics of Democracy," from *Terrorism and Communism* in *The Basic Writings of Trotsky*, Howe, Irving, ed. (New York: Random House, 1963), p. 156.
29. Trotsky, Leon, *The Revolution Betrayed: What Is the Soviet Union and Where Is It Going?* (New York: Pathfinder Press, 1937), p. 128.
30. N. Riabinsky, "New Times—New Rituals," Sovietskie Profsoiuzy (Soviet Trade Unions), No. 19, October, 1965, p. 34, in Lowrie and Fletcher, p. 140.
31. "Zadachi i metody raboty sredi krestian," *Antireligioznik*, no. 2 (1926), p. 27, in Brovkin, p. 95.
32. Quoted in Tuominen, Arvo, *The Bells of the Kremlin: An Experience in Communism* (Hanover and London: University Press of New England, 1983), p. 4.
33. Dimitrov, Georgi, Speech 20 Feb. 1935, Russian State Archive of Social and Political History, (original in Russian), F 546, Op. 1, d 274, ll. 93-96 in Chase, William J., *Enemies Within*

the Gates?: The Comintern and the Stalinist Repression (New York and London: Yale University Press, 2001), p. 97.
34. *USSR—Questions and Answers*, p. 31.
35. *USSR—Questions and Answers*, p. 31.
36. Trotsky, Leon, "The Family and Ceremony," trans. by Z. Vengerovna in "Problems of Life," in *The Basic Writings of Trotsky*, p. 339.
37. Deyneka, Anita and Peter, Jr, *A Song in Siberia: The True Story of a Russian Church That Could Not Be Silenced* (Elgin, IL: David C. Cook Publishing Company, 1977), p. 19.
38. Mironov, B., "In One Word: Shame," Pravda, Jan 22, 1988, p. 3, in Roberts, Paul Craig, and LaFollette, Karen, *Meltdown: Inside the Soviet Economy* (Washington: The Cato Institute, 1990), p. 60.
39. Tarnopolsky, Yuri, *Memoirs of 1984* (Lanhan, MD: University Press of America, 1993), p. 66.
40. Khrushchev, Nikita, *Khrushchev Remembers: The Last Testament*, trans. and ed. Strobe Talbott, London: Andre Deutsch, 1974, in Brown, Archie, *The Rise and Fall of Communism* (New York: Harper Collins Publishers, 2009), p. 253.
41. Quoted in Kravchenko, p. 425.
42. Leonid F. Ilichev, "Formirovanie Nauchnogo Mirovozreniia i Ateisticheskoe Vospitanie" ("The Formation of a Scientific World Outlook and Atheistic Education.") Kommunist, No. 1, 1964, p. 30, in Deyneka, *A Song in Siberia*, p. 38.
43. Quoted in Tuominen, Arvo, p. 134.
44. N. Riabinsky, "New Times—New Rituals," Sovietskie Profsoiuzy (Soviet Trade Unions), No. 19, October, 1965, p. 34, in Lowrie and Fletcher, p. 140.
45. Smith, Hedrick, *The New Russians* (New York: Random House, 1990), p. 143.
46. Vladimir Lenin, quoted by Leon Trotsky, *The Revolution Betrayed*, p. 140.

For more information

www.beyondtherapids.com

Irpin Biblical Seminary (www.ibs-ua.org)

Half of the proceeds of this book will go to support the Irpin Biblical Seminary.

Slavic Gospel Association (www.sga.org)
Hope International (www.hopeinternational.org)

To learn more about persecution of Christians around the world:

Open Doors (www.opendoorsusa.org)
Voice of the Martyrs (www.persecution.com)
International Christian Concern (www.persecution.org)

To learn more about the erosion of religious freedom in the United States and other western countries:

Alliance Defense Fund (www.alliancedefensefund.org)

To order additional copies of this book call:
1-877-421-READ (7323)
or please visit our Web site at
www.pleasantwordbooks.com

If you enjoyed this quality custom-published book,
drop by our Web site for more books and information.

www.winepressgroup.com
"Your partner in custom publishing."

LaVergne, TN USA
15 March 2011
220078LV00001B/8/P